The Aggressive

Management Style

The Aggressive
Management Style

NORMAN KOBERT

PRENTICE-HALL, INC.   Englewood Cliffs, NJ

Prentice-Hall International, Inc., *London*
Prentice-Hall of Australia, Pty. Ltd., *Sydney*
Prentice-Hall of Canada, Ltd., *Toronto*
Prentice-Hall of India Private Ltd., *New Delhi*
Prentice-Hall of Japan, Inc., *Tokyo*
Whitehall Books, Ltd., *Wellington, New Zealand*
Prentice-Hall of Southeast Asia Pte. Ltd., *Singapore*

© 1981 by

Prentice-Hall, Inc.
Englewood Cliffs, N.J.

Second Printing . . . . . November, 1981

Library of Congress Catologing in Publication Data

Kobert, Norman.
   The aggressive management style.

   1. Management.   I. Title.
HD31.K5982   658.4
ISBN 0-13-018762-3

Printed in the United States of America

To a true helpmate,
my Natalie

A WORD FROM THE AUTHOR

The aggressive management style (AMS) is an attack approach to improving the use of your basic management skills. It will help you perform your day-to-day functions with a more forceful drive towards reaching management objectives.

Instead of accepting or working around obstacles to success, the manager with an AMS orientation pushes for solutions which are translatable into action. These include a bagful of bold techniques that are simple enough to be put into practice tomorrow.

Shortcuts (the quick-and-dirty approaches), time-phased implementations, improving control from basic reporting, success and failure accountability and motivation through meaningful rewards and penalties are some of the subjects covered by narrative and illustrations. In fact, the book is profuse with anecdotal experiences and illustrations of results drawn from my almost 30 years of consulting and teaching experiences with managers both here and abroad. These managers are from small companies and from huge industrial enterprises; they view work as seen from the perspective of the first-line manager up to the overview approaches as seen from the pinnacle.

The specific actions recommended in this book can help you stand out from the rest of the corporate "wage slaves" that surround you. This can be accomplished by techniques of AMS that are results oriented, that will apply surgery instead of cosmetic powder. Your bosses should notice reduced indecision caused by procrastination. Certain phrases will become obsolete:

"Let's wait until *all* the facts are in and *all* possible objections overcome."

"Good enough."

"Everything will eventually work out."

"Don't worry."

"Surprise, it didn't happen."

A manager can choose courses of action to avoid unnecessary compromises to eliminate hopeful assumptions in place of factual deductions, unfruitful exhortations in place of constructive support of your employees, and improve the quality of one-on-one relationships to avoid unexpected failures.

Today's managers are seeking results-oriented actions because they know that, in the longer term, their success hinges on aggressive plans brought to a profitable and recognizable conclusion.

I urge the reader to review the table of contents to gain an overview of the aggressive management style. You will see that the techniques of AMS are arrayed against the manager's tasks. In this way, armed with accepted management skills, today's managers can sharpen their use of these assets with their personal, aggressive management style.

Norman Kobert

TABLE OF CONTENTS

15

2 — Improved Managerial Planning Using AMS (Cont.)

3 — AMS Techniques for Planning Your Time Management 77

11 — Relating Motivational Techniques to Your AMS (Cont.)

- *Set an Objective and Develop a Schedule*
- *Monitoring Success*
- *Write Your Own AMS Book*

The Aggressive

Management Style

1

HOW THE AGGRESSIVE MANAGEMENT STYLE HAS WORKED FOR OTHERS

The aggressive management style (AMS) is an "attack" approach to improve your use of the basic management skills of planning, organizing, reviewing, controlling, coordinating, communicating and improving. AMS is a compendium of techniques used by today's aggressive managers to turn plans into actions and problems into opportunities.

All the while, the manager practicing the aggressive management style has a very good chance of enhancing his or her real and perceived value to today's industrial, service and governmental enterprises. I'm sure you have noticed how aggressive managers "get ahead," or are, at the very least, in serious contention for pay increases, promotion and plaudits.

Instead of accepting or working around obstacles to progress, the manager with an AMS orientation pushes for actionable solutions, "quick-and-dirty" approaches, time-phased implementations, reporting and control milestones, success and failure accountabilities and motivation through meaningful rewards *and* penalties. The following pages will show how these AMS techniques have helped managers "climb the corporate ladder," or at least offer opportunities that did not heretofore exist.

SOME HISTORICAL PERSPECTIVES

Great Britain was once described as "a nation of shopkeepers." The British people were annoyed by this put-down, considering that the term implied a "pedestrian mentality," an inability to invoke larger perceptions and perhaps a satisfaction with the simplicity of the status quo.

Since the mid-1950s, the United States could be described as "a nation of office workers." Yet this has not caused any particular arousal on the part of those described. In fact, numerous articles have extolled the virtues of the 20th Century marvel, its service economy and, of course, the nationalistic fact that the United States was the first nation in world history to have more "white collar" than "blue collar" workers.

Human motivation has a way of adjusting to this changing environment. If the way to get periodic increases in pay and position up to the day of that guaranteed, ultimate retirement is to "keep your nose clean" and "don't make waves," the same folks who were able to do this in the factory are now performing this survival tactic in the office.

But, what of the ambitious, the skilled and the manipulative? In a factory environment, one could produce more, get more piece-work pay, be raised to a higher skill level, accrue seniority, become the foreman, etc.

In an office, however, the work count is generally neither available nor even calculable. Measurement is far more subjective. ("That group is doing a good job with just the right amount of people!") Seniority is usually a consideration but not generally a mandated right, and various skills receive approximately the same pay within narrow percentage limits.

GAINING RECOGNITION IN A "ME-TOO" ENVIRONMENT

How to gain positive recognition in a "me-too" environment is one of the objectives of the aggressive management style. Some examples of what will be achieved include:

- reduced indecision caused by procrastination and evidenced by, "Let's wait until *all* the facts are in and *all* possible objections overcome."
- avoiding unnecessary compromises that lead many managers to accept the phrase, "Good enough!"
- eliminating assumptions that "everything will eventually work itself out," which cause the worst of all reports to management, "Don't worry!"

- improving the quality of reports of progress/failure to avoid the bane of most managers, "Surprise! It didn't get done and we missed the deadline!"

If the measure of managerial success is profits or sales, the figures are, of course, affected by inflation. Changing dollar values make these benchmarks far less definitive than the numbers of pieces, parts or earned hours versus the actual hours worked by laborers. *Fortune, Forbes, Business Week, Dun's Review* and *Industry Week* are filled with articles describing top executives who are "turning things around," "defining the market," "re-directing objectives," "improving morale," "organizing the disorganized" and "trimming the fat." These praiseworthy actions must always be completed in time to show some bottom-line progress to the company's board of directors — or the chief executive is axed! In other words, progress among executives is usually based upon a more subjective measure than in a manufacturing area, where pieces and hours are definitive and countable.

For your personal aggressive management style to succeed, you will have to be noticed in a "me-too" environment. To get such high-level recognition, there is no need for you to adopt a radically unusual behavior or appearance. Unlike much of the management style literature that fills corporate bookshelves, this book does not expect you to make drastic personality or dress alterations. The average manager who follows the norm in his personal appearance and behavior traits can achieve an aggressive management style. The AMS is essentially a bagful of bold techniques and results-oriented actions for the average manager of average dress and appearance, who knows he will stand out from the crowd by aggressive plans brought to a profitable and recognizable conclusion.

The actions you take will be based upon the author's almost 30 years of teaching and consulting with managers in the United States and abroad. This book is filled with anecdotes and examples from the author's work in small companies and huge industrial complexes, where he has been able to view the management of work from both the pinnacle and the crevasse.

THE VALUE OF HIGH-LEVEL RECOGNITION IN A "ME-TOO" ENVIRONMENT

Yogi Berra, in his first season as a manager of the New York Yankees, guided the team to an American League pennant, but lost the World Series to the St. Louis Cardinals, managed by Johnny Keane. Yogi was immediately dismissed; Keane got his job and all the players received substantial salary increases. Twenty-game winners, hitters over .300 and home run hitters don't have to win the World Series to be rewarded, but the front office usually has no other measure of managers, coaches, etc. Hence, lack of high-level recognition can have a deleterious effect.

To be positively recognized does not necessarily directly correlate with reward, but it is probably a major input factor. The problem for many managers and office workers is not so much belief in the above statement as it is in how to achieve it. Negative recognition, although sometimes unavoidable, is not desirable. But, how does the average person achieve positive recognition?

In order to uncomplicate the approach, let us assume you are either average or above average in physical, mental and psychological prowess. The purposes of adopting an aggressive management style are: to achieve recognition in promotions and pay increases, but *not* to dominate others or to assert your sexuality or to achieve vindication for the wrong imposed on you (or about to be).

GAINING POSITIVE RECOGNITION

In the following chapters, techniques in practicing the aggressive management style will be described in detail. But, you are cautioned that unless the practice of AMS leads to positive recognition, you will merely be thought of as "aggressive." To achieve positive recognition, both the aggressive act and the perception of the worth of that act must be positive.

Two famous gentlemen from world history provide the rationale for the following:

- "Nothing is more unworthy of a wise man, or ought to trouble him more, than to have allowed more time for trifling, and useless things, than they deserved." PLATO
- "Most men are consistent in their management of self, and consistency is the last refuge of the unimaginative." O. WILDE

Back in the 1960s, a business fad of the era was called Zero Defects. The concept was to look at all quality problems from a zero base; if everyone sought absolute quality perfection, all defects would ultimately reduce significantly. One of the amazing discoveries of that time was the amount of employees who produced "bad work" in order to get the attention of their supervisors. These people found if they produced average work, day-after-day, with an average number of defects, their supervisors rarely even talked to them. But, produce defective work at a higher than acceptable level, and your supervisor's attention — even wrath — was singularly directed towards you. For a person with these kinds of psychological needs, the required recognition is available without any further knowledge of what is presented on the following pages relevant to the techniques of the aggressive management style.

Therefore, the first cardinal rule relative to the practice of AMS is that the recognition achieved be of a positive nature, that it has either an apparent or real advantage to the enterprise and that it is recognized as such by your peers, your superiors and even your employees.

In a Broadway play (later made into a widely acclaimed film, *The Apartment*), a lowly clerical worker timed his departure each evening with that of the boss, hoping to be met at the elevator and thus to be noticed for the diligence perceived to be associated with long hours of work. The clerk's ultimate rise in the company, however, was for renting his apartment to the various company executives desiring female companionship in the privacy of his abode.

This type of recognition, although positive, would not elevate the recipient beyond a minimal level since (1) the contribution could not be publicized, (2) the advantage to the firm is exceedingly minor, although some industrial psychologist may cite improved morale and teamwork and (3) the activity is fraught with dangers from blackmail down to lease breaking.

To achieve recognition, both the act and the perception of the worth of that act must be positive. Since the object of practicing the aggressive management style is increased pay, plaudits and promotion, this positive recognition is a criterion of paramount importance.

EXISTING INERTIA CAN BE A PLATFORM FOR RECOGNITION

The average reader has an advantage, in that he or she probably works in a "me-too" environment. Our correspondence, mode of dress, reverence for the published organization, established procedures, style of meetings and the like fit a mold that is barely altered from Boston to Bakersfield, from Miami to Minneapolis. We are recipients of peer pressure for conformity in office layout, such as room dividers made of potted plants or 5½ - foot partitions allowing for communal conversations and audible interruptions. Then there's the telephone reception (the Centrex approach that bounces the caller all over the office if the primary number is unresponsive or forces the recipient to handle every incoming interruption, including whim calls). Or, you might find this personnel policy: "I'm sorry, Ms. Pippin, but even though you're really superior as my administrative assistant, the wage range is fixed for this position, which is related to *my* position."

In a "me-too" environment, the majority of those confined will meekly adhere and accept. Those employing the aggressive management style will analyze and advocate change for the better. They will look at the firm's problems as opportunities and inertia as a platform for recognition.

A caution here...we are talking of positive recognition for positive results. There is no doubt that you could gain recognition of the company's stodgy dress code by "flashing," "streaking" or "mooning," but this would obviously just be recognition resulting in no dress code change and your dismissal (or arrest).

OPPORTUNITIES FOR RECOGNITION

High-level recognition also involves either a dramatic suggestion leading to improvement or a series of much smaller successes. The latter will probably be the most frequent cause for high-level recognition. If you tie your road to success with the state lottery or oil and gas rights on U.S. Government properties, you might conceivably be successful. For most of us, the road to success for pay increases and promotions is through a series of successes, with the promise that "our well hasn't run dry" or that we've "shot our load."

Most managers are hungry for the employee who at any level aggressively creates opportunities, solves problems and innovatively examines day-to-day acceptances "because we've always done it that way."

Richard J. Kendro, Executive Vice President of the Aqua-Chem Corp., says, "I first try to encourage innovation, then I must recognize it and finally I must reward it. This is not done as easily as it sounds, since the innovative asset is many times hidden in the mountains of correspondence crossing my desk, in comments or suggestions stated at meetings or by employees addressing me in the corridors, at social functions or over the telephone. I must stand prepared to separate the aggressive, positive problem solvers from the aggressive problem presenters; and the solution seekers from the complainers, regardless of the personality or dress code of the employee. Finally, I must reward the positive thinking (and acting) employees within the framework of our corporate objectives, or, if necessary, sanction flexibility to better achieve our corporate goals."

A reader may be thinking, "Boy, if I worked for that kind of a manager, I'd receive instant recognition for my innovative efforts." Perhaps so. If you work in such an environment, the question remains as to what projects, plans and actions can be pursued by aggressive management.

For those of you seeking top-level recognition, the use of AMS involves the selection of plans, projects and actions as well as gaining recognition for these approaches. This is my objective...to demonstrate practical positive approaches to management practices, followed by the recognition of same, in your work environment.

AGGRESSIVENESS MAY NOT REQUIRE ALTERATION OF YOUR PERSONALITY

A great deal has been written in the past five years on the concept of assertiveness, the "I'm somebody!" approach to positive thinking and action. Many have been stimulated and a great many more have read with curiosity and interest...merely as observers.

Assertiveness requires a look at yourself and some important new conclusions to be drawn relative to your attitude, dress, body language and even your social and sexual commitments. One fact, however, is undeniable; everyone finds the subject fascinating. It is hard to resist an approach that asks you to think, "I'm number one," or at the very least, "I'm important."

One of the difficulties, in actual practice, is that a Walter Mitty in your office may fantasize about what he is going to tell his boss, or girl or customer, but can he actually change his personality to maintain that approach? Can we change an army of Walter Mittys into assertive managers? Probably not. Therefore, an area exists for the application of the aggressive management style, regardless of your personality, or alteration of same.

AMS IS A MANAGEMENT STYLE

The aggressive management style is just that — a management style. It is a series of actions designed to provide recognition of the average person working in the average office, regardless of personality, assertiveness or otherwise.

An example may help better define this. Many folks complain of an inability to get things approved by their boss. They say, "His desk is a bottomless pit" such that ideas die when presented in written form. Those same people are put off by the boss who says, "We'll talk about that later," but later never seems to come.

Now, assertiveness training may describe how to camp outside your boss's door, put a pen in his or her hand and force a signature. But, can you do this, given the average person's mildly assertive or mildly passive personality? Is it worth it to confront all or most issues in this way?

CHOOSING THE ACTION TO MEET THE PRIORITY

The aggressive management style would have you choose from a kitbag of management tools and select the appropriate one. For example, I have long counseled company personnel from secretaries to vice-presidents to separate the important from the less important. In this way, one can develop a style for each. In the above-described case, for less important matters requiring your boss's concurrence or rejection, an "If I do not hear from you by Friday, the following will be put into effect..." memo might be appropriate.

In this way, the boss is either informed of a change or may object to it. He or she still has the option, but you appear to be action-oriented regarding less important items. Clients have reported back to me that over 80 percent of the minor suggestions receive "pocket approval" and their bosses have thanked them for keeping them informed. When the idea is rejected or drastically modified, it is not much different a position than one would be in from having received no reply.

For major decisions requiring your boss's concurrence, the above approach may be too impertinent. This is especially true where other data must be reviewed or other inputs weighed by your boss. In these cases, you may try the "agenda visit" approach. Instead of informal discussions between you and your boss, keep a log of your more important work that is pending approval on your boss's desk. Either at a formal or informal meeting with your boss, supply him or her with a copy of an agenda of items requiring approval. As they are covered, cross them out; those without resolution reappear on the next agenda.

The boss will appreciate your organized approach and may try to match this with his or her own attempt to act in a more organized manner. You may also achieve another benefit by getting better results from informal meetings.

ELIMINATION IS THE HIGHEST FORM OF IMPROVEMENT

Of course, the most important principle is one that states "elimination is the highest form of improvement." This concept should be viewed before one even separates the important from the unimportant. Ask yourself, "Do I really need the boss's approval, or am I using it as a crutch for a decision that I can make on my own level?" If you are traversing untrodden ground, you may further ask, "What's the down-side risk if I either make a wrong decision or should have opted for the boss's concurrence?" More on these concepts will be covered in chapters 4 and 9.

Making the aggressive management style work requires an evaluation of self, a change in style (not necessarily in personality) and an action-oriented objective rather than a code of behavior.

THE ATTACK APPROACH IN DAY-TO-DAY MANAGING

In day-to-day managing there are a host of events occurring both inside and outside our control. A since departed manager friend of mine used to heckle his employees with his "guide" to managing that went, "When things go well, take credit unto yourself. When things go badly, blame someone else." He was echoing a long-felt theory that events occur outside our control — for good and bad — so it's just a matter of who gets the blame or credit.

An attack approach to managing isolates the controllables, evaluates the options and develops a strategy for both failure and success. An example may be drawn from the types of traders one sees in the stock market versus those one meets trading commodities. There are fewer "bears" than "bulls" in the stock market even in the worst of economic trends. The newsletters are full of "underpriced stocks" and "values not represented in the price" situations. How many times is there a description of an aggressive policy in shorting a majority of stocks as the Dow-Jones Average tumbles from 1000 to 750? Yet the slightest rally brings out the buyers who were waiting for the break in their charts to "go long." Eternal optimism is a human trait, but like blind bravery, it can be costly.

On the other hand, the most common trade in the commodity market is the spread...buying a contract while selling one. Whichever one is wrong, you sell immediately. You ride and/or pyramid the one that's right. The right one can be either up *or* down in price. Gerson Lewis, a member of the Chicago Board of Trade (among others), is a firm believer in the management principle that, "Losses are the same as gains in how they should be viewed. A manager who rides a winner could be lucky; a manager who creates a winner and understands why, and when to get off, will be a more consistent winner than the lucky manager."

The attack approach requires a manager to review a situation as if it were new. Yesterday's decision may be wrong today. Minimize your losses;

evaluate today's position without the burden of defending yesterday's decision.

FACING UP TO FAILURE BY AGGRESSIVELY
SEEKING SOLUTIONS

A company in a Virginia city had embarked on a participative cost-reduction program. All the employees, including the managers, were encouraged to participate in the program. The plant manager not only approved the program, but had a major hand in developing the details.

As the first ideas started coming in, it became apparent that most of them were requests for major expenditures, many of which were the same as those removed from the capital expenditure budgets in past years. They were removed by the plant manager's bosses because they involved very large debt-commitments.

The plant manager had many options, including:

- keep going with the participative cost-reduction program, but shunt the previously rejected ideas to a side "for further consideration" at some future date.
- push the major expenditure ideas with his bosses with renewed vigor, even though rejection was certain.
- kill the whole program; or, the one he chose. Face up to the problem. He wanted a cost-reduction program, with a "grass-roots" approach, but the requests for improvement were unacceptable, for financial reasons to the higher echelons. He weighed the downside risk of procrastination or total rejection and decided to face up to the problem.

He approached individually all the suggestors who had submitted cost-reduction ideas that involved large capital expenditures, and explained the basics and problems of cash flow and financial planning. For the appropriate ones, he promised resubmission. But, his overall objective was to continue the program with their participation.

The plant manager faced up to the problem as soon as possible and took a positive approach to truthfully explaining the circumstances, while at the same time attempting to regenerate enthusiasm for the program. The attack approach requires this. Face up to your problems as soon as they appear; if no action is the decision, then it is a planned response. Avoid being a victim of your own procrastination. More on the "do it now" approach will be covered in chapter 9.

HOW TO "MAKE HISTORY" IN PLANNING
AND CONTROLLING WORK ACCOMPLISHMENT

There is an old management saying that managers make history while clerks merely record it. I am sure that, as managers, we foster some clerking activities. Some examples may make this point.

When an employee travels to a distant location or seminar or convention, it is not uncommon to require the submission of a trip report. Managers justify this practice as one that either imposes a control on the traveler to be alert or provides the troops back home with a document to review. In actual practice, the traveler looks at the trip report as just another chore to be routinely performed and the folks back home find a rare gem on rare occasions in these circulated reports.

Suppose instead of this exercise all trips were justified on a future value basis and this was pre-agreed with the traveler. Therefore, if the travel was for upgrading the individual's personal skills, only exceptional practices not in present use need be reported. If the trip were to ascertain facts or to solve a particular problem, this objective could easily be stated, and the trip report need not document what everyone knows, but only the exceptional findings or solutions. Finally, what is the everlasting nature of the trip report that it need be reduced to writing? Can a simple oral report to interested parties suffice? In other words, without any effort, a trip report policy can be continued ad infinitum by the clerks, but an aggressive style manager wants objectives to be met and reporting on an efficient and exception basis.

WEEKLY MEETINGS THAT ARE WEAKLY HELD

I remember many years ago telling my secretary I was going to the weekly meeting. Her question was, "Why is it held weekly?" I remember replying, "Because it's held weekly!"

Each week was a "show and tell" affair that required attendance by all managers. Many times we discussed items that we had informally discussed with each other all week long as ongoing business problems. Sometimes we discussed reports that we had already read; sometimes we received information that could have been in the reports that we had already read.

There was a very rough agenda and the meeting *always* lasted two hours because we started at 10:00 a.m. and everyone always planned lunch (business or otherwise) for about noon.

The meeting was an ego trip for some and a bore for others. All failures were "run up the flagpole" so that we could all "throw rocks at the people in the stocks." Minutes were assiduously kept and distributed for comment.

AMS APPROACH TO EFFECTIVE MEETING TIME UTILIZATION

A more logical approach to communications and group action was developed and will be covered in much more detail in chapter 10. The following questions had to be answered:

- Why is a meeting to be held?
- Can, or have we, covered these items heretofore?
- Would a note or memo be an adequate replacement for certain items to be covered?
- What is the value ratio between the time spent and the benefits achieved at the meeting?
- Can the attendees be limited by need-to-know versus like-to-know?
- Can the agenda allow for an item-by-item discussion on a time-planned basis?
- Can each attendee keep track of what is decided and what each is to do? Can reliance on minutes thus be eliminated?
- If a time schedule is generally adhered to, can we encourage staggered attendance?

As managers, we should have been asking questions about the utilization of two hours out of every week. As clerks, we could have kept attending and developed ideas for better minutes being kept, changing meeting times, controlling interruptions and the like. The end result would have been 20 percent less time spent at these meetings (including having less meetings to attend).

Making history, instead of merely being part of it and then recording the acts, requires a bold new look at everything from reports, to meetings, to telephone use, to delegation, to desk organization, to other daily occupations that we perform just because "we've always done it that way."

SIMULATING OWNERSHIP OF THE ENTERPRISE WITH AMS

There are endless examples of efficiencies developed by those who own an enterprise versus those who "just have a job." The employees' first and main thrust is to have a job. Seniority is most important. The avoidance of technological replacement is paramount; unemployment benefits are high on the list of avoidable situations.

The aggressive managerial thrust is to "do better," improve the work environment, expand and advance the enterprise and reward that aggressive manager with pay increases and promotions. I am sure the reader can cite many examples of aggressive managers whose rewards were unemployment. But, by and large, when a manager's view of a situation is that of an owner rather than as a job-holder, the victories generally outnumber the defeats.

Look at some correspondence in your "In" box. How much of it contains semantics to cover a position, justify an opinion, excuse a failure, create an impression or report a problem? How much of it is relative to promoting a new idea, solving an existing problem or recommending a new approach? Perhaps the difference in the answers relates to the attitudes of both you and your employees towards the enterprise itself and your jobs within that framework.

Suppose you were to look at a prospective management action and against all the options assignable thought, "Would I do it this way if I owned this place and it was my money at stake?" Try asking this question when you observe current practices as well.

WITH YOUR MONEY YOU'D MAKE DIFFERENT DECISIONS

A West Coast headquarters of a nationwide service firm spent a goodly sum of money on a very popular and very well-presented employee training program. The employees loved the program, management was happy to have presented a well-received program and the employees went back to their jobs, and did the same things as before the training sessions. If it were your company, would it please you to spend $12,000 just so all your employees could enjoy a good training program?

Would you, the simulated owner, not be happier with

- A program designed for your particular needs, with inputs of specific problems by the prospective attendees?
- A planned follow-up of the training to assure that the principles were understood *and* put into practice on the job?

If you answered "yes" to the above questions, then as a simulated owner you have looked at training not as an end unto itself, but as a means of education toward stimulating future positive actions by your employees.

There is no doubt in my mind that an employee, from the recent graduate to top management, has a much better chance for pay increases and promotions when simulation of ownership is part of the thought process in analysis and decision-making.

USING AMS WITHIN CONSTRAINTS

Another word of caution is in order here. The aggressive management style must be used within the constraints of your talent, personality and level of operation in the company. For this reason, of the many examples of AMS provided throughout this book, a key ingredient is *you*... what *you* feel comfortable in attempting, what *you* consider appropriate from your level of the organization and what suits *your* aspirations.

Therefore, some of the ideas are of immediate value. Some had best be left for another day in your corporate career. Through assertiveness training, new personality traits and dress codes may be helpful to you. The stress on these pages will relate to ideas and techniques which you may adopt within the framework of your present behavioral patterns. But then the pressure is on you to select the comfortable from the uncomfortable. Some cases of failure caused by inaction may help to make this last point.

CASE OF THE FAIRY DUST FALLACY

All of us wish things were better; perhaps we wish *we* were better. A rational person realizes that some wishes could come true with some help from ourselves. Yet it is not an uncommon tendency to watch a situation deteriorate, all the while hoping and praying that things will get better.

Sales managers watch order inputs decline in a previously solid base area; bosses watch employees founder on new projects long past the point of rescue. I watched a parent firm pump millions of dollars into a division whose basic problems had not been resolved for over three years. In another firm, a president's pet project was never profitable and wasn't even close until six years later when the project was sold as a commercial prototype to a giant Midwest firm desiring to enter the field.

The fairy dust fallacy is a technique whereby problems disappear when hit with this cloud. "Perhaps things will get better; maybe they will turn around" are oft-heard approaches. If you're lucky, things will happen the way you dreamed they would...if you're lucky.

AMS TECHNIQUES TO OVERCOME THE FAIRY DUST FALLACY

Within the framework of the aggressive management style, you would be better served to:

- Estimate the probability of success if no action is taken.
- Determine what the down-side risk would be if all or most of the events turn negative.

- Develop alternate courses of action and encourage recommendations. Don't exclude constructive criticism or suggestions that are out-of-the-ordinary.

- Take one or all of the necessary courses of action as soon as the probability of success diminishes beyond an acceptable level, or where a calculated action will definitely improve the probability of success.

- Walk away from losses which are irretrievable. Wait for another day. New losses chasing old losses is a sure road to ultimate failure. Don't waste time on worry or regret. Being right 51 percent of the time is a base that allows for some failures.

PROBLEMS ARE OPPORTUNITIES

Two people who have meant a lot to me in my life are proponents of this theory...problems should be looked at not just as mere problems but as opportunities.

In the confirmation speech he had written, my eldest son Roy talked about the problem Moses faced as he stood with his band of refugees before the Sea of Reeds, today's Red Sea. Moses sent forth an equivalent of a latter day scout, who determined that unarmed civilians could use the reeds to walk upon. The scout also figured that the heavily armoured Egyptians, with horses and chariots, would be stopped. Of course, it would have been more romantic to part the Sea.

Roy's conclusion was that the problem of passage was equally an opportunity to evade the Egyptians. The result is history but the point was impressive. We can get bogged down and even discouraged by problems, or we can view them as opportunities for potential gain.

SEIZING OPPORTUNITIES VERSUS ACCEPTING PROBLEMS

A close friend, Jerome E. Vielehr, President of the Jos. Schlitz Brewing Co., is a model of this philosophy. He has used it in turning around two businesses. If the problem was excessive overhead, he would seize the opportunity to cut costs. If the problem was being locked into a bad situation, he would ascertain that which was salvageable, but at the same time make certain these types of contract clauses would be eliminated for all future work that was bid. If the problem was personnel, he would call a showdown meeting on-site and use the knowledge unearthed as an opportunity to change personnel. If the problem was acceptance of a project, he would seize the opportunity to calculate the projected true variables and present them in the proper format to the right people.

A famous slogan that he has oft-repeated to me is, "I'd like to see all my people make almost any mistake, just *once*. If you haven't learned something from your first mistake then *that* is unforgivable!"

This encouraged his people to expand their horizons and take some chances, but most importantly, to learn something from failure. Jerry's other credo is, "If you don't learn from failure, you pay for it twice; once for the failure and secondly because nothing positive came from the cost of gaining knowledge for future applications."

In practicing the aggressive management style, one can consider problems as opportunities when one can see that we all have problems, but some of us turn them around to some advantage.

CASE OF THE UPSIDE-DOWN CHARTS

Mike Oliver, a commodities' account executive with the E. F. Hutton Company, has an interesting approach to looking at the fundamental price charts. He takes his charts and turns them upside-down. Since we are, as homo sapiens, essentially optimists in the face of natural disasters, wars, pestilence and the like, we tend to think, "tomorrow will be better." We bid work with a firm expectation of getting our share, or more. We postpone layoffs because "things will pick up soon." We don't sell a losing equity position because "it'll turn around!"

Mike turns his charts over because the opportunity to sell has almost as much profit as the opportunity to buy. (The inequality is basically theoretical because commodities won't go to zero. But if they did, that's as far as they'd go; there is no theoretical upside limit.) He knows that a go-no-go decision has as much relevance in either direction, and, therefore, by reversing his charts he tests his philosophy against his basic human prejudice...everything will ultimately go up.

A decision not to buy is a decision to sell, if you really believe the price will go down. Conversely, a decision to sell should really be a double decision: (1) to sell at a price at or near the point it will go down, and (2) if point (1) is correct, to then sell another contract.

NO DECISION IS ALSO A DECISION

Every day we face the same problems in business as Mike does in commodities. "No decision" is a decision not to act. The same rules that apply to making a "yes" or "no" or "maybe, but" also apply. If we have an opportunity to buy inventory at a price break, we may have to override our expensive materials requirement planning system and buy. It would be safer to stick to the system, but the cost of being wrong is the missed opportunity of the price break. If we really have faith in our judgement, why not buy quantities to cover forecast as well as actual demand?

Reverse that procedure. Assume that there is no foreseeable use of two-thirds of an item's inventory. It was bought during an expansion era and orders fell faster than we could cut off supply. Modification is not possible and the supplier is not interested in buying back the excess stock (would you?). Should you hold on hoping for additional business? Should you wait until the end of the year write-downs? Or, should you move to dispose of this stock, even at scrap value, on the premise that cash has an appreciating value and assets have associated depreciating costs?

By reversing a situation, we can test our philosophies under reverse conditions. In many areas of business endeavor, this should create new opportunities for looking at a given set of facts.

SUCCESS BREEDS POPULARITY THOUGH NOT NECESSARILY THE REVERSE

People like to work for winners…those companies and managers who are on the rise. Most employees and bosses would rather be liked than disliked. There is a wealth of information by industrial psychologists that correlates liking work (and people) to performance. The literature lauds the "participative," "understanding," "empathetic," "supportive" manager.

WHY SOME OF US ARE HIGHLY MOTIVATED WORKERS

The question posed is relative to productivity and results, not just "like" and "love." A National Science Foundation supported study[1] investigated worker motivation, productivity and job satisfaction by examining over 300 behavioral science studies published in the United States. They concluded:

- …the key to having workers who are satisfied and productive is *motivation*, that is, arousing and maintaining the will to work effectively — having workers who are productive not because they are coerced but because they are committed."

- "Of all of the factors which help to create highly motivated/highly satisfied workers, the principal one appears to be that effective performance be recognized and rewarded — in whatever terms are

[1]Katzell, R.A.: Yankelovich, D.; Fein, M.; Ornati, O.A., Nash, A., *Work, Productivity, and Job Satisfaction.* The Psychological Corporation, New York, 1975.

meaningful to the individual, be it financial or psychological or both."

Mitchell Fein, one of the nation's leading consultants on improving productivity and "father" of the Improshare Plan, has often stated "When babies are born there is no "M" (for manager) or "W" (for worker) on the bottom of their feet. They are human beings who have the drives for basic types of fulfillment, including job security, recognition, financial rewards, etc."

Can a worker and a manager produce for a boss who is a graduate of the Idi Amin School of Management? Can basic motivation drives be maintained in an adversary relationship? Can an arbitrary, dogmatic and autocratic boss motivate by recognizing and rewarding in a meaningful way?

The jury is still out, but an increasing number of reports indicate that worker motivational requirements, which create commitment, may be in place despite a manager's semi-dictatorial style. If this is so, then a manager who adopts the aggressive management style need not impinge on the productivity of his or her employees, as long as the basic element of motivation and meaningful recognition exists.

RESULTS ARE MORE IMPORTANT THAN MERE EFFORT

Most of us were told in our youth, "Work hard and you'll be a success." Polls are conducted at various times to show the 10 to 16 hours a day worked by successful business and political leaders. The nine-to-five manager or worker is made to feel guilty.

This concept of long hours equated to success would have more validity if it were also related to results. You can spend one hour writing a report or two, but who reads it and takes significant action? You can spend two hours at a meeting and then work two extra hours to develop an innovative idea in the evening.

In the aggressive management style, one realizes that time is an asset just as talent, patents, buildings and the trade name. The purpose of this realization is to understand that, just as it is poor management to waste materials, it is just as devastating to waste the time asset. Chapters 6 and 7 will develop the AMS approach to time management in more detail, but a simple example will illustrate the above-stated philosophy.

WHAT IS UNDERSTOOD IS MORE
IMPORTANT THAN WHAT YOU MEANT

One of the key tasks of anyone in business is related to communications. You soon learn it is more important to worry about what is understood than what you meant, what is read rather than what you wrote and what is heard rather than what you said.

In most office situations one of the key communication devices is the letter, the memo, the report and the directive. Word processing concepts have changed some organizations by providing a new kind of typing pool with more expensive typewriters. The communication documents are created, corrected and reproduced in a much more efficient manner than heretofore.

THE ROUGH DRAFT SYNDROME

To be truly effective communicators in the time management sense requires most people to overcome the rough draft syndrome. In practice, the creator of the document either dictates to a machine or a secretary, or writes a longhand draft. By my personal poll, of over 4,000 secretaries that I have trained in 12 years for Clemson, Rutgers, North Carolina State and for national and international training groups, less than 5 percent of the secretaries stated that their bosses had ever received training or knew how to give dictation! This, alone, will perpetuate the rough draft syndrome.

This syndrome involves the potential communicator being fully aware that everything created has a second or even a third chance at being changed. All reports, letters, etc. can easily be changed with self-correcting typewriters; whole paragraphs can be inserted, rearranged or removed. But what about the document creator? He or she has to read and rewrite more than once.

If the source of the document, the creator, can conceive of performing the communications act *once*, it can make this act much more effective. Learning to give dictation takes four hours of training, much experience and an attitude of, "I'll try to do it *once,* correctly." One learns sentence and paragraph structuring, space visualization and an awareness of the limitations imposed on the reproducer. The reward may be 90 percent or more of all pages reproduced actually going out as originally dictated.

In the aggressive management style, one looks at results achieved as the criteria for success, and effort as an effectively measured tool to achieve it.

SEPARATING EXPERIENCE FROM SENIORITY

About 20 years ago I was working in a steel fabrication plant. While observing a cold rolling of steel plate, I stated to the president standing alongside of me, "Why don't they use the reverse pass as a forming roll?"

This meant instead of 10 forward forming passes, it was possible to use five forward and five reverse passes to achieve the desired shape.

The president's reply was, "I've got 40 years' experience in this field and never thought of that." My response was to point out that 40 years' seniority was not 40 years' experience, since experience connoted new happenings, new insights, etc. A bus driver with 40 years on the job has 40 years' seniority plus six months' experiences repeated 80 times.

If you are exposed to new events and handle them, you gain experience; if you conceive of new ideas based on analyses, even if the idea fails, you have gained experience. However, the repetition of a single accepted event does not add to your wealth of experience.

The above should give a ray of hope to the newer or junior members of our business community. You should not assume that all practices, that have been in existence for long periods of time, have been thoroughly examined for the ultimate improvement. In utilizing the aggressive management style, the better discipline is to question both the new and the tried and true. In chapter 11, some approaches to proper presentation, using AMS, will be covered.

CHOOSING THE RIGHT MANAGEMENT TOOL FROM A BAGFUL OF TECHNIQUES

Many years ago, Warren Alberts who was a vice-president at United Airlines, gave a speech entitled "Techniques Looking for Problems." In this speech he had insightful comments on the purveyors of all sorts of management techniques, who were more interested in selling a particular technique than they were in solving a particular problem.

I remember Warren saying, "If you tell them your roof is leaking, they try to sell you white paint; if you say you want green, they tell you white is a better color. All the while, your roof is still leaking!"

I feel exactly the same way each Christmas while putting together toys for the children. In the department store, the demonstration bicycle looks marvelous. However, you are sent home with a very small box and instructions, sometimes in a foreign language, on how to assemble same. A neighbor of mine believes it is the Japanese revenge for Hiroshima!

Part way through the assembly, I reach a point where the expansion bolt in the steering column is to be added. (For the uninitiated, this bolt passes through the handlebars and into the front wheel collar in the front of the main frame...understand?) After placing this bolt in position, you are required to tap it into place. At this juncture, I ask my 5, 7, 9 or 13-year-old to go into the basement and retrieve a device for this particular operation.

Within minutes, one of my youngsters arrives with a screwdriver! As I start to describe the function of a screwdriver, the child deftly turns the instrument around and starts beating on the steering column expansion bolt with the handle end of the screwdriver.

Sure it works, but surely not as efficiently as a hammer. Many tools can do a job but a key philosophy of AMS is to choose the right one. Therefore, one must know the tools available.

AMS will not be effective in the hands of a practitioner who knows only a few tools of the trade. I am amazed at how many office managers have not studied or even heard of word processing, and how many inventory controllers haven't the foggiest notion of what MRP, capacity planning and shop floor controls are about. There are personnel people who are not versed in motivational plans from flexitime to Scanlon, from compensatory time to Improshare. And how many plant and production managers are unacquainted with true productivity measures?

Whatever your discipline, it is important to achieve credibility by having at least a cursory knowledge of the techniques available to solve your problems. Not having this knowledge may mean you are "using the handle end of the screwdriver to drive in steering bolts." Not knowing the tools available is tantamount to rejecting them, and accepting your present methods is like saying they are the best of what you know to be available.

DEVISING OBJECTIVES TO MATCH COMPLETED ACTIONS

Lawrence M. Mathews, a former partner of mine and a famous lecturer and author in the field of budgeting and cost analysis, was involved on an assignment with me that reached its culmination at a meeting that began at 9:00 a.m. one day and was still going on at 2:00 a.m. the next. Hard and far-reaching decisions were being made based on Larry's recommendations, but at about midnight weariness was creeping over all of us. Since we were attendees, not the hosts of this meeting, we sat it out with the rest, taking mental and physical breaks when possible.

A probing question was asked as the new day arrived and Larry promptly gave a lucid and clearly-structured answer that lasted a full five minutes. Except, it had nothing to do with the question. As Larry finished, the questioner stared, as did the group. I leapt into the fray with a comment that has since been repeatedly played back to me in that company, "Larry gave a great answer, so let's not lose it. Now, does anyone have a question to fit this marvelous answer?"

Ludicrous as the above may sound to the reader, a common practice to avoid is related to the above story. Not only must you be able to choose the right tool from a bagful of techniques, but you should never be caught looking for a problem that fits your solution. This seems to occur when we become so wrapped up in our "terrific idea" that we become blind to criticism and start to match objectives to our completed actions.

FITTING ANSWERS TO THE QUESTIONS

Some further examples may drive this point home. One of my office managers bought a new collating device that collated 20 percent faster than our previous one. I questioned the need for this expenditure (after it was made) and the office manager couldn't understand why he wasn't being praised instead of questioned. He listened as I explained that although a faster collator was desirable it was not an economic gain. I knew that, although the reproduction machine was used 40 percent of the time, the collator was used less than 5 percent of the total time. On that basis, a 20 percent improvement on 5 percent was equal to 1 percent of total time. Also on that basis, a 10-year usage would be required to justify the additional expenditure for the faster collator.

My office manager proceeded to tell me of the lower maintenance costs, the nicer appearance and even about uplifting morale in the office by showing "them" that "we cared." The user of AMS will recognize that a trap to avoid is defending an action by seeking objectives after the fact.

When you are on the defensive, it is difficult to be objective, to approach the logic of your questioner with appropriate answers. Devising objectives to match completed actions will more often than not put you on the defensive.

In chapter 5, an approach to analyzing and bringing ideas to fruition will be discussed. This will keep you on the offensive. As in the Japanese game *GO,* it creates the only chance to "win the game."

AMS MUST RELATE TO ACCEPTABLE
MANAGEMENT FUNCTIONS

The following chapters will discuss AMS, not as a technique unto itself, but as a series of aggressive management actions to help you perform your present management functions. To have an aggressive management style in a vacuum can never be as effective as when practiced to complement the time-proven management skills in any enterprise.

Therefore, AMS will be described as relative to such accepted practices as:

- Planning...for successful action.
- Reporting...for purposes of reaction.

- Review…as a prelude to management control.
- Decision-making…including aggressive risk analysis.
- Problem-solving…with emphasis on where to work (prioritizing).
- Communicating…stressing how understanding leads to meaningful actions.
- Delegation…relative to obstacles within *us*.
- Organizing…lifting implied restrictions of authority.
- Managing Your Personal Office…the desk as a workplace.
- Meetings…fewer and more productive.

There are many accepted management functions that would be too numerous to list here (from directing and/or leading others, to telephone procedures, to working with your secretary) but the purpose of the following pages is to cover as many as pertinent that could be affected by the aggressive management style.

WHAT ABOUT YOU?

Can you test the water without submitting to total immersion, or even drowning? Can you conduct a sample test before committing your present style to a complete overhaul? I believe so.

Start with a concept of your commitment to the goals of pay increases and promotions. Then, select those AMS ideas that

- Relate to existing and known problems.
- Are comfortable for you to adopt with little extra effort.
- Can result in trackable positive improvements.
- Concern the "movers and shakers" in your organization.

Remember, the aggressive management style is just that — a style. Aggressiveness in management style does not require an alteration of personality or dress code. It is a group of attack techniques: simulating the ownership of the enterprise, evaluating the probability of success, converting problems to opportunities, understanding that results are more important than effort, separating experience from seniority, choosing and knowing the right management tools, avoiding determination of objectives to meet completed actions and many, many more. Only you can determine if the results will be worth your effort, but there is plenty of room for small successes and partial accomplishments.

2

IMPROVED MANAGERIAL
PLANNING USING AMS

If you appreciate the rationale I have presented in the previous chapter, you realize that the aggressive management style conforms to the functions normally undertaken by all managers. You should therefore first examine the major management function of *planning*. Within the following pages I will discuss aspects of planning from ways to finding time to plan, to making plans to improve activities, to controlling the results.

As a manager, you must convince yourself that you have time to plan and time to improve your plans. Some companies and governmental institutions spend more time massaging history — smoothing over the past — than finding ways to do things better in the future. You will learn some alternatives, some aggressive planning practices. You will discover that planning without controls is a waste of time, and you will find out how to utilize a simple object like your own desk to practice day-to-day planning improvement.

Using the aggressive management style, you will discover that the highest form of improvement is elimination of the unnecessary, which should always be considered before anything else. You will learn two approaches that will overcome inaction: start in the middle, and overcome all possible objections.

Finally, we will look at *you*, and you will find out why you tend to procrastinate in making plans and, of course, how you can overcome this problem.

LOOKING AT THE FUNCTIONS OF TOMORROW'S MANAGER

Daniel Yankelovich, an insightful interpreter of the American work scene and contributor to *Work in America: The Decade Ahead*[1] wrote in "The New Psychological Contracts at Work" in the May 1978 issue of *Psychology Today:*

"The workplace in America is among the most conservative of our institutions. It has been highly resistant to change, particularly to the successive waves of individualism that have swept over so many other areas in American life. To be sure, at the stratospheric levels of giant corporations, trade unions, government bureaucracies, hospitals and other institutions, individualism flowers for top-level executives. In these great baronies of our society, the self fulfillment needs of those at the top are given full play; but all other employees are expected to conform to rigid rules of group behavior...

In the future, knowledge of how the changed American value system affects incentives and motivations to work hard may well become a key requirement for entering the ranks of top management in both the private and the public sector. If this occurs, we shall see a new breed of managers to correspond to the new breed of employees."

BETTER PLANNING IS TODAY'S REQUIREMENT

Some middle managers can gain the recognition they require by an aggressive practice of the accepted managerial tools of *today*. It would be difficult to find a top manager who would not recognize a middle manager properly practicing the tools of his or her trade, such as routine and emergency planning of the corporate resources, including personal time. Knowledge of human management must be coupled with a knowledge of work management.

For this reason, this chapter emphasizes techniques using the aggressive management style in practicing the most rudimentary management function of planning. Regardless of the wave of the 1980s which will affect the New

---

[1]Van Nostrand Reinhold, edited by Kerr & Rosow, 1978.

Breed Manager's motivational practices, today's manager, as well as tomorrow's, must be an able and recognized planner.

"I DON'T HAVE TIME TO PLAN"

The "clerk" approach to work is just to dig in, sort it out and get it done. And, there are times when this is the only managerial course of action you can take. But, the frustration of seeing the work to be done as a bottomless pit is a most exasperating experience for many managers. These workaholics wind up working longer days, needing more help, offices at home, faster jets, before and after-hours meetings and weekend tapings with resulting spouseless marriages.

B. C. Forbes, of the famous Forbes family, stated in a March, 1977 "Thoughts on the Business Life" section:

"The most successful, highest-up executives carefully select under-studies. They don't strive to do everything themselves. They train and trust others. This leaves them foot-free, mind-free, with time to think. They have time to receive important callers, to pay worthwhile visits. They have time for their families. No matter how able, any employer or executive who in-sists on running a one-man enterprise courts unhappy circumstances when his powers dwindle."

One of the oft-heard cries of despair from executives is, "Delegate? To whom? By the time I tell George what is wanted, I can do it myself. I don't have time to delegate." Yet one of the first steps in planning is to ask, "Why me? Who else but me should be preparing the plan?" In chapter 7 this approach is covered in some detail.

THE "ONLY I!" TO "WHY ME?"
LOOK AT MANAGERIAL TASKS

Two simple tests which I have administered for more than two decades of executive training, may aid you. The first is to put a three column paper on your desk and use it as follows:

1. Label the columns:
    a. "Sample Activity"
    b. "Only *I*" — Make sure you underline the "*I*"
    c. "Others — Specify"
2. At random times (not necessarily so you can establish a statistically reliable sample, but at intervals more closely related to the selection of comfortable observation times, such as say, ten times a day, or at the *start* of any new task, such as answering a letter, placing a call, seeing a visitor,) write down in column "a" a few descriptive words to define the activity.

3. Now, *very honestly* place a check in either column "b" or "c" (or sometimes in both). You will have to *really* mean it when you check the "Only *I*" column. If you check the "Others" column, be sure to "Specify" who else can perform the task.

For an investment of five minutes a day, you will be looking at an analysis of yourself, and your organization, relative to two very important management planning principles: possible delegation of the planning activity and selection, training (or lack of same) of your employees regarding the planning function.

In *My Years With General Motors,* Alfred P. Sloan made a telling point. He had required that no one could be promoted without an able assistant ready to fill his or her shoes. He felt this forced executives at G.M. to place a very high priority on training their replacements for no other reason than to enable their own personal promotions to occur. Obviously the planning skills are taught by more than mere osmosis or filtering techniques.

The famous Cornelius MacGillicudy of the old Philadelphia Athletics (Connie Mack to most) stated, "The first thing any man has to know is how to handle himself. Training counts. You can't win any game unless you are ready to win." He was referring primarily to physical conditioning, but the proper attitude toward work and work habits can be just as fruitful for the office executive as for the professional athlete. Analyzing delegation, training subordinates and prioritization are some managerial preparatory "push-ups."

There is a veritable pyramid of books on management planning, but the worthy ones start by asking, "Why are *you* doing it?" If the answer is "Who else?", start looking at "Why me?" Remember, elimination of a task is the highest form of improvement.

Obviously, if you are a "one man band", beating the drum while cymbals clash at your knees, the sweet potato is pressed to your lips and the marimbas are tied to your toes, the question of "Who else?" seems ridiculous. Your answer will be, "If not me, no one!"

THE 30 SECOND TEST FOR
IMPROVING YOUR PLANNING

The second "quickie" test relates to the above. Let me describe how I have administered this to large groups, because the results of thousands of individuals may be much more dramatic.

In my "Executive Time Management" seminars, which I have conducted for the past 20 years at continuing education seminars for universities, at in-company training sessions and for such groups as Advanced

Management Research (AMR), I am addressing between 20 and 80 people from heterogeneous backgrounds. They are unknown to each other, so that peer pressure is minimized.

I cite the following rules:

- "When you believe 30 seconds have elapsed after I have struck this podium, raise your hand...and hold it up. If you get tired, rest it on someone's shoulder."

- "You are not to look at your watch, to count or to take your pulse. The lapse of 30 seconds is to be perceived, not counted."

I then remain silent. Hands start popping up at 10 seconds, about one-half the hands are up at 15 seconds, three-quarters at 20 seconds and almost all at 30 seconds. Those who have their hands up early look around self-consciously and wonder why the others don't. For those readers who have attended my sessions, there is always the group of disbelievers who cannot comprehend how long 30 seconds really is.

The point I then make is that 30 seconds is long enough to allow the listener to ask before starting any task:

- Who should be working on this?
- Why is it being done?
- When should it be done?
- What method should be employed?
- Where can this be accomplished?
- How much time or money is involved approximately? etc., etc., etc.

The next time you have a planning task, take 30 seconds, and ask:

- Why me?
- Why now?

You may find, as countless others have, that 30 seconds is a much longer time than you envisioned. You can ask some probing questions and you may find a better way than the clerk approach of merely plowing in, sorting it out and doing it. Remember, if you start 20 management actions a day (and probably 40 percent of them are of a planning nature), the 30 second test requires 10 minutes a day. If you don't have that, then you *really* don't have time to plan!

WHO CHOOSES THE PROPER PRIORITY?

Finally, a question of priority always exists. For those of you who have absolutely no one or no organization to use for support, setting priorities is one of the most important approaches to planning. At any given time, the task which you work on apparently has a higher priority than any other task; otherwise, why are you working on it?

Dr. Vincent G. Reuter of Arizona State University states in his speeches on time management, "Efficient personal time management requires both a drive to be more effective and the self-discipline to maintain a schedule of priorities. Unfortunately, when anxiety and stress occur, we tend to neglect the more important items and retreat to the more familiar and less taxing, less important items, where we bury ourselves in detail."

In practicing the aggressive management style, the planning function is of paramount importance, but the first question is, "Why me?" For those who question having the time to plan, I suggest you analyze your concept of time or, more exactly, how much planning, direction and delegation can be performed in even 30 seconds. Finally, prioritization requires a look at how you choose a particular job to be performed at a particular time. In the words of Plato, "Nothing is more unworthy of a wise man, or ought to trouble him more, than to have allowed more time for trifling, and useless things, than they deserved."

OVERCOMING FIRST-PAGE PARALYSIS

I remember an editor of a major publishing house asking me to deliver a chapter of a book. "But," he added, "not the *first* one...preferably a middle chapter so that we can get the flavor of your writing." Aside from the rationale behind this request as he perceived it, this is a helpful technique in the aggressive management style called the "start-in-the-middle" approach.

Many of us are intimidated by a blank piece of paper staring at us or a tape machine with the "record" button depressed. "What's a good beginning? Shall I use an outline? Where do I begin?"

Years ago, I taught myself an approach that I use in preparing an outline. I start with what I know well, what I feel comfortable with, what I have a firm, definite opinion about or where my research, charts, etc. are complete. I "start-in-the-middle."

Literature is full of marvelous advice on how to state your objective, outline your approach, or summarize your conclusions or recommendations. Good advice! But as a human being who fights the natural tendencies of disorderliness each and every day, it is not that helpful when I stare at my recording device's speaker...speechless, alone and feeling a bit helpless.

If it's a request for an analysis and conclusion, I write down the analyses I feel are pertinent to a not yet completely stated objective. If in a later statement of the objective, the analysis is not as pertinent as I first thought, I will reject the analysis. But for the time being, I have *started*!

There are times when I have back-up data, appendices and charts that I feel are *absolutely* going to be in a particular report. I prepare these first, leaving off page numbers to be added during the final collation. Again, I have *started!*

STOP MISSING DUE DATES

There is a side advantage to the "start-in-the-middle" technique, which is that it may help you meet deadlines. Many years ago I had a secretary in the Pan Am Building in New York who was a model of what today would be called an administrative assistant. She had tremendous mental and mechanical skills that belied her advanced age. Yet *we* would miss important due dates.

We decided at one of our "rap sessions" that the problem was more *me* than *her.* She indicated that my dumping all the work required for the first of the month on her desk on the *last* day of the previous month was a more diabolical trick than Dr. No ever envisaged. Yet she knew that portions of the reports and other materials were completed and in my possession.

I remember her poignant request, "Please, *please* give me your completed portions in advance. I'll prepare them without page numbers for later collation. Give me your 'middles'," she pleaded! I wasn't the least offended to discover she was referring to my work, not my body. I have no actual numbers to quote, but after a period of time we felt that my "middles" were giving us a head start on meeting due dates more frequently than before. This same approach can help you feed materials to a word processing group that suffers from underloads and overloads not related to *your* needs and due dates.

AN ALTERNATIVE TO MASSAGING HISTORY

You next need an AMS approach that can help you to move, not to limit your managing by company tradition. The aggressive manager does not confine himself to established routines. In the aggressive management style, that which "is" or "was" is a base for improvement, not the cement that binds you to what is or was. Your job is not to massage past actions. This is not a revolutionary cry to disregard history, but an exhortive call to use base data for future improvement.

President Jimmy Carter, when governor of Georgia, was sold on such an approach to the budgetary approval process. For example, he required his Commissioner of Highways to apply a zero-based budgetary approach to the Georgia Department of Highways. The commissioner had to prepare his budget from the view of the services to be performed, not as a mere extrapolation of the previous year's expenditures. The idea was to break the mold of merely adding to the past, thereby assuming that the past was a model of how things should be in the future.

.   AMS can help you overcome the barrier associated with the comment, "We've always done it that way!" Some examples of using this approach follow.

BIRTH AND DEATH CONTROLS IN PLANNING

When planning any sort of project, always include a scenario for killing it. Obviously, this sets up a control in the planning phase. Resist studying the details of any proposed project until carefully probing why it's needed at all.

A shining example of the aforementioned is in the birth-to-death concept of zero-based budgeting. This approach changes budget-making from a mere extrapolation of what has gone before.

Suppose a department head reports to you by going over last year's numbers and explains why he or she needs more money to improve his or her operation next year. Don't waste too much time questioning the figures. Instead, ask, "Why does that department exist at all? What is the value of the service provided?" If the conclusion is positive, then consider the proposed figures in light of these conclusions.

Likewise, everybody knows how to buy. In some companies, procurement of supplies is a knee-jerk reaction. There isn't nearly enough emphasis on reworking product needs or getting rid of what isn't needed. Scrapping, resale and re-use should be an *ongoing* function in your company, instead of a once-a-year writedown after taking inventory. Can you foster such an aggressive management decisiveness for both the death and birth of the inventory asset?

Most companies have very specific and well-defined hiring policies but only a few have clear-cut *dehiring* practices. How do you get rid of an employee? Is it a practice that can improve the work environment for yourself or others? No policy is also a policy!

If you have an incompetent employee, one who isn't doing the job by *your* criteria, is it easier to hire another employee to help the one that "can't cut the mustard?" Would laying off an incompetent, tardy or insolent employee establish your position with your superiors? Or does it just make good business sense?

Too often two reasons exist for retaining the incompetent:

1. It's easier...less confrontation.
2. The employee has been around for quite a while.

I am not advocating that dehiring is an *only* and desirable solution to your personnel problems. But it should be *one* of your alternatives...along with training, retraining, rap sessions, communicating an expressed interest, transfer, etc.

EXAMPLE OF A BETTER HIRING PRACTICE

An upper Midwest company has an interesting approach. Management recognized that the incompetent employee usually gets by the three to six month probationary, new-hire period and then becomes the tenured employee primarily because:

1. There is no pressure on the superior to dehire the under-achiever during the probationary period, and,
2. After a long period of time, dehiring a long-tenure employee is considered inhumane.

They installed two programs which immensely helped the aggressive managers. First, the decision to retain an employee must be faced after six months with a new hire and annually with *every single* employee. This is done on the evaluation form, where instead of skirting the issue, the following appears:

"Should the employee be retained in your employ? If *Yes* is indicated, a 15 percent or more increase must be granted. If *No* is your reply, contact the Personnel office immediately for dehiring or transfer remedies to commence."

Before the reader visualizes an army of overpaid employees, let me state that this company works in a tightly-controlled budgetary atmosphere. More importantly, think of the competent (and well-paid) group that is fostered.

The second part of their overall plan is a very active dehiring placement program. Company officials estimate that one-third of their personnel budget, including consultants, is to augment the "golden handshake" — providing worthwhile employment elsewhere for dehired employees. How much are you willing to spend to have a vigorous, finely-tuned work force?

EXAMINE THE SOURCE BEFORE DEALING WITH THE EFFECT

Before instituting costly procedures to overcome a problem, examine the source of the problem. Perhaps it stems from another procedure that could simply be eliminated. Companies are like governments; they have more rules than they can possibly enforce. It took a ten-year study to codify federal law, rules and regulations, and we're just a little over 200 years old as a nation!

Do you have various rules defining acceptable practices? Does manufacturing interpret tolerances differently than engineering and sales? Would your customers accept that which you are presently rejecting? Is there an inconsistency in approving expenditures?

I once worked in an Eastern Ohio company with stringent rules on the purchase of capital equipment. Any item over $5,000 had to receive approval from the Capital Equipment Budgetary group, which met every quarter.

In that same company, a junior executive could buy inventory items for the shelves in excess of proscribed amounts, with no more reason than because he felt it was the right thing to do. If a stockout occurred, he would purchase $10-20,000 of additional goods to make sure it didn't happen again, with nothing more than routine approval required.

Is this possible in your firm? If it is, this problem creates an opportunity for the aggressive manager to solve a visible management dilemma and obvious problem...diverse rules for controlling assets.

Ideally, the same people who buy equipment should be responsible for reviewing it for eventual replacement or removal. This is a test of objectivity in requesting the use of the entity's funds.

Assume a paper collator is used 15 percent of the time in conjunction with the reproduction device, which is used 45 percent of the time. What is the true value of buying a collator that works 25 percent faster? What about the new overhead projector that everyone wanted and *needed* last year, but which has been out-of-service for the past four months? Should we fix it or get rid of it? Again, no decision is a decision to retain it. If you had to buy it today, would you? You don't even want to take the route of simple repair. All capital expenditure decisions should be open to question as the course of events changes a situation. No review is also a review.

SOME TRAPS TO AVOID

There are some traps for the AMS practitioner. One is trying to live up to a schedule that, for whatever reason, apparently cannot be met. Impossibility is the death bed of AMS heroes. Intelligence, coupled with valor, will avoid posthumous awards to managers who attack windmills with lances.

The more sophisticated among you will have a tendency to become too involved in complex techniques and methods of problem-solving without stopping to ask whether the problem still exists or is relevant to the cost of the *solution.* This occurs when too much time and costs are spent on inspection and policing procedures. Over 20 years ago, I worked in a life insurance company that spent $10,000 a month to solve a $3,000 per month problem!

Finally, when reviewing plans, always ask for an evaluation of downside risk. Consider the "what ifs...?" Try not to be so committed to a plan that you lose sight of how to separate from it.

ELIMINATION IS THE HIGHEST
FORM OF IMPROVEMENT

That statement was made to me over 25 years ago by Dr. Marvin E. Mundel, one of our nation's leading contributors to the field of industrial engineering. It calls for using a back hoe before a teaspoon to remove dirt, and ultimately asking, "Why are we removing this dirt here and now?"

There are many, many parallels in applying AMS to work planning. We already discussed the questions, "Why am I doing this planning?" and "Why now?" The question before us now is, "Why are we even doing this?"

I have not listed this question first, as well I might have, because, as corporate wage slaves, this may be a rude and discourteous question. It may be difficult to ask your boss, who has called you into his office, "Why are we meeting?" Or, after reading a newly issued agency directive, whip back a memo to the chief asking, "Is this directive necessary?" The employment-wanted sections of the newspapers must be filled with practitioners of *these* approaches.

Yet, innovative questions concerning elimination can always be asked tactfully within our domain. When the effects are recognized, you may then be ready to suggest some improvements to your superiors. The evolutionary process involves pilot testing an idea, tracking and reporting gains, and then selling applications to others.

Paul Le Haye, a leading combustion engineer in the United States and president of Hague International, used a meeting elimination idea during his years as a junior engineering executive. This involved a simple approach to justification for calling high-priced technical people to a meeting. The person calling the meeting had to state the objective of the meeting...not merely to say, "It's the weekly meeting!" All meetings had to have a specific objective(s) justifying the expenditure of the time of his engineers.

Paul figures that 15 to 20 percent of the usually held meetings were eliminated in his department. He also had a meeting substitution list which included such alternatives as: conference call, memo and individual informal meetings. The purpose of listing alternatives was to alert the meeting caller to less costly options. The object of this exercise was to have the meeting caller prove an objective or use an alternative means of communication and decision-making.

During the Korean conflict, I was Chief of Management Engineering Services for the U.S. Army Ordnance Corps in the Pentagon. I observed a seven man-month project to develop a coolant for the medium tank's shock absorbers. The final decision was to eliminate the shock absorbers, which meant the coolant project (the teaspoon) was wiped out by the elimination of the shock absorbers (the steamshovel). A clever reader may think of eliminating the medium tank and so on up the line, including the Department of Defense and the Commander-in-Chief. But, that's the point!

Think "upstream" in planning. Think of elimination of the overriding task; think objectives before improving an action; think alternates; think of delegation, if possible. These are some examples of using AMS in your planning function.

DOING IT NOW BEATS PLANNING TO DO IT

A popular management theory of the 1950s, which was taught to thousands of staff and line managers during that era, was called "Completed Staff Work." The whiz kids at Ford, MacNamara at Defense, and Rickover at Navy all had a hand in refining the significance of staff work brought to completion. As a growing number of personnel became analyzers and advisors to line management functions, a credo was developed to define execution, where persons other than the recommenders performed the final acts. Reports were a means, not an end, unto themselves.

An interesting sidelight of this approach related to aspects of planning as performed at your desk. It was calculated that 75 percent of the tasks coming to your "In" box could be handled immediately. I tested this advice and found it was correct if one could define the word "immediately."

If "immediately" meant within a reasonable period of time, say less than half a day, then this rule was perfectly applicable to my activity and perhaps yours. I found I could reduce planning time (or waiting to plan time) by categorizing the "immediately" label as follows:

1. *Immediately* means do it now, sign it, read it, file it, toss it, or delegate it. Included in this category is anything I could speed read to classify. I have difficulty using speed reading for understanding complicated analyses, but find it to be an invaluable tool for work classification. If I

don't speed read to classify, I may be putting off information of immediate need because "I didn't get around to it yet."

2. *Children's hour* includes items of a little longer duration, such as a letter that needs some information development for reply, a memo requiring a weighing of factors to reach a decision, a tactful response, or none, to a sensitive personnel problem. The children's hour work will be handled sometime in the next 24 hours, during a work week. It is a folder on my desk that I attack during either my creative times of the day or during enforced waiting times...waiting to see someone, waiting for someone's meeting to start (not mine), during travel or other times of forced idleness.

A company in New York City is an amazing institution to visit because a host of people walk around the office with hand carried folders. The managers carry their "children's hour" folders with them as they walk about the offices and work on the contents during forced idleness while away from their desks!

3. *To do* covers the projects to be planned — those long term commitments that require dates of completion (milestones) and much more preparation than for a "children's hour" task that can be completed during the next 24 hours. Preparation of action "To Do" cards and the aggressive use of a "tickler file" will be covered in some detail in chapter 6.

By so classifying work received, I have either forced "work" to eliminate "planning to do it," or have at least performed an immediate categorization (priority) and scheduling of the task. "Do it now" is an especially effective technique for those of you who travel a great deal of the time which necessitates a large amount of work to be done, sorted and/or delegated upon your return. Categorizing it first can help.

THE DESK IS A WORKPLACE

A well-organized work area is a definite aid to the aggressive style manager. It bespeaks efficiency or, at least, action orientation. Now, I know office maintenance requires most managers to clean up their work areas each night, which may mean dumping everything into a file cabinet when the work day ends. But what about during the work day?

I always find it difficult to get executives to admit that their disorganized desks contribute to inefficiency of operation. Their reply is, "I can find it if it's on top of my desk...somewhere." I have seen managers use tables instead of desks so that all materials are exposed on the table top. Some do not use "In" or "Out" boxes to avoid piles of nonhomogeneous matter, feeling safer if every subject is exposed.

There are those whose desks are so cluttered, they use additional surface area behind them, at what is jokingly called "the reference table." If the reference table gets too crowded with material, bridges are built connecting the desk with the reference table. Ultimately, I envision the disappearance of some managers behind their desks, their reference tables and their bridges...last seen wearing a pith helmet, leading a safari in search of some lost (or hidden) paper or file.

A caution here...I have a prejudice about dealing with any stock broker or commodities analyst with a cluttered desk. It could cost you your wallet if an execution of a "stop-loss" or "buy" is lost on his or her desk. In some areas, a cluttered desk can be downright dangerous...financially speaking.

Most executives probably do have the ability of rapid recall. But why rely on it? After all, would that same manager, let's say in a pharmaceutical firm, allow the employee's work area to be so cluttered and disorganized? In the aggressive management style, if we are seeking positive actions from and through others, a good example is expected of us. Would you trust a surgeon with shaking hands as you would an auto mechanic with dirty fingernails? How would you react to an executive exhorting you to become organized, if he or she cannot find last week's directive? Think how frustrated you feel when your ideas are lost on your boss's desk!

WHY SOME EXECUTIVES HAVE CLUTTERED DESKS

Aside from the appearance of inefficiency, a cluttered desk sometimes gives the appearance of:

- procrastination
- indecision
- personal disorganization
- confusion of priorities

In actual practice, I have found three major problems that symbolize or partially relate to the cluttered desk:

1. An inability to delegate. This occurs when that which *could* have been delegated, upon receipt, has now been on the manager's desk for so long that *only* the manager can work on it. It is too late to delegate. See chapter 7 for an expansion of this problem discussion.

2. An inability to complete work. If you keep starting work, putting it aside and starting something else, on more than on an exception basis, you are either very understaffed, unable to schedule yourself for a majority of your work or the recipient of...

3. Frequent interruptions. Now, I believe that interruptions are part of business life. Only academicians, who have never held a managerial job but who are management consultants, will tell you that you should be able to eliminate interruptions. In chapter 3, we will be covering the control of interruptions, which I believe is an accomplishable task, but never the elimination of interruptions.

The straw to break the camel's back is when the overworked executive, with the cluttered desk, has employees working at a much more leisurely pace, during much shorter hours and with much neater desks. No manager likes to be called "stupid" by his or her employees, even if only by inference.

THE ORGANIZED WORKPLACE

What would be an organized workplace and what would it look like for an AMS manager? Well, the desk should be a workplace, depending upon what your job entails. A manager who lives by the telephone should have a console arrangement for both communications and rapid information retrieval. An executive who primarily delegates and then reviews the work of others should have a desk top for analysis, comparison and face-to-face discussion. If personal interviewing is your game, a work area for inconspicuous note-taking and observation is desirable. Frankly, the options are too numerous to even consider; but, if the desk is a workplace, design it for the primary work to be performed.

Let me describe my desk, not as the only way to go, but as an example that may provide some ideas for the reader.

I have an oversize top on my desk because my projects require me to spread work around me for reference. For this reason, I do not have an "In" or "Out" box *on* my desk. They are dugouts in my desk, and when covered, the covers become part of the desk top.

There is no phone *on* my desk. I have a wall phone mounted on the side of my desk with the tape dialer and speaker on an adjacent wall shelf.

The oversize desk top allows for small conferences with three to four people around my desk, since the overhang allows for table-like sitting. There are no other objects or memorabilia on my desk. My desk is my workplace. At the conclusion of any task or meeting, and of course, at the end of the day, my desk is cleared.

All current projects are in folders — expansion folders for the larger projects and vinyl packets for the largest. They are in my right hand file drawer. Completed folders are put in the company files.

Only my secretary can place or remove items from my "In" or "Out" boxes. She examines them two to three times an hour. I use my "Out" box to communicate with her and the outside world. This beats jumping up and down to go to her desk, buzzing her or, even worse, shouting instructions around the wall. I do all of these silly things sometimes, but *only* on an exception basis for a "hot" requirement. A majority of my needs can be covered by the two to three pickups per hour from my "Out" box by my secretary. Of course, this requires a routinized instruction sheet to handle routine explanations of who gets copies, when it is due, and if it is confidential. This approach will be covered in detail in chapter 6.

My "In" box is not for "Hold." Materials for future work by me, or delegation, are disposed of by actions heretofore described. That is, if I classify the item "Immediate," it is worked on "Now." The children's hour folder gets some, and some become "To Do" projects. The "In" box, therefore, is emptied in a matter of minutes. The results of this effort are:

- immediate action, or delegation, of some items
- rapid sorting of work to be performed at a future date. (See discussion of the tickler file in chapter 6.)
- immediate scheduling of all work. Remember, scheduling is nothing more than time-phased planning, so an unscheduled task is really an unplanned task.

The aggressive management style looks at your workplace as a means of making your managerial planning, delegating and decision-making more effective. If assertiveness calls for personality and dress code changes, the least you can sacrifice in order to practice AMS is the cluttered desk.

OVERCOMING ALL POSSIBLE OBJECTIONS

In the corporate conference room of the Gillette Company, there used to hang a slogan, "If All Possible Objections Must First Be Overcome, Nothing Would Ever Be Accomplished." I copied this down about 20 years ago and sent it to the late Mr. John C. Cleaver, founder and chairman of the Aqua-Chem Corporation, and later a director of the Coca Cola company. He promptly had it printed and wall-mounted in his Milwaukee office, but with *my* name appended as the author. Let me apologize to the true author, while stating that this slogan was the cornerstone of John's philosophy of management.

Mr. Cleaver parlayed a Depression bankroll of $3,500 into a more than $100 million value to his stockholders in his lifetime by encouraging objections, but not being paralyzed by the fact that no action can be taken without *some* objections.

From my 35th birthday until the day he died (on my birthday in 1976), John would call me, sometimes just to talk about management philosophy. This wasn't just an academic exercise. He used the philosophy to back up decisions from the installation of a pay plan, to the purchase of equipment, to the acquisition of a company.

John Cleaver expected:

- his legal advisors to tell him all the pitfalls, real or potential.
- his engineers to say, "It hasn't been done yet."
- his plant managers to say, "The shipments can't be made."
- his marketing personnel to say, "We've achieved the maximum penetration."

But, these were inputs for action, not obstacles for paralysis.

Discussion, resulting in heated disagreements, were inputs. Negative progress reports were not obstacles that couldn't be overcome. The rationale for action always involved risk, but if the rewards were adequately compensable, then higher risks could be taken.

Every crap shooter knows this. The "2s" and "12s" pay between 30 and 33 to 1 odds, because the risk on each roll of the dice is 36 to 1 against you. If the return and odds are poor, you shouldn't gamble with serious monies. (In Sweden, the number payoff in roulette is 30 to 1 on a 37 to 1 opportunity.)

The aggressive management style envisages risks. The AMS manager knows there are even objections to "motherhood, God and country." No action should be deferred until *all* possible objections are first overcome, except the rare occasion when life or death is involved. (Doctors, like weathermen, will even give you probabilities of success.) Remember, no action is an action to take no action. The mark of an aggressive manager is taking action or making a decision appropriate to both the risks involved and the rewards expected.

ESTABLISHING DUE DATES IS NOT SCHEDULING

"When" something is due or wanted may be entirely independent of when it *can* be performed. Making the distinction can aid your planning.

I once was in an office in St. Louis when a secretary walked in on her boss to announce that she was leaving for the day. She produced six items the boss had required for *that day*. She announced that she'd completed four, had to leave immediately and would complete the other two in the morning prior to the boss's arrival. As she left, he gasped, "Those were the two I wanted for tonight!"

There are those among you who will say:

- "It's her fault; she should have stayed and finished them all."
- "It's the boss' fault for not telling her he *really* wanted those."
- "Don't worry. It'll get done tomorrow."

But what are the rules? Is it a matter of boss loyalty? Personal responsibility? Better communications? Pay and overtime? Personal relationships?

I believe it is a matter of basic rules, which if adhered to, do not involve "flag waving" or personality analysis. These rules are:

- Unless inferred or unimportant, all work given to your employees requires a due date. "Please get me some staples" implies compliance within an hour.
- The boss establishes the due date by decree, negotiation, or agreement with a recommendation.
- Only the boss can change a due date.
- Employees schedule themselves, by knowledge of past performance, an estimate of new work as it relates to previously performed work or a "stab in the dark."
- Employees who find out about a due date that *cannot* be met because of a lack of resources, unavailability of information, unrealistic target date, unexpected event, conflict with other work, etc., must notify their boss as soon as this is known.
- Only the boss can change a due date.

The above system works well with the rational manager and employee.

For example, I used to have a work scheduling meeting at 1:30 p.m. each day with my secretary. By that time of day, she pretty much knew where we stood and what could happen the rest of the day. All of my work is requested with a date *and* time appended thereto. (Example: "Tuesday, a.m.," or "Friday, before 3:15 p.m.") The work is supplied at various times by tape, over the phone, by work request, etc.

On any given day, the workload may be more or less than what can be accomplished to satisfy the requested due dates. If less, my secretary will so report and say Good-bye. If more work than resources available exists by her estimation, she will tell me. I then review my requested due dates. My comments may be:

- "I must have this at 4 p.m. today. Get some help if you can. Otherwise see me and I'll see what I can do. Can I help? But, I *must* have this.

- "If you can complete this item by 10:30 a.m. tomorrow, let it slide till then." *My* decision to change the due date.

In practicing the aggressive management style, rules can be most helpful. In this case, our rule is that the boss sets and revises due dates. The employee schedules as best he or she can, but is charged with advice and/or recommendation if the schedule does not satisfy the due date. Put in your own work planning rules, but state them and make the rules the base from which you may vary. Without rules, everyone does the best he or she can; but, more often than not, this will not be as productive as a more formal, stated approach to planning or work accomplishment.

ARE YOU SELLING OR ARE THEY BUYING?

The venerable chicken and egg dilemma (Which *did* come first?) provides the manager with an opportunity to test his or her plans against the criteria for success. First of all, "What difference does it make whether the chicken or the egg came first?" is a better question than, "How much will it cost to find out?"

Conversely, if the question reversal allows you another view of an existing objective, this is very worthwhile. Example: A Midwest farm implement manufacturer wanted more (and more profitable) sales. Concentrating on more profitable sales, the manufacturer installed a sliding commission arrangement, rewarding sales of high profit items at a greater rate than for lower profit (and loss) items. The result was hardly measurable from an analysis of order input.

The company came to a very interesting conclusion, which was, "People bought what they wanted, despite what we are selling." If we consider what people are *buying* to be more significant than what we are *selling,* this could open up new planning vistas. The company embarked upon a whole new selling program, with emphasis on determining what the individual customer wanted. Sales emphasis was slanted *from* the "heavy-handed closing" *to* the concept of selling solutions to customer problems. The company proceeded to tie this philosophy to sales management training for its sales people, emphasizing techniques of eliciting customer requirements so the potential customer became part of the solution. Most people tend to buy *their* recommendations rather than *yours*.

For the AMS practitioner, some philosophy is pertinent here.

- View your planning according to your knowledge of the objective. Review alternate plans by viewing new concepts of how to achieve these objectives.

- Review objectives. Do you want cost-reduction or profit improvement? High return or low risk? Or, is the problem that you want both, and your planning reflects this dichotomy?

"SURPRISE; IT'S NOT DONE"

One of the most traumatic reports received by managers is, "Surprise! It's not done!" The womb of security is suddenly pierced. "But, I thought everything was okay." At this point, some folks start scrambling for excuses, "fall guys", "Band-aid" solutions, quick-and-dirty approaches, an emergency meeting, lots of shouting, etc.

Like the equity traders who always expect the market to go up, managers more likely than not expect schedules to be met. There is a feeling I call, "implied completion," when you don't hear about a failure. It is an assumption of success.

Perhaps this is better than the minority of managers who feel like Chicken Little about *all* projects. They feel "the sky is falling" on every one of their projects and require constant reassurance and a massive reporting complex. They confuse information with control and reporting with action.

Somewhere between the optimistic and pessimistic approaches, you can establish controls in the planning phase to prevent "Surprise!" This will be more fully developed in chapter 4, but is being covered here because controls should be considered in the planning phase.

The use of milestones, or progress completion targets, can be one of the answers. Discuss and agree to these milestones with your people in the planning phase. If it is a matter of problem-solving, use the defined steps along the way to keep abreast. (See chapter 5 for defined milestones in problem-solving.)

Dudley Bryant, vice-president of the Clarke-Gravely Division of Studebaker-Worthington, states, "All projects worth planning are worth breaking down into accomplishable parts. My people know that I know and track progress on projects. Together, we are controlling our plans by planning our controls."

Look at your current projects. Do you know the milestones? Are they informally or formally understood by others? If not, you are a prime target for, "Surprise; we aren't that far along!"; or, "No, we won't finish on time!" Surprised? Now, go give *your* boss *his* surprise.

QUALITY IS ALSO PLANNED

Professor Gayle W. McElrath, of the University of Minnesota and Fellow of the American Society for Quality Control, used to say to me, "One of the first tenets of quality assurance is to understand that quality is not inspected into a product or service; it is only observed in that state after having gotten there by the actions of workers, vendors, transporters, equipment, et al."

Many a surprise can be eliminated by the act of sampling the quality of work along the way. However, as Professor McElrath stated, inspection is not correction; it is notification.

Coordinate your checkpoint sampling with aid and advice relative to:

- quality of facts versus assumptions and opinions
- quality of rationale or conclusions drawn from the above facts
- quality of alternatives considered
- quality of recommendations as they fit within the parameters of the problem scope and the company objectives
- quality of the "King's English" used

This last point used to plague me. I found there were times I was so busy fixing the semantics, paragraph and sentence structures, that I then had to reread the report or plan for business logic. To help overcome this, I required a "best effort" regarding the "mother tongue" at the project check points. In this way, I not only was training my people, I was also assuring the quality of the English along the way. This last point allowed me a better biew of the "trees" instead of being befuddled by the "forest."

KNOW THYSELF

The reader at this point is seeing some problems that may seem insurmountable...one of which is that criticism is required in order to practice the aggressive management style. Correction is sometimes looked upon as criticism. Questioning the status quo can be a criticism of those who practice, or who devised, that which is today's method of operation.

As stated in chapter 1, pick those techniques in the AMS bag that suit you. Test the water. Don't start with evaluations that impinge on others, but stick to those which affect you and only you.

Dr. Howard Wilson, a well-known West Coast industrial psychologist and author of *Understanding People,* talks of three types of maturity relevant to understanding ourselves. The first is chronological maturity, where-by we grow older accumulating experiences each moment (unless we can move faster than the speed of light). Second, we experience intellectual maturity, that which involves separating facts from assumptions, prioritiz-ing them and drawing conclusions from this knowledge. For our purposes, I have limited the more detailed discussion of intellectual maturity to the above.

Finally, there is emotional maturity...how we react, based on how we feel about events, perceptions, hurts (both real and imagined), ourselves, others, etc. An emotionally mature person can separate a reasonable response from vindictiveness, perception of self from ego satisfaction, constructive comments from embarrassing criticism, etc.

An aggressive management style requires a closer look at that which attacks the premise and changes the practice. If the reader is unable to constructively criticize himself or herself as objectively as possible, and is totally alienated by any discussion involving questioning the status quo, a prerequisite to adopting AMS is assertiveness training, perhaps preceded by Life Orientations (LIFO)® behavioral pattern analysis.

For the uninitiated, assertiveness training involves looking at:

- Your behavior, whether it be passive, aggressive, indirectly ag-gressive and/or assertive.
- Responses, including fight, flight and manipulations.
- Childish misconceptions, as related to your personal bill of rights.
- Communications and responses, including win and lose possibilities.
- Learned relationships, from commercial and authority to equal.
- Persistence, coping with criticism, giving directions.
- Eye contact, physical gestures and facial expressions.

The concept is to develop you as "number one", commanding — not demanding — respect and authority. For the reader who has gotten this far and has trouble visualizing the implementation of AMS, training in as-sertiveness may be a prerequisite.

Stuart Atkins' Los Angeles consulting firm, which developed LIFO, defines four basic management styles:

- Conserving/Holding
- Supporting/Giving
- Controlling/Taking
- Adapting/Dealing

From a battery of about 75 questions, a dominant management style and secondary ones are analyzed. From these analyses, Mr. Atkins and his associates develop approaches for the manager to utilize for self-understanding and for improving communications with other personalities in the organization.

The foregoing are prerequisites for those who have come this far and feel frustrated. We have described some aggressive management actions, and a few readers cannot find one that fits his or her style comfortably. Since the next nine chapters are more of the same, I feel this is a good point to find the 10 to 15 percent of you who have been dragged forcibly into the role of manager. A thousand deaths a year await you until *you* know *you* and can comfortably manage your people.

The techniques hereinafter described are looked at by 85 percent of you who are managers, such that some will be discarded, some modified, some will be swallowed whole. "Knowing thyself" always has been a prerequisite to effective managing; AMS is merely a group of techniques to aid that manager.

I DON'T HAVE TIME TO MANAGE

This chapter began with the plaintive cry, "I don't have time to plan!" I believe this is equivalent to saying, "I don't have time to manage," if one assumes that planning is a major function of managing. As human beings, we may agree with a philosophy but perceive and practice something else. For this reason, a cornerstone of AMS is an extension of "know thyself" ...it is knowing how you spend your time, not just how you perceive of it being spent.

Many companies and government bureaucracies adopted the management-by-objectives approach, which gained popularity in the early 1970s. The success of these programs over a long period of time depends on many factors, but the primary ones seem to be:

- a dedication to the concept by *all* levels of management
- a system of "bench mark" controls, both progress and financial, to assure that the planning is successful
- the proper allocation and application of management time in proportion to the value and priority of your objectives

Programs that fail become "paperwork games." Managers learn the acceptable "buzz words" and play them back as objectives. Sometimes, specific projects are chosen and passed off as next year's objectives, even though they may account for only 40 percent of the total time budgeted (or allocated) for the entire function.

The major point for the AMS person is first to know himself or herself. Set total planning goals, assure they fit within the organizational goals, develop priorities and establish controls to carry them out. In other words, regardless of the management-by-objectives approach practiced in your environment, from "none" to "playing the game" to total dedication, there are advantages to choosing some form of personal commitment.

An example will make this point. A financial officer in a New England enterprise listed his major objectives for 1977 in a random order. He then reviewed the list to both prioritize and weigh these functions as to his forecasted time commitment. The list looked like this:

	1977	
	Plan	Actual
Financial planning and relations	10%	2%
Credit, collections and insurance	10%	17%
General and cost accounting	20%	4%
Budgetary planning and control	20%	31%
Tax preparation	5%	6%
Internal audit	5%	1%
Systems and procedures	10%	0%
Fund management	10%	21%
Data processing	5%	1%
Financial counseling and *other*	5%	17%
	100%	100%

The "Actual" column was derived in a manner described in the next chapter. Granted that priorities do change during a year, this analysis showed a marked difference between plan and actual...different enough for the financial officer to rate himself "D" for 1977 in time management for planning.

A listing of his major goals and objectives was then compared with his boss's:

Your Ranking		Boss' Ranking
1	Introduce new labor control procedure	4
7	Put in new government contract cost controls	3
3	Change physical inventorying verification	6
8	Weigh LIFO change and get approval	2
2	Eliminate parallel system on verification of receivers	8
5	Prepare better graphics for division presentations	7

Your Ranking		Boss' Ranking
9	Recruit and/or train your potential replacement	5
10	Rearrange your office	10
6	Reduce number of people reporting to you to four	9
4	Close E.O.M. reports within two days; quarterlies in three	1

Obviously, an in-depth discussion of relative priorities with your boss is called for by the above. Assuming this is settled, how do these priorities fit within your *time* utilization? Do they fit? If not, you may wish to revise your time allocation plan.

The steps in planning time control are:

• Find out how you are currently spending your time and on what categories of work (See next chapter for procedure.)

• Match this against your job objectives, which should be evaluated with your boss's objectives for your function.

• Develop procedures to reduce or eliminate time spent on less-important tasks.

• Add this saved time to be spent on more important tasks.

• Keep checking on a regular basis to see that this goal is being attained.

The technique to use for measuring your time use will be covered in the beginning of the next chapter. For now, realize that your perception of time for planning to meet your objectives may not be that closely related to its actual utilization.

Oscar Wilde said, "Most men are consistent in managing their time, and consistency is the last refuge of the unimaginative." A much simpler statement of this philosophy was stated by Peter Drucker in *The Effective Manager,* "The effective manager knows where his time goes."

This chapter related the aggressive management style to the planning function. Starting with elimination as the first step, through desk control, the do-it-now approach, overcoming objections, due dates, scheduling, milestone controls, quality planning, personal evaluation and time management, the thrust has been to apply AMS for positive, and perhaps dramatically different, results. If you remember that the average manager spends about 40 percent of his or her time on planning, taking a small step in this area can be more rewarding than a larger step in other areas that are less significant.

3

AMS TECHNIQUES FOR PLANNING
YOUR TIME MANAGEMENT

Where will the AMS manager get the time to explore the new planning approaches or even technical advances in his or her field of endeavor? The 30 second test described in the previous chapter will help on a day-by-day planning improvement basis, but where can a manager get great chunks of time to plow back into the improvement function?

In the following pages, a time analysis technique little used in today's offices will be described. Approximately 2½ minutes a day is all that is required to adequately know how you are now spending your time. Interruptions will be viewed not just for elimination, but at the very least, to be better controlled by the practicing AMS manager.

Imagine the frustration of high level executives who plan, but are not sure, except through costly and time consuming data retrieval systems, whether their plans are being put into effect. To overcome this, a technique for matching the actions required to meet these objectives to the time commitments will be described. Coupled with this will be the description of a technique for determining relative priorities to be resolved on a daily or project-by-project basis.

Failure to accomplish plans will be viewed from the aspect of pre-determining down-side risks before failure, so that one can plan for failure ...facing up to potential problems as a mature management approach to real life. Finally, since all problems are not equal, a technique for determining the dollar value of opportunities for improvement will be examined.

EXHORTATION VERSUS PRACTICAL TIME ANALYSIS

Over the past 15 years, many intriguing books and articles have exhorted the manager to make better use of his or her time. The sameness of the approaches is such that if you've read one, you've read them all.

You are exhorted to study your time-wasters, keep a diary, analyze your motives, delegate more responsibilities, use your secretary as an administrative assistant, have better meetings, use the telephone more effectively and organize your daily calendar.

The programs are very appealing. Everyone would like to be more efficient; there is no business or social stigma attached to admitting it; the approaches to improvement aren't more than one step above good old common sense. After stating it in this way, the reader is now asking, "What can the manager practicing AMS do that will result in more effective time management?"

I suggest three answers to this question:

1. Try to find out *objectively* how you are now utilizing your time. Ranking your personal timewasters or keeping a personal time diary are examples of *subjectively* analyzing your management of time.

2. Accept better time management as *one* of your goals. Its significance is only as important as it relates to your major activities of planning, organizing, delegating, communicating, doing your specific job, reviewing, controlling, coordinating, improving and the like. Choose those techniques in time management that have a significance towards enhancing your *management* activities.

3. *Prioritize.* Separate the penny ideas from those with dollar impact. Spend more resources where the payoff potential is greater. Either reject or minimize low value problems and solutions.

PERSONAL DIARIES ARE A WASTE OF TIME

I have met countless executives who have kept personal time diaries of either time use or interruptions. A minuscule few still keep them.

They started to keep them because it sounded logical. A diary would show the executives how their time had been spent so that areas for improvement could be pinpointed. But, in actual practice their use diminished because:

- The analyst started to develop a document of what he or she either suspected or really knew.

- The initial impact required changes that were either made immediately or were improvements too difficult to implement and/or too costly to contemplate. ("Ask the boss *not* to interrupt me one hour each day? Wow!")

- Interruption time was either not documented or a separate interruption diary had to be maintained.

- The diary writer felt the entries covered only a small fraction of total time use during a varying and seasonal year of events.

- A cumulative look at all the entries was difficult to achieve through summarization of uncategorized raw data.

- The time spent in collecting the data, recording the entries and summarizing seemed to consume more time than it appeared to be worth, after the initial impact of analysis and quick improvement.

- Some of the installed time management improvements could not be documented as timesavers, but the installer did "feel better and more efficient."

As stated in the credo of the aggressive management style in chapter 1, there must be positive actions taken that result in positive long lasting results, not just quick improvements that make one feel better for a short period of time. Therefore, I suggest keeping a time diary only for the initial impact...to correct the obvious.

Many of the objections to diaries listed above can be overcome through the use of activity sampling (also called work sampling and ratio delay studies). As titled, the technique involves sampling, not a running documentation of all events.

WHY ACTIVITY SAMPLING WORKS BEST

For the purpose of time use analysis, sampling categorizes observed events. The randomness of the observations, coupled with the validity test of the sample, will provide the manager with ratios of time spent representative of the true population of events. Of course, there are rules to be observed, but they are logical ones.

Why activity sampling?

- A valid sample over a long enough period of time will be more representative than a detailed time diary taken during a short period of time.
- Interruption time is documented as an independent event that will be uncovered and measured in a random sample. I always thought I spent 30 to 40 percent of my time on the telephone...the black tumor in my ear! Actual sampling showed this to be 14 percent of my total time. It just *seemed* like more!
- Being sampled by someone else should have a higher degree of validity than keeping your own time diary.
- Sampling is a much less time-consuming task than keeping a diary. For years my secretary used an average of 2½ minutes per day in sampling my activities.

STEPS IN SAMPLING YOUR TIME UTILIZATION

The steps involved in conducting such a sampling study are simple and adequately described in management literature.

First, select *any* categories you desire or feel appropriate for the type of work you perform. In the beginning, you will tend to have many more categories than you will need for the purpose of improving your management time.

You will also have many misconceptions about your time's use. I thought I spent vast amounts of time training and instructing my staff. Over a full year's study (16 hours for analysis in that year), I found that figure never got over three-quarter of one percent!

You will underestimate, and perhaps even omit, such obvious categories as "Idle" and "Personal." Chances are you will lump "Indirect Work" with "Direct Work." Some explanations here:

- "Idle" consists of time spent on nonwork activities, such as a discussion of the Monday night game on the tube. If you feel this is for morale-building, set up such a category. Idle gossip is "Idle;" getting coffee, dozing or daydreaming are "Idle."

    Unavoidable delays, such as waiting for information or people, might be "Idle." Personal time, checking on your child's temperature or calling for a house painting estimate is "Idle." Let me repeat; *you* select the categories. The above examples are merely for your consideration.
- "Direct Work" is all of those tasks a manager is required to perform, such as planning and improving.

- "Special Activities" are functions that could fall into any of your categories, but you have selected for special study. At various times in my career, I have studied my time spent on the telephone, with visitors, at meetings or doing work that could have been delegated to my secretary (administrative assistant).

- "Indirect Work" is work performed supportive to your main tasks, which are described as "Direct Work" or included in "Special Activities." You may be getting office supplies, arranging your own travel, delivering a message to George or getting material from the files. These are tasks requiring a pay scale well below that for which your main tasks ("Direct Work") are remunerated. I'll admit it is fun to run the reproduction machine, read the airlines guide and fill the staple gun...but, why you? If the reader runs a one-man office that question might be begging an obvious answer. But for the vast majority, "why you?" And for such a large percentage of the time?

- "Absent" is a category that is needed because, although you are in the office somewhere, the observer isn't required to look for you. When we cover observation techniques, the need for this category will become more obvious. For the time being, consider this observation as being necessary in the sample to account for 100 percent of your time. You could consider prorating this category's occurrences across all of the other categories, but this doesn't add to the knowledge we are seeking about the actual use of our time.

The next step is to select random times for observations. This selection takes about 15 seconds each day. (Remember the 30 second test in chapter 2?)

The best sampling of you is by someone else — your secretary or a member of the staff that can afford two-and-a-half minutes a day. Only if such a person is lacking should you consider yourself as the observer.

For years I have used the white pages of the local telephone directory to select random times. The observer turns to a random page each sampling day and selects the last four digits from about 10 numbers. I use 10 since it makes for easy division, but this is not a statistical criterion.

Look at the last four digits and discount all first digits larger than "1." (See example below.) Modify all remaining numbers to the 60 minute clock, such that 380 equals 4:20. Use the "24 hour clock" concept for numbers starting with "1," so that 1428 is 2:28.

Disregard all times outside normal working hours (unless you're sampling yourself) or when observation would be impossible. Since "10" and "11" will be rare numerical occurences considering the nature of random numbers, I use "6" to represent "10:00 a.m. and "7" to mean "11:00

a.m." when they appear as the second digit. Example: 9621 will equal 10:21, and 0718 will be 11:18.

Example:

Telephone Directory

Sample Page

Phone number	Selected Digits		Observation Time Selected
384-8231	231	=	2:31
522-2716	716	=	11:16
391-1441	1441	=	2:41
781-3983	983	=	10:23
521-1080	1080	=	11:20
393-4348	348	=	3:48
419-5607	607	=	10:07
521-1551	1551	=	3:51
384-0894	0894	=	9:34
521-2434	434	=	4:34

10 Numbers

If you're wondering how these 10 numbers were selected and converted in 15 seconds, remember you only have to write down the numbers in the last column.

If you're sampling yourself, place each number on a separate 5" x 7" card, then sort in ascending order of time. If your observer is selecting the times, have him or her just rearrange the times in that ascending order on a single sheet, as shown below:

9:34
10:07
10:23
11:16
11:20
2.31
2:41
3:48
3:51
4:34

Observations will be recorded at these times during the day. We're seeking a guide to time use, not a scientific study for reaching an earthshaking conclusion. The times are a guide, not a number that will wipe out the day's data if missed. Be logical.

If you are sampling yourself, keep the cards face up on your desk. When the sample time arrives, place a tick mark next to the appropriate category as observed. If someone is sampling you, this is what he or she will do.

The observation should be instantaneous, otherwise you may start doing work as soon as you hang up on your complaining girlfriend. If the sample time occurs while on with her, this is "personal time" (even though you were using your most businesslike voice to explain why your wife's birthday is more important than her time needs).

Activity Sample Form

CATEGORY (Select and Use Any)	4/18 DATE		4/24 DATE	
	Observation	Cumulative Percentage	Observation	Cumulative Percentage
1. Direct Work				
a. Communicate				
b. Plan				
c. Control	XXX	30%	XXXX XX	45%
d. Improve				
2. Indirect Work				
a. Get Supplies				
b. Arrange Travel	XX	20%	— —	10%
c. Travel Time				
d. File Retrieval				
3. Special Activities				
a. Telephone				
b. Visitors	X	10%	X	10%
c. Meetings				
4. Idle				
a. Choice				
b. U.D.	XXX	30%	X	20%
c. Personal				
5. Absent	X	10%	XX	15%
CUMULATIVE TOTALS	10	100%	20	100%

After two-and-a-half minutes per day on 4/18 and 4/24, you should have 20 observations. Random days may be used. I try to have between 10 and 12 days a month sampled, so about three days a week are sample days.

When I am sampled, I do not know the times used by the observer. If you feel the numbers are being prejudiced by your self-consciousness, disregard the sample observations for the first couple of days or weeks.

On 4/18, the "Cumulative Percentage" column is derived by dividing the number of observations per category by 10; on 4/24 the cumulative total of observations per category is divided by 20, and so on. The "Direct Work" category sample percentage equals 3 (from 4/18) plus 6 (from 4/24) divided by the total sample size 20 to equal 45 percent.

WHEN DO YOU KNOW THE SAMPLE HAS A HIGH DEGREE OF VALIDITY?

At what point do you start feeling the sample is valid enough to represent the true population of occurrences? There is a marvelous square root formula to answer this question that depends on the confidence you desire in your answer. The more consistent each day's sample is to all of the other days, the smaller the number of observations required.

For our purposes, I have found that a plot of the cumulative values by category is more than sufficient for time measurement needs. As you can see, the curve gets flatter as the cumulative sample size increases, until it becomes obvious that a massive shift in observations would be required to move a cumulative figure of 400 observations.

On a practical basis, I have found that after 300 to 400 cumulative observations, the percentage for any category will not change significantly. I end the study and start another one, which will last another 300 to 400 observations. The grand total of time spent sampling over this three month period is one and a half to two hours! If you cannot afford this time during the next three months, forget this approach. See Figure 3-1.

You now have a fairly reliable statistic on time use, cheaply achieved, but reasonably useful. Decide on improvements in your time management to increase your "Direct Work" from 45 percent. (If "Special Activities" include direct work, add 10 percent.) The ratios will surprise and perhaps discourage you.

After instituting an improvement, start a new sample to measure the difference. If you've really improved, not just put in a "cosmetic change" so you feel better about your time management, it should be reflected in the new set of observations. Don't stop. Keep investing one and a half to

CATEGORY: DIRECT WORK
(PLOT CUMULATIVES)

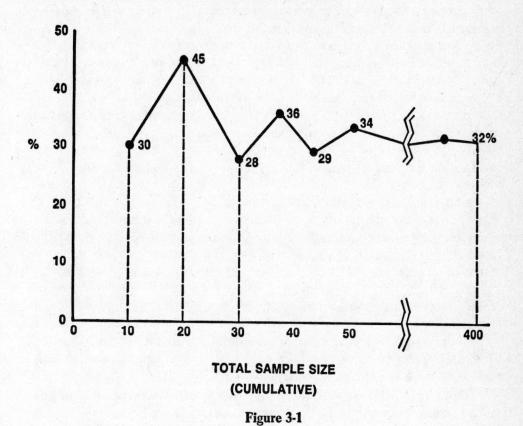

TOTAL SAMPLE SIZE
(CUMULATIVE)

Figure 3-1

two hours every quarter year to monitor and improve the management of one of your more valuable assets — time.

INTERRUPTIONS ARE PART OF BUSINESS LIFE

Much has been written to denounce interruptions. The assumption garnered from reading this literature is that one can almost eliminate interruptions by better discipline in management. Kings and certain chief executive officers are interrupted only when they want to be. If this book were for those chosen few, circulation would barely exceed 500 in the entire World.

In actual practice, I have found that interruptions, even those based on a fairly-structured exception basis, are and probably always will be a part of an executive's life. It is therefore far better to assume that interruptions will continue; but, the aggressive management style envisages that they be reduced in quantity and improved in quality.

Look at your activity sample. How many of the categories are under your control? For example, on a whim or because of a need for information not of *immediate* requirement, a call or visit is made to your office. Let's evaluate the causes and some cures the AMS manager may consider.

Some interruptions are a direct result of your stated and practiced management style. You are an "open door" manager...at least you strive to be. You want every one of your troops and every visitor to feel free to drop in and see you. Any time? On any matter? Let's look at some of these visitations.

Can you determine if the interrupters are using you as a "crutch?" They could make the decision themselves but would rather you do it for them. See if you encourage this by needing the ego builder of being the omniscient one, the only one allowed to make decisions. Is your concurrence even necessary? Have you placed the decision level too high for every situation? Would a delineation of decision levels by work category free you from many "penny concurrences" so you can spend more time on "big dollar approvals?"

Is the interruption informative? If so, did it warrant the time urgency of an oral statement made by you? Could a brief note have sufficed, which you could have read at your leisure?

Does your office layout encourage the passerby to drop in with idle talk? Do you encourage the information interruption by asking for it? Did you express an urgency to receive the information that was not warranted? "Tell me as soon as the credit is cleared for the Jones order." Can you make a distinction between "need to know *now*" and "would like to know at your convenience?"

GROUPING INTERRUPTIONS

Can interruptions be grouped so various people can see you at the same time on the same subject? Or must they see you individually?

See page 88 for an example of a diary I kept back in 1956 as a junior executive. You will note that two hours and 45 minutes were consumed by interruptions. Assume at least half the time was direct work; this still leaves a lot of time that could have been better planned or used.

Can you encourage your employees to group their questions and discussions in their meetings with you? Don't *you* do that in your folders of work to cover with *your* boss? Every secretary worth her pay keeps a signature folder, file and comment folder, schedule or diary in readiness to go over with you. She has grouped the work by types of action required. (The work is probably also prioritized.)

Why not set an example by covering multiple subjects on visits and telephone calls to *your* employees' places of work? The Pygmalion Effect, written about so effectively by Dr. Sterling Livingstone of The Sterling Institute, indicates that many employees emulate their boss's characteristics, both good and bad. If you avoid unnecessary interruptions of your employees and reduce them by grouping requests, telephone calls and visits, they will begin to utilize this same practice.

Are you interrupted because your previous instructions were not understood? More on this will be covered in chapter 6. The evidences of poor communications do appear in interruption analyses. When people don't understand, they will sometimes come back and ask for clarification; more often they will avoid, postpone, do partial work or none at all. Poor communications are, primarily, the sender's responsibility.

Are you the recipient of those who come to you unprepared, causing your involvement in unnecessary detail and questioning? The solution to this may take quite a bit of time in training (and retraining) your employees. Indicate the desired status and form of progress and problems brought to you. Show by example the kind of questions that *you* expect to have answered. Define a completed stage or task. The composition of some of these milestones in problem-solving will be covered in chapter 5.

Learn to control personal interruptions. Say *Yes* when asked if you're busy; say *No* to those who bypass the chain of command in order to speak to you. Distinguish between social and business courtesy requirements.

If you are in your garden planting tulip bulbs and a neighbor drops by to ask, "May I speak with you?", it would be downright rude to exclaim, "Go away; I'm busy planting!" In the office, if you're busy and the company busybody asks, "Did you hear about Harriet?", it would be quite proper to say, "No, I haven't; but I can't be interrupted now. Let me get back to you." There is a different code of social behavior required in the office than expected socially.

Although interruptions are a part of business life, the aggressive management style requires a diminution of their quantity and an improvement in their quality. Even *your* boss will appreciate your efforts to reduce his or her interruption time. Discuss your plan with your boss and emphasize the positive work results that will accrue.

DATE: 3/18/56

A Personal Interruption Diary

Interruption	Time	Description	Comment or Possible Improvement
1	9:04-9:18	John gave out cigar for new son	Shorten time
2	10:00-10:08	Charlie needed help	Did he really?
3	11:41-11:43	John called me to confirm meeting next week	Sec'y could have taken info.
4	12:00-12:11	Charlie still needs help	Did I give good enough info the first time?
5	1:16-1:19	Mary wants next Wed. off	How about a note?
6	1:28-1:36	Mary needs concurrence signature	Could have been grouped with #5 above.
7	1:55-2:11	Charlie needs help again	Consider replacing Charlie.
8	2:39-3:18	George has wife problems	39 minutes!?!?
9	4:12-4:41	Attend weekly meeting chaired by yourself	Why is it held weekly?
10	5:01-5:36	The boss needed "hand holding"	Can I be honest with him?
TOTAL	165 minutes	Interruption time	

"GOPHERS" CAN HELP

An insurance company in New Jersey instituted a time management training program for all of its clerical personnel, bosses, secretaries, clerks, technical people and salesmen. As part of their training, they were shown how to conduct an activity sample of their time use. More than 50 secretaries sampled their activities and were amazed to see almost one-third of their total time was consumed by interruptions to perform "Indirect Work." This "Indirect Work" consisted of "get supplies," "deliver mail and memos," "reproduce copies," "retrieve lost files" and the like.

The composite picture of all the secretaries was studied by the Administrative Assistant Committee. At the same time, this insurance company was advertising in the papers for 16 new secretaries for the expanding organization. The Administrative Assistant Committee approached the vice-president of Personnel (Human Resources) and suggested the recruitment of six "gophers" to "go for this and go for that" instead of the 16 new secretaries. They felt these six "gophers" could work for the present secretarial group to allow them to do "more secretary-type work" (their words). After one year, the program was so successful, the company split the annual savings from hiring "six gophers" instead of 16 new secretaries with the existing secretaries.

The point is that if you can analyze time utilization of a single manager, think what it can mean if an entire group is analyzed. Is the American answer to more work more "hot bodies," or should we invest in "cleaning up our act" so that new employees are brought into a better work environment? An AMS orientation leans toward the latter option.

CORPORATE OBJECTIVES SHOULD LEAVE
THE BOARDROOM AS PRACTICES

A Policy Planning Committee of an upper Midwest conglomerate had the board of directors and the chief executive officer review and approve the following philosophies. From these, all company executives were then asked to develop their next year's objectives and strategies based on these philosophies. After receiving approval, these strategies were then to be prioritized.

A sample of the approved philosophies follows (author's emphasis):

1. High marketing expenditure of *time,* money and effort for lower quality products in the line would have little positive affect on profits.

2. The "stronger" divisions of the company should seek acquisitions for vertical integration; the "weaker" divisions should not spend much *time* on this type of acquisition.

3. Only a minimal amount of *time* should be spent on research and development for any product with a "weak" market position. Copying the competitors' products and services would be a better strategy than inventing them during this coming year. More *time*

in research and development should be spent on those products having a "strong" market position.

4. Our costs of products and services, relative to the value received and price paid by the customer, are the backbone of our profitability. Therefore, next year 50 percent of all research and development *time* will be devoted to cost reduction studies on existing products and services...

The reader will note that the asset of time was clearly mentioned in the statement of these philosophies. Of course, there is no direct link between the expenditure of management time and success, but there must be *some* correlation. Agreed, some progress can be made in "a flash" with little effort and a lot of luck. But for most of us, carrying out a board philosophy at the operating level is very closely related to some time commitment.

The obvious question posed to the reader is, "Are you matching the use of your time to the priorities and emphasis placed on certain projects by the policy-makers in your work environment?" Do you know these priorities? Here is where another surprise awaits you when you perform an activity sample.

I firmly believe a manager practicing AMS must not only know how he or she spends time but should be able to match this to stated or perceived objectives. This is the way to make time management work in your managerial environment. Everything else that just makes you feel better is a cosmetic approach.

DEVELOPING PRIORITIES IN A
NONQUANTITATIVE ENVIRONMENT

No one doubts that more money is greater than less money. But, would you prefer a Lincoln or a Cadillac, Candice Bergen or Farrah Fawcett, Athens or Copenhagen? Now we are into subjective selections depending on numerous weightings given to many factors for consideration.

As a manager, there are many events that plague you; some merely deserve "pin-prick" status. Let's make a list of some of these and examine them to ascertain priorities for solution or disregarding.

1. "I spend hours on the *telephone;* I feel like I have a black tumor in my ear."

2. "I keep solving the same problems over again. Here comes one of my employees with the *same questions again.*"

3. "I wish I could *delegate* this job to Natalie...but by the time I show her how to do it, I can do it myself."

4. "Here goes another 'search safari.' Why can't we *retrieve files* in a more efficient manner?"

5. "Another *meeting*...this one will last until the mid-morning meeting."

6. "*Visitors* seem to put my office on the 'plant tour.' Can't they go see someone else or see me for shorter periods of time?"

7. "Here comes another *crisis*. How can I put a *priority* on it instead of having a continuous bout of *'firefighting'*?"

8. "I had to listen to Audrey's *personal problems* so I didn't get around to setting up my Sunday golf date with George."

To improve your practice of management, it is obvious that you should work on *all* of these problems. But, a priority approach is generally more productive.

An accepted technique is called triangulation (coupling and pairing are also commonly used words to describe evaluations of combinations and permutations.) Of the eight problems listed above, there are 28 $\left(\dfrac{8^2 - 8}{2}\right)$ comparisons that would have to be weighed. Look at this graphically:

Triangulation (Pairing)

```
1   1   1   1   1   1   1
2   3   4   5   6   7   8
    2   2   2   2   2   2
    3   4   5   6   7   8
        3   3   3   3   3
        4   5   6   7   8
            4   4   4   4
            5   6   7   8
                5   5   5
                6   7   8
                    6   6
                    7   8
                        7
                        8
```

$$\frac{n^2 - n}{2} = 28 \text{ pairings}$$

Circle Count	Weighted Ranking
1	
2	
3	
4	
5	
6	
7	
8	

You will note there are 28 pairs of comparisons possible from these eight problems. For example, suppose you compare #1 ("hours on the telephone") with #2 ("same questions again"). If you feel #1 is more important a problem than #2, circle #1 on the chart. Perform this test for all 28 possibilities and the completed triangulation might look like the following:

Triangulation (Pairing)

```
①   1   ①   1   1   ①   1
2   ③   4   ⑤   ⑥   7   ⑧
    2   ②   2   ②   2   2
    ③   4   ⑤   6   ⑦   ⑧
        ③   ③   ③   ③   ③
        4   5   6   7   8
            4   ④   4   ④
            ⑤   6   ⑦   8
                ⑤   ⑤   5
                6   7   ⑧
                    6   6
                    ⑦   ⑧
                        ⑦
                        8
```

Circle Count		Weighted Ranking	
1	3	3	7
2	2	5	5
3	7	7	4
4	2	8	4
5	5	1	3
6	1	2	2
7	4	4	2
8	4	6	1
	28		28

Item #3 ("delegation") is weighted twice as much a problem as #7 ("crises"), #8 ("personal problems") or #1 ("telephone"). Item #5 ("meetings") and item #3 ("delegation") together account for one half of the weighting of all your perceived and actual problems. Items #2 ("same questions"), #4 ("file retrieval") and #6 ("visitors") seem negligible compared to the five others and should be attacked as low on the list of priority and time consumption for solution.

A simple ranking is never as meaningful as a weighted ranking. The magnitude of the relationship of a manager's problems may be as significant as their relative rank to one another. The listing is not an end unto itself but a guide for future corrective actions. For that reason, weighting of factors is an important tool for AMS practitioners.

PLANNING FOR FAILURE

This subject has been mentioned heretofore in both chapters 1 and 2 under such terminology as downside-risk evaluation and failure control from reviewed data. The purpose of bringing it to the fore again is to relate this planning approach to the empathy one should feel towards the affected party.

A case in point relates to a manufacturer of pressure vessels. The manufacturing lead time is six weeks from forming the shell plate to final assembly. The customer usually places an order about five months in advance of need. Between eight to 10 weeks of the requirement date, the firm ship date is fixed by agreement. The customer awaits shipment and prepares for same on this expected date.

Not too infrequently, delays occur in the manufacturing process, such that progress of the product moving through the manufacturing process is slowed. Sometimes it becomes evident the ship date will be missed. What to do? Inform the customer? Hope and pray something will happen? Hope that fairy dust will be sprinkled on the product and Gepetto's dream will turn Pinocchio into a real live boy?

The commonly used approach was to wait and see if they really would miss the ship date. A large majority of the missed dates were then uncovered during the last week of the original schedule. Now, the manufacturing folks call the salespeople, who, in turn, call the customer to say the ship date will be missed. The customer is now both furious and helpless.

The customer has sat through 10 weeks of being relatively happy, expecting on-time delivery. The reader might say, "Why didn't the customer check?" Two reasons why this wouldn't have been an effective approach are: (1) the manufacturing concern's salespeople would have confirmed the on-time delivery either by lack of knowledge of the potential miss or because they, too, were hoping and praying, and (2) customers don't usually expedite every order they've placed, but do follow-up on an exception basis.

A better approach, now used in this company, works as follows:

- As soon as there is definite, incontrovertible knowledge that the promised date will be missed, manufacturing must inform sales. That is their job. Only sales can alter the promise to the customer (or lie to them).
- As soon as sales has this information they must so inform the customer.

What's new or different? Won't the customer still be disappointed? Of course; but there are degrees of disappointment. And, advance knowledge of an event, sad or happy, allows others to replan. Remember the last time you ordered a large piece of furniture and were promised first Saturday of April delivery? You plan for the delivery by staying home. At 11:00 a.m. on Saturday, a call informs you that delivery will be made next Thursday. At this point, you start to rant and rave. Suppose you were called a week earlier, which is probably when this delay was first discovered by someone at the shipping facility of the supplier to your furniture store.

Failure of plans should be a minority occurrence (less than 50 percent), but in any management of any enterprise it is a fairly large minority. The AMS approach is to ascertain failure as soon as possible, inform the necessary parties and thus replace the hope and pray approach with "immediate honesty."

It will hurt to practice this in the beginning, but in the long run, your style will be recognized as both honest and refreshing. Plan for failure; don't fail to plan. In analyzing your time management, see how many times firefighting interruptions could have been avoided by planning for failure.

PLAN TO FACE UP TO YOUR PROBLEMS

One of the techniques used by the Plains Indians to kill buffalo was to use a lure (sometimes a young brave). The idea was to get the buffalo to start running toward the lure. In so doing, the buffalo were fooled into jumping off a cliff (while the lure hid beneath the ledge). The Indians recorded the amazing fact that literally scores of buffalo would follow the pack over the precipice.

I am not inferring that the average manager blindly follows orders or conforms to the regimen of the work environment, unquestioning as he or she "goes over the cliff." But what about traditional thinking, such as, "We've always planned this way, always analyzed this way, always done it this way." If it's logical, keep going, but don't assume it's logical because it has always been done that way.

An example or two will demonstrate the validity of questioning the logic of time spent on both analysis and improvement.

About half of the manufacturing concerns I work with as a management consultant have more dollars invested in inventory than in labor or equipment depreciation costs. Their main objectives are profitability, long-term growth and return on investment. If inventory is one of the major investments, it would then seem logical to assume that a majority of management time is consumed with increasing output relative to inventory or maintaining output while reducing inventory.

I find their major effort is usually more directed towards control of the asset (counting it, locating it, verifying it, moving it, buying it, storing it, etc.). Some of the systems available today even ensure the propagation of past performance by using the data of past operating capacities and procurement lead times in the newer scheduling and reporting formats.

When they work on scheduling problems, should these managements place greater emphasis on equipment and manpower utilization, or should they zero-in on efficient inventory scheduling? A firm in Scotland that makes telephone handsets spends 38 minutes of labor and equipment to produce one handset, and a handset is being worked on (work-in-process) for two weeks! This means the materials are "sitting" for 39 hours and 22 minutes waiting for 38 minutes of work. Where would you emphasize these managers spend their time to increase return on investment?

I once chided an Ohio company for running a peculiar looking warehouse. They quickly shot back, "Kobert, you were in our manufacturing plant!" You could have fooled me. Three-quarters of the floor space in the "manufacturing plant" was devoted to inventory and one-quarter to operations. I replied, "You have a warehouse with some manufacturing going on in-between the inventory!"

In the aggressive management style, you should be able to seek problems (opportunities) that deserve your planning and improvement emphasis. How successful would you be if you worked on the real problem instead of "following the buffalo herd over the cliff"?

The foregoing sets the stage for another principle.

MANAGEMENT AID IS MORE EFFECTIVE THAN EXHORTATION

There is an army of executives who demand and expect better performance merely by asking for it. But that's only one side of it. Vince Lombardi would exhort the Packers and Redskins, but this was coupled with the innovative strategies of pulling guards, very mobile line-backers and special team "kamikaze" training.

"Cut costs" is an exhortation. Aiding in a cost effective study is usually more productive. "Sell more" is also an exhortation. Analyzing marketing strategy relative to position, product and logical penetration will more likely increase sales.

Management should aid not only in defining objectives but in isolating key factors for analysis and solutions. Coupled with exhortation, this is a sound approach for a results-oriented manager properly managing his or her time. Everyone can and is a critic, but aid in the planning phase is a more fruitful occupation.

One of the easiest to describe and most effective tools is the Pareto Approach (also called Emphasis Analysis and A-B-C Analysis). This technique was introduced by the Italian economist, Vilfredo Pareto, in his paper *The Theory of Maladjusted Statistics* in 1896. In his analysis of the gross national product of nations, he noted that a *small* change in a significant area of a nation's economy can have a significant effect on the GNP, while a *large* move in an insignificant area of the economy could hardly be noticed. A 5 percent drop in auto sales is far more dramatic than a strike of all lawn gardeners that isn't settled for six months.

A cost analysis of products and services usually turns up the same principle. Twenty percent of the services account for 80 percent of the profits in a bank. One-third of the budgetary accounts correspond to 70 percent of expenditures. Twenty-seven percent of the parts are in 70 percent of the dollars of inventory. A typical Pareto curve is shown in Figure 3-2.

As such, if one could concentrate appropriate time relative to the value of the endeavor, a different set of priorities may evolve for the AMS manager. Since there are generally more problems to resolve than time or talent available to resolve them, a manager who is more selective with his or her time can be a more effective overall manager.

The way to view the Pareto curve, then, is to view the problems as opportunities. The following chart depicts the 10 to 50 percent opportunity curve based on the Pareto principle. In some areas of opportunity, a 10 percent savings or gain would have to be offset with as much as a 50 percent reduction of cost in other areas. (See Figure 3-3.)

Utilizing the opportunity curve, a manager can direct both his and his employee's efforts to more productive ends. In time management, it can help provide a reverse ratio...to try and spend more time on the 80 percent cost factors. A 10 percent gain would be more significant than a 50 percent loss in the areas of insignificant cost factors (and probably im-

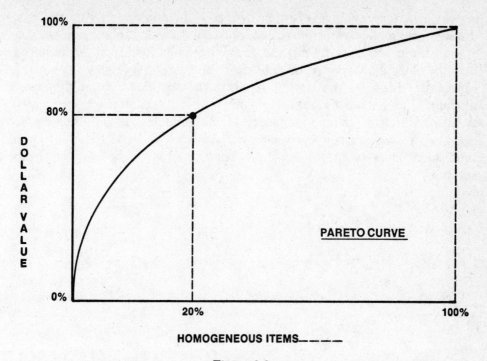

Figure 3-2

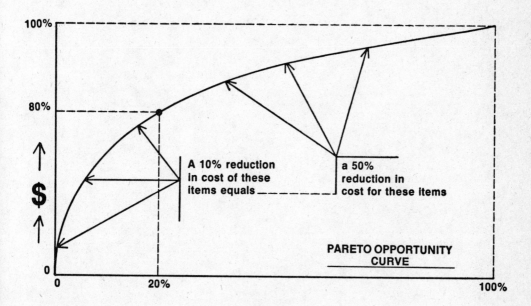

Figure 3-3

probable areas for saving 50 percent). By providing an opportunity analysis, management makes employee action more effective than mere exhortation.

In the practice of the aggressive management style, you are required to study objectively *your* management of *your* time as it relates to your job objectives. Prioritize and try to separate the significant from the insignificant. Understand the causes of interruptions and attack these causes as they relate to your time management. How much time is related to the emphasis placed on you by overall corporate objectives? Finally, match time spent in solving problems to opportunities to be derived from solution.

4

STRATEGIES AND TECHNIQUES
FOR EFFECTIVE CONTROL
USING AMS

As stated in both chapters 2 and 3, one of the most unproductive of management actions is planning without controls. In the following pages, the manager desiring to practice the aggressive management style will be taken through examples of both success and failure control, the strategies of replanning, schedule-miss reporting, and isolating history reporting from action-oriented control of your plans.

KEEPING THE "MONKEY" WHERE HE BELONGS

It is important for managers to know (and practice) the difference between review and control. When a manager walks up to his boss and says, "We have a problem!", his boss might well reply, "*We* have a problem?" The manager is presenting a problem to his or her boss and hoping:

- the boss has a solution
- the boss will accept the problem as his or her own

William Oncken in his famous *Harvard Business Review* article called this the attempt to transfer the "monkey" from the manager's back to his boss'. He went on to describe how "monkeys" are transferred, as well as the care and feeding of the "monkeys."

Let's change the scenario. The manager says to his or her boss, "We have a problem and...

1. Here's what I've done." You at this point hear about a solution within the parameters of action for that level of organization. You are receiving a report that is informational. (The time urgency of this reporting was discussed in the previous chapter.)

Or,

2. Here's what I recommend be done." Only the boss is authorized to act, but instead of just being presented with the "monkey," a recommendation is provided. One step further might be taken after the boss agrees with the recommendation, such as, "Good. I've prepared this action request memo for your signature based on your expected approval of this recommendation." Or, "OK. I'll make the necessary arrangements to put the recommendation into effect."

The business world is full of critics and problem presenters; analysis followed by recommendation, coupled with a completed action orientation, is what is required of AMS managers.

PLACING PRIORITY ON CONTROL RELATIVE TO REVIEW

Herbert Rounick, Chairman of Charlotte Ford Corp., in New York City states, "I can review anything at anytime. Control requires a different priority; it infers concurrence or acknowledgement of what has gone before and a proscribed or inferred action to proceed.

"If my controller reports an overrun in an estimated category, I do not have the freedom to do a leisurely review. I must look at causes and effects, call for action or do nothing...but, if I choose to do nothing, it is a planned action. The key point is that the priority for a control action is much higher than for a review. The time factor is the major difference."

USING SPEED READING TO CATEGORIZE ACTION REQUIRED

As discussed in chapter 2, a major advantage of training in speed reading is that it allows you to categorize letters, memos and other written or printed documents. Consider this when reading Herb Rounick's comments.

One of the major distinctions between review and control is the time factor for action (or reaction); the *decision* to act or defer action can be arrived at almost as soon as the paper hits your "In" box.

Use your speed reading to separate control items (high on the time priority list) from review items (low time priority). This time priority distinction can aid your AMS by organizing your replanning actions. See the "Children's Hour" and "Desk is a Workplace" segments of chapter 2 for a physical manifestation of the above-stated philosophy.

CASE OF THE MANAGER TOO BUSY REVIEWING TO CONTROL HIS ACTIVITY

A procurement director in a major Southeast concern was besieged by problems, personnel, boss dissatisfaction and a general feeling that he was not doing his job. I spent time showing him the review factors of his job as well as the control factors.

As I defined the problem, it became larger than even he had somehow envisioned it to be. In frustration, he shouted, "I don't have time to control my activity, I'm too busy reviewing today's problems!"

Like many of today's managers, he was besieged with reports designed to provide information on which he had to react. The problem was that the action information was mixed in with the review data. There were some management-by-exception reports, but even these required manual prioritizations before action could be taken.

We listed the five major situations the procurement manager and his employees had to consider based on data review. In priority order (and oversimplified for this discussion) they were:

1. *Stockout*...No supplies were either available or committed to other use that could immediately be procured at any price. Emergency supplies had to be sought to overcome calculated losses in processing and manufacturing delays.

2. *Expedite*...Some stocks were at a dangerous level caused by an order being late in arriving or partial receipts being diminished in regular use. Actions had to be taken to prevent a stockout.

3. *Order now*...The requirement to order items had been triggered. Orders placed in this time frame had a more than reasonable chance of being received in plenty of time to meet anticipated demand. (The percentage of on-time *receipts* is related to a firm's service level, which is the percentage of on-time *deliveries*.)

4. *Do nothing now*...Reviews were made on a routine basis on major cost items, price and volume changes, procurement lead time variations, new products or substitutions, supplier quality and reliability, etc. Any one of these items could have required either a routine or cursory review at a low-priority time or, by exception,

have been of a high-priority order. The exception should have been handled on a high-priority time basis; but, for 85 to 90 percent of the inventoried items, "do nothing now" called for a cursory review.

5. *Obsolete,* if possible...these were the items that could have been disposed of, or where quantities of the total might have been eliminated. These actions were related to an overall management plan calling for "write-downs" in the good years and no action in the lean ones.

The reports were then redesigned for the department on the basis of the above categories. Now, everyday the "stockout" and "expedite" items are analyzed to assure no alternate courses of action have been overlooked. As required, the "order now" items are isolated by the materials requirement planning system. The "do nothing now" and "obsolete" items are never printed out on the old-fashioned thick inventory status reports. If you'd like to know, the information is immediately available; but to print everything, (both action and review material piled together), does not aid an AMS manager.

The purpose of the above exercise was to ration the use of a sense of urgency on a timely, priority basis. Isolating review and control items was the key.

DECISION RISK EVALUATION STRATEGIES

In an insightful look at risk-taking rewards and penalties, David Viscott[1] points out some valuable rules to follow. For our purposes here, the following are significant in controlling your plan:

- Know the boss involved.
- Don't count on being 100 percent successful.
- Don't misplace your emotions.
- Do take time to correct mistakes.
- Do list everything that can go wrong — and why.
- Do list everything that can go right — and why.

For the aggressive management style to work, a plan does not receive *less* attention after it is proposed, altered and accepted. "Surprise!" is the reward for those managers' naivete.

If you are monitoring a plan, not just by asking, "How's it going?",

---

[1]David Viscott, M.D., *Risking,* Simon and Schuster, 1977.

but by seeking and even simulating problems, chances are you'll pick up deviations sooner, just because you will be looking for them.

Dr. Viscott points out that you can make lists of items that can go both "wrong" and "right," such that determinations can be made as to the likelihood of either change or stability. Those items that stay the same remain predictable...either for or against your plan's success. Concentrate on the variables that can become liabilities.

The lessons derived from this approach are:

- plan for success *and* failure
- monitor your plan
- concentrate on risks to success that fluctuate in their affect on your plan
- replan when the original decision factors have varied *significantly*
- monitor the new decision (plan) as you did the original one

OVERCOMING THE "PRIDE OF AUTHORSHIP" SYNDROME

Sounds simple? Well, it should be, but a prerequisite might be to wipe out ego that causes blind commitment to emotion. Assertiveness demands that you take a position and, through words and actions, command yourself (and others) to agree and follow. The aggressive management style requires that firmness and commitment today are based on today's condition. Tomorrow's data, actively monitored, may create a need to act decisively to alter the original commitment. The only qualifications are:

- establish the original plan on as objective as possible review of the risk factors
- treat the changed commitment like the initial one — right for today's factors, but conditional on a new success and failure list

Before you jump to the conclusion that I am preaching for a new breed of managers, whose plans are as changeable as a weather vane off Cape Hatteras, let me say that you should concentrate on factors that vary *significantly* from that which was used to establish the plan. A determination of significance is therefore paramount to help avoid "whim" changes to plans.

When you list the factors in a plan, list what a significant change would be:

- a quote that is $8 higher, without an offsetting gain in other economic terms.
- a substitution of an unknown talent for a known skill.

- an ally that has turned completely hostile.
- an event that was not thought significant in the original plan. For example, when the United States decided to sell wheat to Russia in 1974, someone later found out it had to be shipped to seaports and transported in grain freighters! The disasterous logistics planning could have led to a plan reversal, if such a contingency was considered.

The above list can be as *long* as your imagination or as *short* as your blind commitment to the initial plan. The essence of control is an objective reaction to a truthful review.

MAKING UP YOUR MIND

The essence of plan control (as in decision-making) also relates to the fine art of making up your mind. Should I or shouldn't I? Flip a coin; roll the dice. How do you decide, even when all the factors are stated in as cold and objective a manner as possible?

A widely held view today is that planning and decision-making are "arts" that can be learned, refined and developed far beyond the scope of those 1930s business books that called for good, old applied imagination and intuitive feelings that come with experience. Today's thinking is that the main ingredient is the weighting of inputs and objectives. (See the triangulation approach described in chapter 3 as an example.)

What do you really desire as a result? Personal gain through recognition? Improved positioning of the company's product? Elimination of an undesirable condition (undesirable to you)? A better society?

The College Entrance Examination Board (CEEB) in its decision-making seminars places initial emphasis on personal values to gain insight into the decision-making process. What are *your* values that *you* bring to the quest for the best decision? Are you motivated by altruism, money, gregariousness?

Your personal values do not necessarily add or detract from practicing the aggressive management style, but you should be able to distinguish between making decisions and solving problems. Problem-solving seeks the correct answer while decision-making seeks the best method, says the CEEB.

Decisions are based on such "pillars of your mind" as:

1. Familiarity, which is more comfortable than the unfamiliar
2. Possibility, which always seems more attractive than perceived impossibility ("That can't possibly happen!")

3. Importance, as weighed against your concept of unimportant

4. Useful and necessary, as distinguished from your personal prejudice regarding useless and unnecessary ("All reports should be in blue folders; no one takes them seriously in yellow folders"), and

5. "I can discount my emotions and arrive at an objective decision"

POSSIBLE DECISION-MAKING STRATEGIES

Four possible strategies then evolve to be used in making up your mind. They are:

- *Wish.* To apply this strategy, think of what you really want and disregard the probability of success or risk involved. "The price of our bid is proper because we need this business at this price." There is the chance that the wish will come true, which gives weight to the next "wish decision."

- *Safe.* Take very few risks and seek decisions with a high probability of success. Such a decision may also avoid the necessary risk one may have to take to achieve a breakthrough. As Dr. Joseph Juran, the guru of quality assurance, often stated, "High risk leads to the possibility of high gain and sometimes breakthroughs." Vasco De Gama found a sea route to India by never leaving the sight of the West African Coast; Christopher Columbus lost sight of land on the first day out and achieved a navigational breakthrough.

- *Escape.* This strategy attempts to minimize the occurence of the maximum downside event. If you are seeking promotion, it is possible that you see the worst disaster as discharge from employ. Therefore, you would strategize your promotion, gather facts and prioritize decisions...all with an eye to achieving the promotion with a minimum exposure to being fired. You create escape positions to assure retention of your job in case "George" becomes your boss or your present boss misinterprets the overtures you've made for promotion.

- *Combination.* This approach mixes the Wish and Safe strategies by combining your values with your wishes, and your alternatives with your probabilities for success.

No doubt my prejudice for this latter strategy has evidenced itself in these last two chapters. The aggressive management style envisages a conscious effort to match your wishes for pay, promotion and recognition with a safe strategy that considers down-side risks and alternative courses of action in controlling a plan.

EXPOSING YOURSELF (AND NOT GETTING ARRESTED)

I believe the answer lies in a combination of "what really is" and an aggressive and conscious effort to attain "what you desire." In the business entity, the confusion exists between what you desire and what you are told to desire. Some examples follow:

- "The managerial ladder is for those who 'keep their noses clean' and 'don't make waves'."
- "Longevity of service is a major element considered in personnel advancement and provides for job security over less senior employees or outsiders."
- "Knowledge of the intricate details of how the work is performed today (and those changes that were tried and failed) is a prerequisite for advancement."
- "Tracking down and compiling problem statistics is, by itself, a recognized skill for a potential manager."
- "Having the ability to perform, to an acceptable degree, all of the tasks of *your* employees is an asset without peer in gaining the support of your employees and recognition from your bosses."
- "You will be much less faulted for an inability to solve an unexpected plan problem than for submitting a nonspecific and incomplete plan (or budget) in the first place."
- "A well-documented event (such as minutes of a meeting) is far better received than an informal, though effective, corrective action taken without receiving adequate recognition."
- "Presentation *always* improves content."

I could continue indefinitely with such quotes. Some of the above are acceptable and trackable dogma in some of your work environments, as *you* perceive it.

Yet, every one of you know of exceptions to the above. To these exceptions, the following terms might be applied by the observer:

- Lucky!
- Right church and right pew.
- A fluke!
- Slipped through the net.
- He (or she) had "timing."
- She has a definite outstanding physical advantage.
- Exceptions are not the rule.

- Probably a compromise.
- Politics at work.
- He's "cute" and is always kissing...
- Probably related to somebody.
- Secret nepotism at work.
- Looks and talks like a manager.

My point here is to state that it may be worth "exposing yourself," instead of an outright "acceptance of the dogma" and thus "rejection of the exceptions." Test the water; try a zero-based plan in a small area; disregard a safe (or wish) strategy in a test area, where taking a risk might never result in a catastrophe. Build a plan with tight controls to trigger action, not just another reported problem without solution.

MOTIVATING YOURSELF

Of course, there will still be observable frustrating situations, people who advance through luck, looks, or longevity or plans that, luckily for the "wisher", worked out. But more and more, management is viewed as accomplishing tasks, whether the motive is achievement or power.

Alice G. Sargent, a consultant specializing in managerial behavior, development and effectiveness and author of *Beyond Sex Roles,*[2] stated in the October 1978 issue of *Management Review* that management accomplishes its tasks through "building a set of relationships between boss and manager, manager and subordinates, and manager and peers...This kind of communication requires interpersonal skills and concern for relationships. As a result of this emphasis, affiliation (human relations) may become important."

Thus, managers may be motivated to achieve growth through building on closer interpersonal relationships, whether or not they perceive this as their interest. However, some folks have difficulty in becoming more collaborative and less competitive, and become more aware of others' needs than in the need to gain control of the situation.

In my opinion, the reason newer management styles (consultative and participative) are not more widely used or accepted is that they have been introduced on the "total immersion" basis, where you convert the organization, train and change everyone from their practices to their very thoughts. Yet, the biggest successes have been in the less all-encompassing areas:

---

[2]West Publishing Company, 1977.

- a new sales approach
- better productivity suggestions from some workers
- reduced absenteeism
- better feelings toward each other
- molding a small group into a supportive staff to help others achieve their goals

Again, test any theory of improved management in a micro area, a small step, a minor project, a few people, one management decision. It takes very little to motivate for an apparently minor change...compared to changing a personality or attitude.

I may not agree that my employees are interested in anything but putting in their time, doing a minimum of work, getting paid and "getting the hell out of here." But if I have a specific project or problem, regardless of my attitude (or prejudice) toward them, I may ask for their ideas. By testing the water, I don't have to change my attitude towards them, and I don't have to ask for their ideas or participation on *everything* (yet).

Small successes even in minor areas are a better start than emphasis on major breakthroughs in personnel attitudes and actions in the larger arena. Success breeds success and can act as a personal motivator to future "revolutionary" acts, especially in the area of changing attitudes and managerial style.

Finally, you will probably find that the greatest single motivator of you *is* you. Trying out an academic concept in a small, insignificant real work, real world area may be the way to achieve a small positive success for you to build on.

CREATORS VERSUS MAINTAINERS

The reason so many of us continue to accept our present method of planning (and control of these plans) as an inertia difficult to reverse, may be due to the "inherent job that the Lord has for us." We cannot all be bosses, let alone top managers or good motivators.

The acceptance and use of this knowledge — to breed better management teams — is a concept held by Gene Davidsmeyer, Vice-President of Finance of the Kroehler Furniture Company. He believes that all of us have traits for creating and maintaining. Whichever is dominant establishes our label as creator or maintainer. Gene believes it is the function of a good manager to classify and then to utilize these skills to attain the organization's goals, as well as to gain more satisfied employees.

Think of the job you would have to do to change all the maintainers into creators. That doesn't mean the maintainers won't receive creativity training (and the creators, maintenance training), but the development and training will be to develop more "crossover" abilities when required, and more appreciation of the tasks and motivations of the other group.

Appreciation is a good example of the "small step" you can hope to achieve. If maintainers receive just an appreciation of creative approaches, some applications will come forth. How much success can we expect if we try to convert all maintainers to the creative process?

Whatever group you are (or perceive to be) affiliated with, the concept put forth in this chapter is that you can "wet your toes before jumping in" or try some ideas without ever risking total immersion. No action whatsoever may be the least desirable alternative.

WHY PROBLEMS PERSIST WHEN THE SOLUTION EXISTS

This subheading is extracted from an article so titled in the November 1977 issue of *Currents,* provided on United Airlines longhaul routes by the editors of *Boardroom Reports.* It is quoted here, again, because it so adequately expresses the frustration of so many managers; namely, the problem persists even though the solution exists. I'm sure many a political leader feels this same frustration.

Four ideas were put forth in this article by the author...me. (A masthead writer, unknown to me, wrote the article's title, hence my modesty up to this point.) The primary reason for nonacceptance of the solution is in the failure to sell it to the people who will use it. Seems obvious, but a surprising number of managers omit this step.

- "It's a good idea and it should sell itself."
- "The advantages are obvious."
- "If I were them, I'd buy it. Looks good to me."

I received sales training many years ago and will always remember the slogan that was in front of the classroom, "We Don't Sell; They Buy." This type of empathetic feeling would be quite a valuable help in the way you structure your sales pitch for a new idea or modified approach to an old suggestion:

- "Let me show you what this can mean to you personally."
- "These are the advantages that I perceive you will realize."
- "If I were you, I'd look at it this way."

I am not suggesting you verbalize the above, but if selling involves what the other person is buying, these are thoughts around which you could build your presentation.

IF IT'S WORTH DOING, IT'S WORTH FORMALIZING

The second reason solutions exist but the problems persist is because the new way of doing things has not been formalized, either by specific written instruction or by incorporation into mandatory operating procedures. It is so very easy to accommodate a suggestor by giving lip service to a better idea, trying it for a short period of time, then dropping it and drifting back to old habits. Of course, one of the key elements is to follow-up, but this will be covered next. Right now the premise is: if it's worth doing, it's worth formalizing.

In my early 20s (during the Korean War) I was given a special assignment at the Picatinny Arsenal in Dover, New Jersey...find out why the returned ammunition boxes could not be reused, shipped to another Army installation or simply burned. My assessment of the problem and recommended solution were heartily accepted by the Branch and Division chiefs. Two months later, the problem still existed.

A fellow engineer, my cousin-in-law, Irv Florman, suggested I incorporate my recommendation in a directive to be signed by the Division chief. This directive was signed and issued within a week and became the modus operandi that left open no options for indecision.

Since that day, I always provide the action instrument with the recommendation:

- a recommended procedure is submitted with this procedure, ready for signature and issuance, appended to the analysis.
- a proposal has the acceptance statement or signature space easily available for the needed approval.
- a recommended organizational change has the new setup attached in the form to be issued.
- a new form is not just proposed, it is designed and the printing order is sent along.
- a suggestion for a purchase should contain the purchase order ready for initialing.
- if you are recommending a reply to a letter or memo, or providing information for same, why not put the reply in the completed format of an answer?

As a boss, it often crossed my mind when I agreed to a proposal, "Now what do I do?" I could ask for a letter to be prepared or prepare it myself.

Think how much I appreciated receiving the recommendation with the action instrument. I could still reject or modify...but the proposer in-cated he or she was action oriented. As stated in chapter 1, a pillar of the aggressive management style is the efficient application of a positive and recognizable management action. Clerks record history; managers make it!

FOLLOW-UP OR FAIL

The third reason that plans and solutions fail is related to that oft-stated phrase, "Plan your controls and control your plans." To keep a new method alive, it is necessary to build in a periodic check for a reasonable period of time after installation.

The follow-up could be on a sampling or an exception basis. Look for deviations. A caution here...before you shoot them down out of hand, see if the new variation has merit. If it does, give credit to the innovator and modify your plan. Remember, "People will make their own plans work in preference to yours." By giving credit for an innovation, you will be asking your people to make *their* plan work.

The fourth idea for assuring that control of the plan is in effect is but a variation of the third one above...establish your follow-up on an excep-tion basis. As a manager, it is impossible to control everything. However, in the planning phase it is worthwhile to establish your expectations *and* those deviations from plan that should be brought to your attention. As stated in chapter 2, "Surprise" can be a very traumatic word to a man-ager's ears.

The establishment of these controls provides another advantage to the AMS practitioner, in that it forces the planner to consider downside risks and contingency plans "up front." While establishing acceptable or un-acceptable deviations from the plan, you should be forcing yourself to con-sider alternative strategies, before unexpected events force panic decisions at a later, less opportune time.

CASE OF THE FAILED SUGGESTION SYSTEM

Two cases will make this last point. One deals with a cost-reduction idea that failed, another with a control system that didn't control.

A Virginia plant of a vending machine company established a cost-reduction system with a great deal of inplant and media publicity. The workers were told of the rewards of pay and job security that awaited them when their suggestions were adopted.

Management ran a contest and the winners were not only to receive cash but recognition before their peers. No one spent any time or funds to indicate to the workers where and how to look for savings. The plant manager said, "They ought to know!"

After three months the winners were announced. Since the company was committed to a prearranged publicity campaign, these winners had to receive plaudits for the following:

- A maintenance man suggested that the floor wax be diluted with water to gain twice the floor coverage.
- An accounting clerk recommended that the adding machine tapes be reversed after use to allow the other side to be utilized.
- A truck driver suggested that the drivers clean and wash their own trucks before taking them out.

I would have loved to have been privy to the losers' ideas, considering that the three above were winners!

The plant manager stated that, although very little was done to reduce costs, employee morale was significantly boosted, and, "on that you cannot put a price tag." The world is full of people who:

- change the objective to meet new or unexpected results.
- accept surprises without learning from them for future planning, and
- claim that "feeling better" leads to higher productivity; that recognition alone is motivation; that exhortation need not be coupled with "how to" in order to cut costs, improve quality or increase productivity.

Suppose instead, the plant manager had included in his planning:

- the prospect of noncooperation, the downside risk of going ahead.
- the need to test the plan in a small area before failing in front of the whole operation. .
- what to do if the results were infinitestimal or even negative.
- some methods, procedures and cost-effectiveness training, either informal or formal.
- tie all actions to the objective, which was cost-reduction, not publicity.

Let's look at another example of poor control.

LAST TO KNOW BEING THE ONLY ONE THAT COULD CORRECT

I provided management consultancy in a company that was dedicated to the concepts that:

- if you can account for everything, you have control.
- an accurate report is worth all the money invested in the "control system", which report by itself will improve management.

Unfortunately, the control data were offered such that most of management time was spent insuring that history was repeated…that which had happened before would become the criteria for success for future activities. The budget and associated expenditures were all judged against these criteria, such that requests for deviations were "stone-walled"… requests for new technology, equipment, skills and even the updating type of training were tabled.

An example of the foregoing was in their approach to handling schedule misses on the production floor:

- The data processing system provided the first notice of a missed schedule, for whatever reason, to a Management Information Service Center two miles away. Actually, the knowledge that the schedule was missed had to be calculated by the actual data being compared to the planned schedule data.
- On the following day, a missed schedule report, a massive exception document, was issued. By 10:00 a.m., on the day after the schedule was missed, the general manager received this report in his office. If he was there to receive it, he could question the schedule misses immediately.
- On noting some of the major deviations, the general manager called in the section foreman regarding that schedule miss.
- The section foreman on most occasions would say, "I'll find out the problem."
- Upon ascertaining the problem, he or she would come back to the general manager, who would ask, "Well, what should we do? What's the effect of this on our overall schedule?" The section foreman had various answers, but the best way to sum up all of them would begin with these words, "Don't worry!"

As you can see, the last person to know about the variation is probably the only one who can do something about it — the section foreman. Much evaluation time is spent checking on history, "What happened? What shall we do?"

Now, think about establishing a control system where the *first* person to know about variations from plan (such as a schedule miss) would be the party most likely to take an effective action based on a timely evaluation. A portion of practicing the aggressive management style relates to using control data for action, not just for accountability.

Let us take this situation a step further. If you practice the AMS, consider establishing control of the plan, so that significant variations (precalculated) are not only reported on an exception basis to the party who can best react, but may also require:

• Notification of the variation to the responsible party (in the case described above, to the general manager) detailing the actions taken. This may eliminate another management nemesis, the word, "Surprise!" ("Surprise, the order is late!, Surprise, the material isn't here!, Surprise, we forgot to tell you!")

• Notification of the problem, *coupled* with a recommendation for solution or amelioration of the situation. In other words, don't just be told, "We've got a problem!" Have the potential recommended solution as part of the reporting procedure. As described in chapters 1 and 4, an implementation memo for signature could accompany the suggestion. If the boss says, "OK," what is the action authorization instrument required? Why not provide it with the recommendation?

In AMS, one presses for information for control, notification *first* of a party best equipped to evaluate and act, and finally, reporting or providing for action to that party at the appropriate action level. This approach will separate the reporters from those who are action oriented in the management control area.

INSPECTION AND EXPECTATION

There is a management adage that "you are more likely to receive that which you inspect rather than that which you expect."

A case study will depict this philosophy. In an Illinois company a meeting was held each week to plan the next week's activities. The meeting was chaired by the operations manager, who would "go around the room" and encourage the various attendees to disclose their weekly plans. Some of the managers:

• told the boss just what he wanted to hear ("Don't worry!")
• documented their plans in minute, specific, written detail (while sweeping to the grand fallacy.)
• made very conservative, understated forecasts (hoping to win kudos for beating their goals.)
• played it "straight" (and found that the glory went to the "foggers.")

Minimal contact was maintained during the subsequent week. As the first order of business for the next meeting, the weekly results versus the previous week's plans were discussed. The review:

- was easily handled by "the silver-tongued orators" who could explain any variation from plan...no matter how wide a deviation.
- was most appreciated by those whose plans had succeeded since they practiced that famous rule for getting ahead, "Take credit if things go well... no matter whether (or not) it is deserved."
- was merely a matter of finding out and accusing someone or some group whose inefficiency was inexcusable. These folks were practicing that other famous rule for political advancement, "When things go poorly, blame someone else!"

All of the plan versus actual data was distributed to the recipients just prior to the weekly meeting. On one occasion, a "game" was secretly requested for one week, whereby all of the "actual" data were multiplied by a 1.2 factor. This increased all hours, costs and other actual inputs by 20 percent. Let me repeat that only a few of us, and the data processing personnel, were privy to this knowledge.

The effect of this imaginary 20 percent increase was to throw about 40 percent of the results over the projected plan...due dates showed as being missed, cost overruns were shown as rampant, etc.

At the start of the next weekly meeting, the first ones to take the floor were the silver-tongued orators. They explained away every variation. (Quite frankly, they were so good that even I, the perpetrator of the phony numbers, was almost convinced of the reasons for the failures!)

After the "excusers" came the "blamers." They blamed everything on someone, from the president of the United States down to an old unfulfilled request for more people in Mail and Reproduction. Everyone put on an outstanding performance, using all the right buzz words and excuses that had succeeded in the past.

Could this happen where you are employed or in your department? Have you spent all of your time and effort in better planning and reporting, such that control is a game to be mastered through writing and elocution skills? Would false data be just as acceptable as a base for solution (or excuses) as reliable data?

DEFINING ACCEPTABLE FAILURES

As stated in chapter 1, the basis for the aggressive management style is the truthful though aggressive approach to foster positive results. Look at your management style and see if the following steps can improve your control:

- Define the control points in your planning phase. (See chapter 2.)
- Define the acceptable variations from plan, and plan alternate courses of action should failure either be imminent or reported to have occurred (chapter 3).
- Establish the priorities for follow-up, since you don't have the time to control everything. Remember, managers have more problems to resolve than time or talent available to resolve them. (See chapter 3 for prioritization approaches.)
- Remember that data can be sampled so that errors in significant reporting areas can be unearthed (instead of accepted). Many companies do a physical inventory count of one-twelfth of their inventory items each month. In this way, inventory errors are uncovered throughout the year, not just by "Surprise, we've run out!" or finding out you really have a two year supply at the end of the year. If you have 5,000 different stock items, this means you will physically count 18 items per day for verification. That may add up to 30 minutes a day spent to avoid, or to have to explain away, a variation.
- Don't be trapped by the artificial nature of preset times. A week, a month or a reporting period are arbitrary time frames to give a framework to accounting people (and the budget and tax people). Events and progress usually follow a much more random time pattern. A weekly report may be perfectly logical for a highly repetitive operation. This time frame, however, may have little significance in the construction or office arenas where long cycle and not easily described or measured activities occur. These types of activities are more readily controlled by milestones — definable stages of review reported on a timely and actionable basis to the party authorized to act. (See previous subhead discussion on management control.)

If the above managerial approaches are being utilized, planning and control meetings will be less fun than those with only "silver-tongued orators," "excusers," "blamers," and "surprisers." In the long run, the AMS practitioner will probably be happy to substitute the rewards of pay and promotion for "Surprise!"

In AMS, one strives to foster action through control. The strategies of failure and success control relate to preplanned actions that are spurred by review and reports. In practicing the aggressive management style, the distinction between reporting for the sake of reporting has been analyzed, so that the AMS practitioner can see the distinct advantages of seeking appropriate actions instead of excuses.

In the next chapter a special form of planning and control will be studied...managerial problem-solving. The basic premise of the AMS will be expanded to cover those managerial steps required not just to define the problem but to install a lasting solution.

PROBLEM-SOLVING WITH AMS

Allowing that the practice of the aggressive management style is most productive when applied against the functions a manager generally performs, we now proceed to discuss problem-solving leading to decision-making using the AMS. To duplicate the wealth of literature in the problem-solving field would not serve a useful purpose; to apply an AMS approach to this body of accepted knowledge is the purpose of this chapter.

PROBLEM-SOLVING UNDER PRESSURE

No discussion of problem-solving can have validity without referring to the landmark work in the field, *The Rational Manager* by Kepner and Tregoe.[1] Their book and training methods have excited managers throughout the world to rethink the seemingly obvious approaches to the logic practiced in problem-solving.

One of their most telling points (and selling points) is that "...the pitfalls of problem analysis and decision-making are almost certain to increase whenever a manager is under pressure...It is precisely at this time, when people are clamoring for action, when he (or she) doesn't have all the

[1] McGraw-Hill, 1965.

important information he thinks is needed or all the resources he would like to have, when time is short — it is precisely then that the manager most desperately needs an efficient method for handling problems and decisions. Indeed, any method that doesn't work under such pressures cannot be considered worth trying."

The strategic planners use the term "unpredictability" to describe planner problems under pressure. Here the pressure is longer range involving a new advertising campaign, divesture of a product line, new plant expansion, product introduction, new legislation, etc. The test of the managers' problem-solving abilities are measured against such factors as:

- How would you operate if business fell off 25 percent?
- What would you do if lead times for replenishment of vital stocks not only got longer but supplies became unpredictable?
- What will be the plan when the new legislation takes effect on March 15, involving new energy considerations in construction?
- Who will manage the enterprise upon the demise of the founding father and guiding light?

If your answer to all of the above is, "Don't worry! We'll make the appropriate decision, at that time, by weighing the best possible alternative courses of action;" then your answer to problem-solving is, "We'll do the best we can when we have to make a decision to solve a problem."

The purpose of this chapter is to explore the advantages of understanding and employing a set of tools for problem-solving that provides for a better response then that stated above. It is to motivate a manager to develop an understanding of the concepts underlying problem analysis and solution, such that under either long or short term pressure, the manager has a systematic approach that:

- allows him or her to know where in the problem-solving approach he or she is. Is information missing? Is a question unanswered or unasked? Has the relevant been separated from the irrevelevant? Whose input is lagging?
- enables him or her to redirect resources, change emphasis and otherwise react in a logical way to the task of pressing for an answer or reaching a decision — not just because of the time frame pressure but because the problem-solving logic drives that manager.

This approach then evidences itself in your subordinates. They begin to develop a competence in these areas through their observations of your approach to problem-solving. In the compression chamber of management under pressure, when all levels of management revert to a preset approach, this will "prevent the crew from rearranging the deck chairs on the Titanic" or "worrying about egg production while the hatchery is on fire."

WHEN THE SOLUTION COSTS MORE THAN IT'S WORTH

The AMS recognizes that the only solutions are practical ones that achieve positive results. Practical includes economical, whether this be measured on the basis of return on investment or the value of making people feel better about their work and the environment.

The two basic problems to overcome in practical problem-solving are:

1. The solution may cost more than the solution is worth.
2. The solution doesn't solve the problem.

The following example makes these two points.

An Upstate New York manufacturer of plumbing fixtures was experiencing a loss of expendable tools of the magnitude of $1,000 per month. After a three-month study, a system of controls was instituted, which had the effect of cutting these losses to about $750 per month. However, the control system cost $375 per month to administer. My suggestion (sarcastically) was that it was cheaper to let them continue stealing the expendable tools!

Obviously, this case study demonstrates the age-old problem-solving approach at work. Weigh solution alternatives (in this case only one was advanced by a "silver-tongued" orator) and *choose the best one at that time.*

This case not only exemplifies and oversimplifies the traditional approach, but it also demonstrates an area where a decision reversal is possible. What if the same company had to solve a problem under pressure of time or imminent, exaggerated loss? Could a "shoot from the hip" solution be reversed without first causing serious loss? Is your company's comment about a bad decision arrived at under pressure, "Well, it was the best we could do under the circumstances."

The British General Staff decided in 1915 to break the stalemate on the Western Front by a massive offensive in the area of the Somme River. About 300,000 casualties were suffered in the first week of that offensive, which failed both militarily and in geographic gain. However, to prove the decision was right originally, the British Expeditionery Forces lost another 200,000 men over the next two months before calling the whole thing off.

Most managers do not make such dramatic decisions that involve life or death, even of the corporate entity. But consider what tools you are using today to decide:

- The effects of future inflationary pressures on the business. Most of us underestimate the cumulative effects of inflation. We attack cost increases with price rises. Do we spend as much time and effort on productivity increases, cost analysis and reductions, motivation and incentive schemes, reducing investment such as in inventories, etc.?
- The cost of factors not heretofore relevant. Before the Arab oil embargo of 1973, it was most common to order and state "ship cheapest." In today's environment, alternatives must be calculated. Employee benefits, governmental regulation regarding health and safety, the collapse of the dollar's value, etc. all add "new" costs to our base for decision-making.

When is any of the above relevant? Do we wait until it rises from the swamp and bites us in the posterior before we react? And is our reaction based on a problem-solving approach, not just an expedient one? Although we may not be dealing with human life, a problem-solving system will generally lead to a better decision than a "shoot from the hip" response (no matter how experienced).

PREJUDICE FACTOR IN DETERMINING CAUSES AND SOLUTIONS

In my opinion, too many managers begin problem-solving with a prejudice as to:

- what the cause of the problem is, and
- what can be the expected solution, or
- a failure to recognize that a problem exists that should be solved.

Alex Osborn introduced the concept of brainstorming in his best-selling classic, *Applied Imagination*[2]. He reasoned that the creation of a vast myriad of sources and resources for solution would eventually lead to less "prejudiced" and better solutions. If "noninvolved" personnel from the clerical staff could be shown some technical or production problems, they would supply solutions promulgated by their very remoteness from the problem and the prejudices thereby incurred. Some of the ideas thus forwarded would be less "prejudiced" by preconceived notions of solutions.

Although the prejudice factor may be removed regarding cause and solution, the main feature of this approach was its novelty...people like trying to solve creatively other people's problems. The free-wheeling approach to problem-solving also involved participation of many people, whose opinions were never before sought out.

---

[2]Scribner, 1953.

However, aside from the participative involvement feature, there was no guarantee that the group would drive on to an appropriate solution; or if they did, that a valid course of management action would be derived.

The creative problem-solving approach created a wave of books and articles both pro and con. Most of the positive discussion centered on:

- new sources of ideas
- sharing of problems and rewards for solving them ("If you make me part of the problem, I'll be part of the solution by helping make *my* ideas work.")

The negative conclusions regarding creative problem-solving were summed up by Bernard Benson in *"Let's Toss This Idea Up"*[3] where he derided brainstorming as "potluck group-think" and "cerebral popcorn." Many others, like Kepner and Tregoe, feel that a systematic step-by-step approach has a higher chance of:

- recognizing the problem areas and causes
- establishing objectives and potential actions
- weighing alternatives and downside risks
- establishing priorities for implementation

As stated in the beginning of this section, "too many managers begin problem-solving with a prejudice as to what the cause of the problem is and what can be the expected solution, or a failure to recognize that a problem exists." I believe the way to overcome this prejudice is to have both a problem-solving logic *and* the creative participation of others, but only to the extent that this creativity is channeled within the discipline of problem analysis and decision-making. In this way, creativity is encouraged within the problem-solving methodology so that the prejudice factor is diminished, where the solutions are strained through the weave of the problem-solving procedure.

PROBLEM-SOLVING TO SOLVE PROBLEMS

All the thinking on problem-solving today points to selecting the problem to be resolved as a first step. If this sounds terribly basic to most of the readers, consider the teachings of just 25 years ago that started with "gather facts" as the first step. I remember asking, "of what?" and being told, "Gather the facts regarding the problem presented to you." Had I

---

[3]*Fortune,* October 1957.

been more clever, I would have then asked, "Why are we working on *this* problem?"

Today's approach is to first select a problem area. Herbert Simon[4] laid the groundwork for management simulation by showing how the human mind and a computer might look at data when comparing what was planned or expected to what did occur or what exists. He described a problem as a deviation from a standard of expectancy and the cause of problems as some unplanned and probably unanticipated change. A case study will help describe how this approach aids in selecting the problem area.

SELECTING THE PROBLEM AREA

A vice-president of an Indiana company noted a rapidly increasing value of the company's inventories. Without any other action being considered, he issued a directive that limited the dollar value of both purchases and receipts for all manufacturing required components. He assumed:

- inventory increases were due mainly to purchasing excesses
- the deviation from the expected norm was due to uncontrolled purchasing
- the resolution was to limit procurement
- limiting purchases would, by itself, reduce the value of inventory

What really occurred was that a manager under pressure moved to the easiest and most evident area for solution. But was that the problem area?

Two-thirds of the inventory value was in work-in-process...inventory that had accummulated man and machine hours and costs. Half of the remaining inventory (one-sixth) was in finished goods awaiting shipping releases, and another one-sixth was in raw materials. The vice-president assumed if he controlled raw materials procurement that the inventory would go down.

The reverse occurred. Because mating parts did not arrive for work-in-process inventories, these inventories rose; since these work-in-process inventories could not be pushed through to completion, production management kept the work force busy building with whatever parts were available. Thus, the raw materials inventories shrank faster than before while the more costly work-in-process inventories grew even larger.

The aggressive management style envisages a planned action based on selected management analysis leading to a positive result. Assuming

---

[4]*The New Science of Management Decision-Making,* Harper and Row, 1960.

the rapid growth of inventory value is a high priority problem based on a major deviation from the expected, the vice-president could have determined (or have it determined for him) that the problem area was work-in-process:

- by the size of the present commitment or by comparing the investment in work-in-process to the expected norm. Is it the absolute value that has increased or the percent of the total inventory investment?

- by understanding that procurement is a "reaction function"... reaction to the diminution of raw material supplies, acceleration of the demands of the manufacturing schedule, inefficiency of the scheduling function to balance capacity to material supply or the increasing variability in the time for replenishing stocks.

- by considering that the opportunity for solution is related to the size of the problem area.(See chapter 3.) If 65 percent of the inventory value is in work-in-process and 15 percent in raw materials, a 10 percent reduction in work-in-process (7 percent) would have to be equated to a 50 percent reduction in raw materials inventories... to equal the same 7 percent. A 50 percent reduction in any area of problem-solving is rare, but a 10 percent savings in a major area of concern is a reasonable and achievable objective.

- by isolating what the deviation from acceptable *is* and *is not.*[5] The increase in inventory *is* in dollars, not in number of different items stocked; it *is* in work-in-process, not in raw materials or finished goods; and, most importantly, it *is* caused by poorly balanced scheduling, not by over-zealous reaction in the Procurement Department.

Therefore, a manager under stress can still overcome the prejudice factor by a rational approach to determining the problem area.

EFFICIENCY LAW FOR EXECUTIVES

Dr. Alex Reuter[6] claims that executives under stress tend to gravitate toward simple problems whose solutions are evident and easily defined. The choice of the problem area for an executive under stress sometimes is limited to:

- the obvious
- the easily solvable

---

[5]A basic distinction made in the Kepner-Tregoe Approach, *op. cit.*
[6]Professor of business management, University of Arizona.

- the one that requires the least commitment or down-side risk
- that which involves the least amount of time, cost, concurrence or commitment by others

As stated earlier in this chapter, if one has a problem-solving procedure, an executive under stress can fall back on this systematic approach just as easily because:

- it has worked before
- it's comfortable because it's not new
- determination of downside risk is only one of the factors to consider ...not the only one
- proper selection of the problem area can overcome the prejudice factor in predetermining both the cause of the problem and its solution

Since most enterprises have more problems to resolve than time or talent available to resolve them, the proper selection of the problem area can reap another efficiency, that of efficiently applying management time and talent to maximize solutions.

PROBLEM SELECTION TO MATCH BUCKS TO BANG

A few examples should make this latter point.

A maraculture product's costs were closing in on the market price for fishing in the open seas. Three-quarters of the cost were composed of the variable costs of direct labor and materials. Of the 18 items included in these two categories, one of the items, feed cost, accounted for 54 percent of the total direct costs (41 percent of the total cost). An eight percent reduction in this feed cost by a "buy or make" decision was equivalent to about four percent in product profit. An 88 percent reduction in power used (an improbability of the highest magnitude) would provide the same results. Yet the same amount of technical manpower was allocated to both areas of cost (problems)! Surely management should match bucks to bang!

Another example involves the cost-estimating function of a construction operation. If the estimate came in too high, management would decree, "Cut the cost 10 percent so that we put in a responsive bid!" Across-the-board cuts of 10 percent were mandated.

This meant both the conservative department putting in a reasonable estimate and the "free-wheeling" manager who put in a padded estimate had their estimates hacked by 10 percent. It didn't take long for the various managers to learn to "play the game"...put in for all you can get: you'll be cut by a percentage anyway.

A better approach involved determining the 22 percent of the items in the estimate that caused 70 percent of the cost. Management time was expended in these few areas to seek shortcuts and savings.

This self-same approach is evident in the next case. A manufacturer of coated fabrics for the auto industry produced these products on 21 different final assembly lines. Both Quality Control and Inspection staffed these lines on the basis of one inspector per line and one Quality Control person per three lines. Yet, the yield (good product as a percent of total yards produced) figures indicated that 52 percent of the rejected material came from four out of the 21 lines. A dramatic effect on quality yield was achieved by reallocating Quality Control talent and time to match the problem, not the number of lines.

Finally, a financial controller of a Midwest concern had a serious problem of cash flow (and float) to contend with, which he had inherited. Realizing that cash commitments are a function of cash size *and* the time that cash is committed, he analyzed the cash flow as shown in Figure 5-1.

He then found out that a very disproportionate amount of time was spent on pursuing accounts receivable, speeding up the billing and collections process, etc. When he realized that 83 percent of the cash float was in the time committed to preparing and processing an order, he reallocated his manpower to match the size *and* location of the problem.

These are examples of the positive effects of adequately defining the problem area by matching bucks to bang.

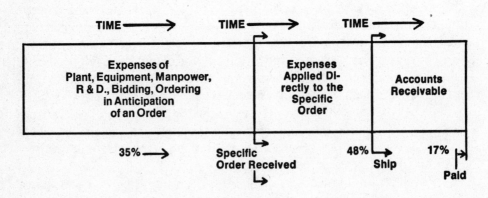

Figure 5-1

DEFINING YOUR EXPECTATIONS

Assuming the selection of the problem area has been accomplished, what are management's expectations or criteria for success? In practicing the aggressive management style, one must:

- match bucks to bang
- select areas of opportunity
- establish reasonable objectives of accomplishment within these parameters

Some of the biggest problems that managers complain to me about are related to:

- "That's not what I wanted."
- "Good solution to the wrong problem."
- "Great problem-solver if I stay with him or her all the way to conclusion."
- "What problem did you solve?"

As stated in chapters 2 and 8, management must constantly be looking at the objectives they have communicated to others. Remember, "It's not what is said that counts; it's what is heard." "It's not what is written; it's what is read." "It's not what you mean; it's what is understood." In chapter 7 these principles will be expanded as they relate to the practice of delegation in using the aggressive management style.

This step in problem-solving — defining your expectations — is exceedingly important not just for delegation and improved communication but also because many times solutions become evident while establishing objectives. Some solutions will be evident, but discarded; obvious conclusions are isolated as the only ones that meet the criteria for success.

A reverse-twist story can help make this point from my own experience as an employee in a U.S. Army arsenal during the Korean conflict. An engineer was sent to observe an operation of crimping cartridge cases on high-explosive shells. The boss wanted to reduce the number of personnel exposed to the hazards of working in that area. After a two-week study, the engineer devised a plan to *add* two more people in order to *increase* production by 19 percent!

Obviously, a specific, understood statement of what constitutes problem solution can be misinterpreted or even disregarded. But, I do not believe in any one who works for me on a problem who cannot repeat what the agreed objective consists of in specific detail. If memos and reports are frustrating to understand, see if the writer has clearly stated the criteria for success. Is this your understanding of the objective?

ESTABLISH LIMITS OF EXPENDITURE

The selection of the problem area and the establishment of the criteria for success, in reality, establish the limits for the expenditure of resources for solution. Granted unlimited time, money, skills, plant and equipment, you could probably solve every management problem. If your typewriter breaks, it would be easier to replace it than repair it, but at what cost? During the 1930s poor people really believed the radio comedian who said, "Rich folks trade in their cars when the ash trays are full."

Down here on terra firma, the aggressive management style requires a logical limit on the commitment to problem-solving, which is likely to be dictated by the value of the solution — be it cost, morale or safety. No operation in an office or plant is completely safe. The cost of the floor surface is more likely to be related to safety and durability in the plant, or the beauty and maintenance in the office. The limits of expenditure are related to these obvious criteria for success.

Even the creative problem-solving approach needs limitations. By my criteria, the greatest negative factor I have seen in the unstructured, brainstorming approach, is the vast amount of time spent in weighing ideas where the solution may cost more than the problem is worth to have resolved. Hence, this step in problem-solving is both obvious and important.

GATHER FACTS AND ANALYZE THEM

In practicing the aggressive management style, a positive approach to gathering facts follows the previous problem-solving steps. A manager, practicing AMS, gathers facts:

- As they relate to the statement of the problem — the criteria for success.
- Relevant to the limits of expenditure as well as utilizing the following practices:
  - The cost of gathering extraneous information should be weighed against the future value of this information (and future costs of regathering this information).
  - Separate "need to know" from "like to know."
  - Consider sampling data or observations, rather than total dedication to every detail of information being collected. If a computer report consists of 200 pages of 25 lines each of ran-

domly printed information, a sample of one item per page (four percent) may tell you what you wish to know in general enough terms about *all* the items.

- Since most data are gathered at random, a logical grouping (analysis) is a vital prerequisite to a meaningful evaluation of this data.
- Separate the pertinent from the merely interesting (and it helps to know the difference).

In solving a quality problem, the Quality Assurance Department knew that the critical costs of losses were evident in 10 percent of the product failures. They conducted a 400 percent sort and analysis to find this 10 percent. A consultant took this 10 percent of rejects to the customers' incoming inspectors, who proceeded to pass 43 percent of the rejected items by the supplying company! What are the facts as they relate to the problem of quality losses? How should these facts have been gathered? Gather facts relevant to the problem statement.

CASE OF THE UNMANNED DESKS

An insurance company was examining the manning (and womanning) requirements for its Query Department. Queries were received from policy-holders relevant to their policies, beneficiaries, cash values, etc. The only place where these queries could be answered was from the employees' desks, which held inquiry terminal screens. There was no direct work activity that could be performed away from these desks.

A two-month activity sampling study showed 53 percent desk utilization. Assuming 1½ hours of personal and idle time as normal in an office environment (20 percent), this still left two hours a day of unmanned answering stations in the Query Department. The company turned down the manager's request for a 10 percent increase in personnel and invested that same amount of money in work scheduling and control, as well as in supervisory training.

The insurance company had:

- gathered data relevant to the staffing problem.
- used sampling to gain a more representative view of the work versus idle time.
- drawn a conclusion based on an analysis of the data relevant to the size and cost of the problem.

This is a good example of gathering facts relevant to the nature of the problem.

CREATIVITY HAS ITS DAY

As discussed earlier in this chapter, a fundamental schism exists between the creative problem solvers and the structured devotees. I have found that the best of both worlds converge at this point in problem-solving *after:*

- the area for solution has been selected.
- the criteria for success have been established.
- expenditure limitations have been expressed.
- facts have been gathered and grouped for evaluation.

Given the above, brainstorming, creative participation or even using a "quiet time" in your office are of maximum value. The objectives and limitations for "free and sometimes wild" thinking have been set. Both experience and virgin ingenuity can be used. Constructive criticism can be defined within the limits of the problem-solving objectives. Directed creativity so constrained is usually far more constructive than random brainstorming (you may miss the big breakthrough, but you'll solve many more day-to-day problems on a logical basis).

A caution here...make sure the proposed solution meets the criteria for success heretofore established. This may mean rejecting or shelving some "fantastic" ideas. Assign the proper priority and responsibility to these rejected gems, but solve the problem before you as an imminent priority. The aforementioned concept is obviously overridden by a safety or exceptionally costly problem that may be unearthed.

If possible, try out the solution on a limited or pilot basis, so that a small financial exposure may turn up necessary modifications prior to any total commitment. Remember, consider the downside risk...the risk of failure.

SELLING IS NOT A DIRTY WORD

Managers have said to me, "A good idea sells itself." They forget to add the word "ultimately."

In practicing AMS, an unacceptable idea is one that is not sold. The reasons may vary from inappropriate and unworkable, to untimely and premature. These are not sold for obvious and valid reasons.

But what of good ideas, logical solutions to known and costly problems? Can we rely on the theme, "Good ideas sell themselves?" It would seem that if this were true, Stephen Foster, Thomas Edison and Alexander Bell would have had glorious years in their youths wallowing in recognition, money and acceptance.

Unfortunately for today's managers, good ideas must still be sold; solutions to problems are not readily accepted based on logic, cost, quality or even safety. Yet, the myriad of books and articles on problem-solving and decision-making give scant notice to this phenomena.

To one wishing to apply AMS to the problem-solving method, I recommend two concepts in the following sections that, among others, may be easy to consider and apply. As stated in chapter 1, there are a host of skills one is exposed to in assertiveness training, but our objective is to provide aids to those who cannot practice "power" and "I am someone" poses, but would like some help within the framework of the average, nonassertive personality.

I'LL BUY MY OWN IDEAS BEFORE YOURS

The first of these techniques is a very old approach that focuses on making the person to be sold part of the solution. The theory here is that people are more prone to buy their ideas than yours. The object of the aggressive management style is to achieve recognition for positive actions taken; however, the first thrust is to have sold a positive action to be taken, then to receive recognition.

A proposal is shown in "rough" to the potential "buyer"; a question is asked, help or advice are elicited; comments are encouraged on a test or pilot area. As soon as any aid is given, try to incorporate it in the solution; give credit to the potential "buyer." You have now made them part of the problem resolution. You have incorporated their ideas (at least some of them) and they have become part of the solution.

This approach, I believe, is better than coldly requesting concurrence, which works real well for minor requests (such as the "If I don't hear from you by Friday..." technique described in chapter 2). However, for major proposals and projects, selling by involving the potential "buyer" is one approach that works.

SELLING PEERS AND SUBORDINATES WITH "SIMMER TIME"

To sell your peers or subordinates may require a modification of the above described approach. Here, you are not just requesting concurrence or approval, but are many times asking for commitment, since acceptance of the proposal will subsequently require the "buyer's" time, effort and some degree of enthusiasm.

In these instances, I recommend the "simmer time" approach. Broach the idea informally. Let some "simmer time" pass and ask if they've given the idea any thought. If they have, discuss their inputs on a positive basis, seeking some constructive criticism, some germs of ideas, some insights that you may have overlooked. Incorporate their thinking in the formal proposal, mention their input and give credit and thanks where appropriate.

Using "simmer time" allows for the fact that your first contact with the potential "user" may result in a negative reaction, which is a normal "knee-jerk" response implying:

- Why are *you* requesting a change in the "status quo?"
- *Your* solution may be a criticism of *my* present practices.
- Is it change or does the solution mask some other less obvious motive?
- I have some ideas, too! I can also think!
- If that's what you want, I'd better buy some time to think about it!

"Simmer time" envisages any or all of the above as possible; so instead of a mandated solution being told to peers and subordinates, an informal discussion masks the introduction of the idea and elicits ideas during the "simmer time." This is a better approach than trying to change a "knee-jerk" "No!" to a meaningful "I'll try" by the potential "user."

Even when a manager is under pressure, he can buy a lot more acceptances by potential "users" if the "simmer time" is but a few hours in one day. Obviously, "simmer time" is a most inappropriate selling device when "the barn is afire"...but is an appropriate approach in a majority of selling situations involving peers and subordinates.

BE FLEXIBLE NOT BRITTLE

Another acceptable word that has crept into the dictionary of useful management terms is "compromise." A generation of managers in the 1940s and 1950s related compromise with a 1938 picture of Neville Chamberlain returning from Munich waving a signed document by Messrs. Hitler, Mussolini and Daladier, whilst proclaiming, "peace in our time." Compromise was related not only to "give-away" but also to a "non-macho" management style.

Industrial psychologists and laymen thinkers, especially Blake and Moulton[7], Hertzberger, Rensis Likert and MacGregor, gave rise to the concepts of people orientation, participative managerial style, motivation through understanding and communication, involvement, etc.

More recently, transactional analysis (TA) has provided managers

---

[7]Blake, Robert R. and Jane S. Moulton, *The Managerial Grid,* Gulf Publishing, 1964.

with some useful insights on understanding and using human behavioral patterns. Each person is viewed as a parent (critical and nurturing), an adult (problem-solving, rational thinker) and a child (free, natural, adaptive, rebellious, manipulative, creative). Behavior is analyzed for understanding, modification or elimination of negative or negative invoking traits.

Selling depends on the interaction of buyer and seller, whether the buyer perceives the advantages of the proposal or is rejecting or accepting the proposer. The manager must combine his or her adult problem-solving mode with "supportive" (nurturing) of a parent and the creativity and spontaneity of a child.

I call the technique that fits the above in selling solutions, "Compromise," which involves:

- listening to the "buyer's" problems with acceptance of the solution as presented and actively seeking an accommodation.
- negotiating a solution instead of forcibly stating your position and awaiting the "buyer's" reaction.
- building in the varied experiences and priorities that may have escaped you in your subjective drive for a solution.

Compromise is not weakness. It calls for managers to increase their understanding of themselves, others and the nature of interactions. As Franklin D. Roosevelt once said, "It is much easier to make war than to make peace." Compromise is a useful tool in selling solutions, but difficult to apply by the "macho" manager.

GETTING CREDIT FOR PROBLEM RESOLUTION

By working with and through others, I stated that the main thrust is to sell a positive action, by having the "buyer" accept through involvement (participation), use of "simmer time" or compromise. Yet the practice of the aggressive management style also requires recognition of you by others, as either the problem-solver or the installer. The drive for a "sold" solution is paramount, since little credit adheres to the failed problem-solver who mournfully complains, "If they had bought my idea, we would have been successful!"

Credit is achieved by:

- a recognition of the positive result in a series of problem resolutions inaugurated or fertilized by your efforts (This is the ideal.)
- a follow-up note thanking all who participated...written by you.
- a report on the success of the solution, tabulating the savings, the participants and the successes (on your letterhead).

- a call for additional ideas to augment the partially successful installation...to then be forwarded to you as coordinator.

But, the first AMS step in selling is to drive to solution. Credit taking is a subtle acknowledgement of the participants to the success. The alternative is either to receive no credit where deserved, or to strive to take credit for all your efforts, which may result in both successes and failures. But who wants credit for failures?

FINALIZE AND FOLLOW-UP

Chapter 4 dealt with the philosophy that controls and makes plans work. So too, problem solution without finalization, follow-up, evaluation and control, may be a less than worthy management endeavor.

Finalizing a problem solution requires utilizing whatever procedural formality exists in your work environment. The objective is to make it very difficult to slip back to the "old and comfortable" ways (pre-solution). Finalizing may involve:

- a written procedure "dipped in the cement" of a procedures manual or standard operating procedure (SOP).

- an announcement to one and all by letter or memorandum over the signature of the highest placed officer you can persuade to sign.

- a statement with supporting "nods of approval" at an important meeting.

- a "Hail Mary" distribution to everyone even remotely involved, such that a drifting back to the previous action or procedure may require a similar notification to be acceptable.

Follow-up is merely a designated selection of a sampling time in the future, in order to see if the proscribed problem solution is still in effect. Remember the statement in chapter 3, "You are more likely to get that which you inspect rather than that which you expect." Also, if you accept that problems are noted as deviations from an accepted norm, during the follow-up determine the reasons for deviations from that which was sold and finalized. If a deviation of significance exists, you must now recycle to steps one through three:

- Is this a problem or is the deviation acceptable?

- Am I still meeting the criteria for success or should I modify my original objective in light of current circumstances?

- Gather the facts as they relate to the deviation, etc.

A case study will demonstrate how follow-up succeeds. A fractional horsepower motor manufacturer experienced three problem operations that were causing a 17 percent rejection rate in final assembly. This rejection rate varied only minutely from a range of plus or minus two percent (15 to 19 percent rejection rate occurred 96 percent of the time). In fact, there were technical personnel who actually congratulated themselves on their startlingly accurate forecasts of rejection.

A detailed study of the first operation revealed that seven out of nine operators were exactly following the written procedures. It followed that there was a direct correlation between the rejection rate and the two out of nine operators who did not follow the proscribed procedure.

On the second operation, there were four possible acceptable procedures, which the operators could choose to follow. They randomly chose *all* of them. Meanwhile, an analysis of the third operation showed that eight out of 11 operators were not following the established procedure... but had actually developed a better one. Thus, three out of 11 who were following the established procedure produced most of the 17 percent defectives from that operation.

Moral:

- Follow-up is an investigation of what is versus what you expect.
- Correct and train operators or modify the procedure in light of the follow-up information.
- Installation and data collection are not the final steps in problem solution.
- Problem solution may also involve, in the planning for installation phase, establishing contingency plans to cope with failure — partial or total. Consider downside risks and their probability in scheduling installation of the solution.

EVALUATE AND CONTROL ON AN EXCEPTION BASIS

Finally, evaluate and control the solution to see that the projected savings and/or benefits have been achieved. Solutions are many times sold on the basis of projected savings, but the prognosticators are not evaluated and rated at some future date.

Hence, approvals may be given for projects because:

- It sounds about right.
- It was backed up nicely by charts, curves and a thick appendix.
- The presentation was super!

- What can we lose?
- It's better to take a positive action than to reject an impassioned plea for action.

CONDUCTING A POST-MORTEM

In practicing the aggressive management style, a very handy evaluative tool is the "post-mortem"...the planned evaluation of savings or benefits achieved versus those prognosticated and sold to the approvers.

A good example is the capital audit. In preparing capital budget expenditures, I have seen managers decide what they'd like to have and then drum up the reasons to back up that decision.

The request then goes to a capital equipment budget committee whose personnel decide for or against the project on the basis of:

- Does it sound good?
- Are the projected savings reasonable for the requested expenditure?
- Is the proposal well written, in that its premises answer all the questions we might ask?
- Do we have the money to spend?
- Is that division's contribution worthy of recognition?
- Let's put a "No" in with the approvals to show we're even-handed.

A post-mortem approach adds another question, "What is the track record of the requesting party or organizational element in planned savings versus actual savings?" A post-mortem (or capital expenditures audit) usually turns up those who propose but cannot produce.

The very existence of an evaluation process can have an ameliorating affect on the planning, forecasting and problem-solving functions. Consider how much management time is spent in weighing a project's worth and priority, relying on the proposer's promised savings and time frame for same.

CONTROLLING THE SOLUTION

Controls should be established (see chapter 4) over the installation of the solution by the normal reporting or budgetary control system. This is to ensure continued and effective use of the solution as envisioned.

Wherever possible, controls should be on an exception basis, so that out-of-control deviations from acceptable come to the fore for management action.

MANAGEMENT IS A RESULTS CONTEST

Management is a results contest, not just a report writing, personality contest. The payoff for any project is not just in the "cuteness" of the solution, but in the effectiveness of the installation.

Problem-solving techniques are guides to trigger a structured response to the drive for solution. The test of the practicality of the problem-solving technique is when the manager is under pressure. The solution should not cost more than the problem is worth to resolve and the solution should solve the problem.

In practicing AMS, the manager must overcome the prejudice of beginning with a preset idea of what is the cause of the problem and what can be the expected solution. Yet, creative approaches to problem-solving are most valuable as practiced within the framework of the structured problem-solving steps.

The first step is to define and select the problem area. This step helps the manager match bucks to bang in establishing the criteria for success and the limits of expenditure.

When facts are gathered, restraints are established by both the criteria for success and the limits of expenditure. The evaluation of these facts brings creativity to the fore in problem-solving.

We next concerned ourselves with selling the proposed solution because the "buyers" are both our bosses and peers as well as our subordinates. Since people tend to favor their ideas over ours, the "simmer time" and compromise approaches were presented.

As stated in chapter 1, one of the cornerstones of the aggressive management style is to receive credit for the accomplishment of positive solutions. Ideas on receiving such credit, after installation, were presented on a shotgun basis...choose the pellet that strikes you.

As in the preceding chapter, plans without controls are as treacherous as solutions without finalization, follow-up, evaluation and control.

We may all wish we had a better system for problem-solving, but the state-of-the-art has brought us a long way from the days of the "shoot-from-the-hip" problem solvers. As in the famous Polish saying, "Veneer can be added to wood but the wood has to be there in the first place." Build from today's status of problem-solving; a lot of business thinkers have brought us this far, so why repeat the mistakes of the past?...instead, build on them by "putting veneer on wood" that exists.

6

AGGRESSIVE ANALYSIS
OF COMMUNICATIONS

No book on management style can be complete without revealing the author's concepts on how to preserve and improve communications. An offshoot of these concepts appears in a major portion of any discussion on delegation (which will be covered in chapter 7). Therefore, in practicing the aggressive management style, the main thrust of this chapter will be to provide self-analysis and self-improvement tools to turn your plans into actions by others. Communication and delegation techniques are means to this end and will be so treated.

By adopting a results approach, the manager practicing AMS may:

- communicate without being "loved" by the recipient.
- have work carried out precisely and on time, even with a minimum of personal contact.
- relate the value of communications and delegation to the value of the particular task to be performed (action-orientation for positive results).

SENDER MUST HAVE EMPATHY WITH THE RECEIVER

Of all of the writings on communication and communicative skills, nothing is more basic or pertinent to the action-orientation AMS promulgates as the slogan, "The sender must have empathy with the receiver." In practice, this means it is more important to concern yourself with:

- what is *understood* rather than what you *meant;*
- what is *heard* rather than what you *said;*
- what is *read* rather than what you have *written.*

When querying managers who are frustrated by their employees' lack of performance, it is not uncommon for these managers to state:

- "That wasn't what I *meant!*"
- "I *said* I wanted it finished by Tuesday!"
- "I *wrote* that I required an answer as soon as possible; when will that happen?"

Some managers even assume righteous poses indicative of the feeling, "I'm communicating; why aren't they listening?" Perhaps assertiveness training can make managers feel that their aggressiveness must surely be communicated to the recipient and therefore act as a call to action. *Perhaps?*

I propose that the aggressive management style is best served by a practitioner so action-oriented that his or her drive to communicate is best served by a prejudice towards what the receiver hears as a higher priority than the bombast of what was said. The sender must have empathy with the receiver.

WHAT OUR BOSSES TEACH US

Dr. Sterling Livingstone stated in his writings on the Pygmalion Effect that most of us learn management styles from our bosses. If they are autocratic, participative or assertive, there is a good possibility that we will emulate them, on the assumption that if it's successful for them, it may work for us.

Some will view the particular style of their bosses as weak, ineffective or domineering, depending upon their ability to compare the style with others that may appear more successful. We also compare our boss' style to that which we've read about or heard about at seminars, professional societies' conventions or at social or outside gatherings.

What we are looking at is the style versus the result. If it is a successful approach, from our viewpoint, the practicality of adoption becomes significant. If we match the observed style to failure, we'll react accordingly. All of the above relates to styles of management, including styles of communication.

If the boss puts everything in writing, we tend to. If all oral decisions are treated with less regard than written ones, we tend to first make the decision as to importance, then state them or write them out. If the boss's method results in missed communications, forgotten due dates and partial completions, we may then apply our own management style to improve the results.

The point is that we learn our management styles from either emulating successful managers' traits or developing appropriate techniques from their failures. But, the measure of our judgement is related to their style versus our perception of results.

OBSERVING A GRADUATE OF THE
IDI AMIN SCHOOL OF MANAGEMENT

Let me tell you about a boss of mine back in mid-century, named George. George was discharged from the Marine Corps and was still holding his swagger stick when I met him at a meeting to present him to the staff. His opening remarks were filled with the usual buzz words of 1950s management: "teamwork," "strive for excellence," "we're as good as the weakest link," "brainstorm the problems," and "you're all important to me." He punctuated each phrase by smashing the swagger stick on the table top.

Some of the group were intimidated; some motivated by the call to company "nationalism"; some inwardly sneered and smirked at George's posturing mannerisms. No one was unaffected. Everyone was curious to see this management style in action.

A week after this introductory meeting, George summoned me to his office. I later found out I was not being singled out for this "honor", but that George could better dominate his employees from his office than from seeing us in ours. In any event, he made a simple request. "I want the absenteeism report on my desk on Monday at 8:00 a.m." ("Bang!" went the swagger stick on the desk top.) P.S. — The request was made at 4:30 p.m. on Friday by this endearing man!

I worked over the weekend and did complete the report on Sunday night. On Monday, at 8:00 a.m., I marched into his office, only to be told by his secretary that he informed her on Friday night he wouldn't be in until Tuesday.

On Tuesday, he came in but didn't ask for my report, so I didn't volunteer it. On Wednesday, he called to ask if I'd completed my work on his requested report. I replied, "Yes. I'll bring it right over." Without a word he accepted my offering, even though it was two days late.

Did he realize I was late? Did he remember he had asked for it on Monday at 8:00 a.m.? Did he control only that which he remembered? Was his original communication of time merely a pose for asserting his authority? How should I play the game in the future?

A month later, George asked (demanded, if you include the pounding of his swagger stick) for another type of report to be submitted on the following Wednesday. I thought, "Maybe he means the following Friday," and performed accordingly.

I guessed wrong. George never asked for that report again!

The climax of my career while working for George came when he demanded an equipment utilization report five days after the end of the month. Five days after the month ended, he hadn't asked, but I hadn't done the report either. Ten days after the end of the month, he did ask for the report. I responded with, "What report?" He countered, "Why, the report I asked you to prepare!" My reply was, "You didn't ask *me!*" He left at this point. I left one year later, of my own accord and for other reasons.

Note that this last time George remembered the request for the equipment utilization report. What he couldn't quite recall was when it was due or who was to do it.

The communicator (George) failed in both communication and delegation not because he wasn't specific but because his control of the communication was nowhere as precise as the request. The sender had empathy with the receiver but the receiver also received another message, "He doesn't really mean it." If the objective of the aggressive management style is to communicate to achieve positive results, rules should be adhered to for *both* adequate communication (and delegation) as well as follow-up and control.

COMMUNICATING SPECIFICITY

Let's start with a list of items that might be a mental check list to assure communication. Tie this list to a specific rule, "What they read is more important than what you wrote," by applying the check list to specific outgoing mail, memos and notes going out of your "out-box" (or your secretary's).

Is the task to be performed (being communicated to the receiver) specific as to:

- *What* is to be done? If you are communicating with a senior member of your staff or of the organization, a note that says (or infers), "handle this" is sufficient. For a less than senior member of your organization, about half the time the following may occur:
  a. The recipient may come back and ask for clarification.
  b. He or she may do nothing or postpone action.
  c. They may do something or merely part of the job.
  d. They may perform wrongly, requiring rework.
  e. Many times, those who do not understand become antagonistic towards the requestor.

As stated earlier in this chapter and in chapter 3, many managers complain about "never having the feeling they've put something to bed." (Like the couch's down pillow, when you push down on one side, it comes up on the other; so you push down on the other side and the original side rises!)

See if you can categorize interruptions caused by an unspecific, "What is to be done?" in your next activity sample. (See chapter 3.) A more specific "what" can help you communicate *once* for effective action by the receiver.

- *Why* it is to be done? Reasons lend credence to requests that require some initiative. You can tell a drill press operator to drill the holes to a specification without a "why?" You can ask the word processing typing pool to produce a report, without a "Why the report is being written." However, examine the requests that require some initiative or creative thinking on the part of the receiver; a "why" for these folks is a definite specificity to enable you to communicate *once*. It will also help prevent solutions that "kill the patient to cure the cancer."

- *Who* is to do it? Unspecified responsibility gives people the feeling that if everyone's responsible then no one's responsible. Think about the last time you went to a meeting and the boss said, "We've got to cut costs!" You thought, "Well, I'm doing my job; I hope the others shape up and do theirs." As you look through your "Out-box," see if you have been specific as to who is to do what. It will save a lot of personal trauma that is felt when your subordinates reply, "Did you mean *you* wanted *me* to do *that?*" Granted 50 percent know without it being stated. What about the other half who have to guess you mean them? Remember, in practicing the AMS, our whole thrust must be to encourage positive action in an efficient manner, by a party we wish to have act.

- *When* is it to be done? By applying realistic deadlines, we allow others to plan. In chapter 2, this principle was expressed in a case study of the secretary who mistook priority establishment with scheduling herself. I believe it is the sender's responsibility to establish or, at least infer, a due date. The recipient melds this assignment into the schedule of all work to be accomplished.

If the date appears realistic in terms of the existing workload, all well and good. If it appears unlikely that the requested due date and priority description can be achieved, the receiver must notify the requestor as soon as possible with an alternative date. Only the requestor can change his or her due date. Hence, the specificity by the requestor starts the above-described cycle.

The routine use of any of the above-required specifics, or those following, will be covered in the discussion of "To Do" cards and "Work Request" forms. Specificity is an "apparent burden" to the uninitiated that can be reduced through routinization.

- *Where* is it to be accomplished? This is a specific of limited applicability. Most times "where" is obvious. However, I have found the use of this specific very helpful in assuring the maintenance of confidentiality. I request certain items be "handled," such as typed, researched, or even the file held, "In Your Office Only." I have found that confidentiality is assured not just by stamping and sealing, but also by defining the only area where the information can or should exist. However, as stated, this specific has very limited applicability.

- *What* are the *factors* to consider? This is a must when training new employees or opening a new task for resolution. Sometimes you may have been the only recipient of the factors to consider, by hearing them from your boss. By defining the parameters of the work, you not only save time for your employees, but you also give them the benefit of the effort and thought that has gone before.

Describing a limitation for investigation and consideration is an economical specific. Can it be expressed orally? Is it important enough to be communicated in writing? In the previous chapter on problem-solving this was discussed in the importance of both stating objectives *and* defining the limits of expenditure to meet the criteria for success.

- *What organization* or *personnel* must make commitments of manpower, machine time, space, etc.? Have you or your boss requested these commitments? Have they been given? Again, this specific is not universally required.

- *What* are the *politics* involved? Who must be sold? Who can be told?

The list of questions to bring specificity to your communications is endless. The purpose of giving the reader the above list was to trigger a thought process. At first blush, it looks like quite a list, a larger than necessary time-consumer. Perhaps the "cure" costs more than the "sickness" is worth to cure.

What is being suggested is that specificity can improve action by the receiver. Therefore, the rest of this chapter will be devoted to using this principle in practice...such that one can see that, if specificity is built into the routine of communicating, delegating, assigning and controlling, the task becomes less arduous than an individual effort of thinking through the questions of, "what, why, who, when, where, etc.?"

THE TICKLER FILE FOR AUTOMATIC FOLLOW-UP

About half the managers I speak to, in the United States and abroad, keep some form of tickler file (also called "bring forward file", "suspense file", "schedule time-jogger)". This file consists of at least 31 slots, folders or spaces to account for the dates of the months. Additional folders may include overflows for annual quarters, accounting periods or critical path milestones. (See Figure 6-1.)

For the uninitiated, this file is kept by the manager or by his or her secretary. Instead of marking up the little desk calendar with due dates, keeping separate notes, letting papers pile up in a "hold box" (sometimes the bottom of the "in box") or making priority piles on your desk, the tickler file is used.

As papers flow across the manager's desk, those that require delegation and follow-up work that can be postponed until further data are received are put in the appropriate file date folder for recall. This folder may also include meeting notices, promises made to you (remember my boss, George?) or calls that were to be made and received. Instead of the informality of relying on personal recall ability, the file is an automatic mind-jogger.

The purpose of mentioning the tickler file at this juncture is to cover three previously described principles:

- communication should be specific.
- delegation without control is less effective than with control.
- routinization of both specificity and control should be sought.

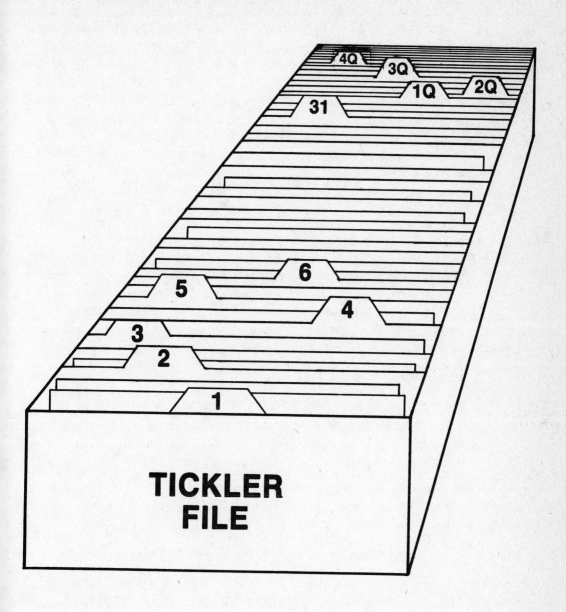

TICKLER FILE

Figure 6-1

SPECIFICITY WITH ROUTINIZATION AND CONTROL

Figure 6-2 shows a delegation that is a good example of both routinization and controlled delegation at work. The form depicted is a "To Do" card (which I much prefer to a "To Do" list, for reasons that will be disclosed in chapter 7). Note the specificity of "what", "who" and "when." "Why" was not included because this was part of a project that all had been involved with for quite some time. My secretary notes the 3/20 and 3/25 due dates in my tickler file folders and dispatches the assignment.

If the work is to be performed by me as a personal assignment for a future date, this, too, is entered in the tickler file. A start date is added to trigger the appropriate response from me at the proper time as I perceive my personal work schedule.

Queries concerning the assignment (delegation) to others are always welcome. The "To Do" card can never be considered the last word regarding the information I might be able to provide. It is an admirable framework...the "bones" on which we "hang some skin." Questions arise that I had never considered; unforseen problems with the original assumptions arise. But the queries fit within the framework of the procedure for meeting objectives with specific assignments being communicated and a routinized control system in effect.

It takes about one minute to prepare that "To Do" card, which really isn't that much time if you consider:

- the specificity is put in writing (the formal communication).
- the card becomes a work authorization (delegation).
- the follow-up is procedurized (the control is established in the planning phase as envisioned in chapter 4).

Obviously not all assignments should require "To Do" cards. A majority of assignments merely require a notation of the expected completion dates to be entered in the tickler file.

FORMALIZING THE INFORMAL COMMITMENT

For many managers, the tickler file is a recipient of written communications only. This need not be. My tickler file has over 250 entries at any given time...about one-third to one-half are letters, memos, minutes and the like. The majority of the entries are a formalization of informal commitments.

Suppose you pass John in the hall and ask him, "When will I see the final copy of the Apple Report?" John may reply, "Friday, the sixth, at the

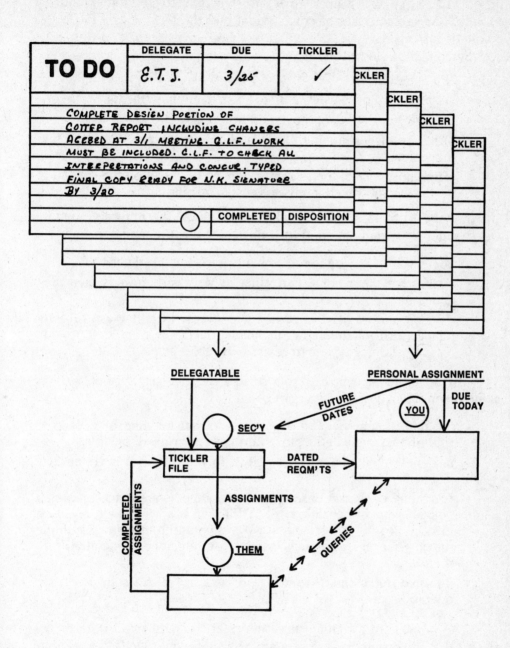

Figure 6-2

latest." The usual follow-up is to try to remember this commitment; try to recall the subject, date of commitment and the person who made the commitment.

Some of the readers will say:

- "I'll remember."
- "A good employee will live up to his or her commitments."
- "I forget some, but not the important ones."
- "Are you suggesting that I keep tabs on everything? Who's got that much time?"
- "If we miss a date, then I remember; so I control on the exception principle...however, lately we've been missing a lot of due dates."

For the 10 to 15 seconds it takes to jot down the informal commitments and have them commited to your tickler file, the manager may:

- be freed from having to remember a myriad of due dates.
- assure that the average performer as well as the others meet due dates.
- develop a routinized, automatic follow-up to either assure compliance with volunteered or mandated due dates, or at least provide an early warning system to advise of trouble spots.

The tickler file may be used to formalize the following type of business commitments, at a cost of 15 seconds per entry:

- the oral commitment to a completion date or time by a peer or subordinate made in the office during an informal discussion.
- informal statements made by visitors to your office or in restaurants and bars.
- telephone conversations, where commitments are made on which you or your organization rely. "I'll call you with an answer on Friday." You could remember, but it could be in your tickler file (or on your messy calendar page if you remember to scratch it on there).
- informal statements at meetings, of actions which impinge on your operation.

The purpose of assigning these informal commitments to the tickler file is to assure a routinized control and to free the manager's "think" time for more creative and positive thoughts other than remembering every commitment.

A final idea here. If the tickler file is controlled by your secretary as shown in the Figure 2 diagram, not only are entries made by and through her, but commitments met can cause her to automatically relieve the tickler file. In this manner, when the tickler file folder #6 is given to you on 6 April, you may see *only* those commitments that have *not* been met (including your own).

TYING ANSWERS TO QUESTIONS

In chapter 1, a case study described a situation where a marvelous answer was given to a question that wasn't even asked. The composer of that answer really needed someone to match a good question to his good answer!

Have you ever received a response to a question you are not sure you asked? Have you ever had to dig out your memo, minutes of a meeting or other letter correspondence to match an answer you've received to the question?

If you have, think about how efficient it looks to receive the answer with the question. For years, such devices as "Reply-o-grams"© have existed where the answer and the letter were part of the same form. I don't believe they gained the popularity they enjoyed in the 1950s because the form was three or four-part and of a size that did not allow for either easy handling or filing (even in the tickler file).

But, the idea was a good one. What seems to be catching on today is to have the answer either typed or written on the question itself. The reason for this seems to be the profusion of copying machines, which allow the asker and answerer to respond quickly to a request and have a copy of the question and the answer readily available through the use of the reproduction machine. To reduce the cost of reproduction, notes are being appended to letters and a majority are not reproduced by the answerers, on the assumption that to keep a copy without a rationale for recall may be a redundancy.

The managers practicing this procedure, however, still feel quite apologetic about the informality of their appended reply, most times in longhand, on the requestor's missive. This apologia is most common in answering letters from the "outside." Note the statement, "I felt you would prefer promptness to formality" on the sticker used by Twentieth Century-Fox CEO, Dennis Stanfill, when referring to his handwritten answers appended to letters.

TWENTIETH
CENTURY-FOX
Film Corporation

Because we wanted you to have...

A
QUICK
REPLY

I have written a note on your letter.
I felt you would prefer promptness
to formality.

DENNIS C. STANFILL

In practicing the aggressive management style, you should establish your action-orientation for positive results by both appearance and action. I believe that answering many requests with the reply appended thereto establishes this type of aura. It proclaims your desire to communicate...to get an answer to the requestor in the quickest, most efficient manner possible, while at the same time informally documenting the question and the answer.

A SIMPLISTIC APPROACH TO ASSURING COMMUNICATION

A technique will now be described that at first blush might be rejected as exceptionally simplistic. Therefore, I will preface the description of this technique by setting the stage for a more objective decision by the reader.

If you have an employee in your office to discuss a problem, the employee may arrive with a pen and pad to take notes of the discussion and the actions agreed to be pursued. The following might be the reactions of managers to employees taking notes during their discussions:

- "Good worker; I can rely on what we decide to be done to be completed, since it's in her notes."
- "Can't that dummy remember anything?! When they take him out of here, feet-first, we'll find all his notes in the files with the actions never completed!"
- "I wonder if his notes match my notes."

- "It's so disconcerting to talk to the top of her head."
- "Doesn't he know this is just an informal discussion?"

But, the purpose of communication is to have the receiver understand what you mean, to "hear" what you "said." Positive action must flow from the understanding of the communication, which is the premise of this chapter. Hence, why not give the receiver the communication? Why rely on his or her note-taking? How long would it really take? Weigh that against the benefit of good communication.

Suppose at the end of an informal discussion, you gave the following handwritten note to the other party (ies) at the meeting:

11/30/79
1. Arrange to finish Claude's role in the Green Study by 12/11.
2. Green Study, when complete on 2/1, will be given to Claude for concurrence at that time. Concurrence required by 2/10.
3. Claude, in the meantime, will be assigned to the bid work under Harriet's direction on 12/12.

It will take you about one minute to write this note. But the sender will be assured of the proper message being received by the receiver. If these decisions are preordained, the message could be written before the meeting or in place of it!

What is bothering most of you right now is that it seems so childish, time consuming or overbearing to give an employee a written request. But is it? As a test, I will sometimes ask a group of 40 delegates midway through a conference that I am conducting on, say, "Time Management," "Please pass your books forward; I am going to collect them." It is rare that I get anything but resistance, coupled with a loud chorus of groans.

The group had received a 137-page set of seminar notes and was in the midst of adding their personal notes to those provided. The point I am making is that, because the seminar notes were provided, the delegates:

- felt secure in receiving all that was presented, even though their minds might wander during the 12 hours of instruction over those two days.
- had merely added their "meat" to the "bones" of the notes...which

consisted of transposing general principles to the specific techniques required for application at the delegates' individual work areas.

- were relieved of trying to sort out the principles, outline and major thrust of the program, which was already documented in precisely the sequence to be followed by the presenter.

Does the reader consider this note preparation childish or overbearing? Of course not! So, let's consider the *sender*. What do *I* desire?

- All delegates will have the same basic notes. If left to their own, there is no assurance that 40 notes by 40 note-takers would have captured the emphasis, thrust and objectives of the speaker. Some would be organized. Some would miss the obvious, the relationships, the conversion of philosophy into techniques.
- The free-flow of ideas, arguments and questions is made possible by the "freeing up" of basic note-taking time by the receiver (the delegate). Just copying my slides in the dark would be a major task. Don't you wish all your school professors lectured from predistributed notes?

Now, the reader may say, "Okay I'll agree there are advantages to note distribution as an aid to communication, but it is not a logical choice for *every* discussion!" Therefore, the argument against providing the communication is economics, only. To this I'll agree.

If the message is important enough to warrant one minute of your time to assure communication, and more importantly, positive action by the receiver, put it in writing. Even if the decision is reached at the meeting, take one more minute to write down what was agreed. The note is not only now a specific that can be referred to by the receiver, but becomes the basis for follow-up when the sender puts it in the tickler file.

A very simplistic approach has been presented to improving your communications...getting the receiver to take a positive action, one that is controllable by the sender. It is not a new idea, but it is an idea that most managers reject on the first threshold of introduction. Try it. Count the times you may diminish the symptoms of poor communication, previously described in this chapter:

- return visits for clarification.
- postponed action or none at all.
- partly performed actions.
- wrongly performed tasks.
- antagonism towards the requestor.

GROUP EXPLANATION HAS ITS VIRTUES

The aggressive management style includes ideas that have been brought forward in previous decades, but through disuse or misuse have crept into the cobwebs of memory. One of these techniques that was a pillar of management thinking in the 1950-60 era was that communications receive less distortion the less times one has to repeat the message, the less time between the original message and the receiver's action, and the less people who have to interpret and pass the message on to other recipients.

This philosophy still applies. Wherever possible, avoid the "chain" communication and encourage group exposure to the message. This provides:

- all to hear the same thing at the same time.
- everyone with the ability to hear the questions asked and the explanations received.
- the group with a knowledge of what is *not* required as well as *what* is required by the communicator.
- less distortion to be received by the parties required to act...the advantage of getting it "straight from the horse's mouth."

Considering the above advantages, the group explanation *should be avoided:*

- where the cost and geographics of group gathering versus communication objectives do not make sense.
- where the time frame does not allow for this approach.
- where the subject matter cannot make much of a difference, even if wrongly communicated from individual to individual.

Finally, group presentation coupled with a written communication being provided to that group, makes for the most assured transmission in practicing AMS. The limitations are logical, but that should not veto the drive to increase applications of an old, recognized tool of communications for action.

This chapter was designed to select the communicative techniques that fit the aggressive management style. They relate not just to communications, but to performing that management (and human) function for purposes of promulgating positive management action. What is understood, heard and read takes priority over what is meant, said or written. Most of us learn these communicative techniques from our bosses, rejecting what we perceive to fail and practicing what appears to work. We judge style with result.

Specificity is both a logical and a required technique to assure the recipient "gets the message." But control of the request is just as important with managerial planning and problem-solving, as discussed in chapters 4 and 5. A tickler file and routinized dispatch of work with "To Do" cards may help both your specificity and your communication (or delegation) control.

Since not all communications are in letters, memos or the like, this chapter also covered the advantages of formalizing informal commitments …the advantages to both the sender and the receiver.

Further aid to communications can be achieved by tying answers to the questions asked, to assure the action-orientation posture. Finally, a simplistic approach was put forth…that of providing a written missive to the receiver in lieu of relying on his or her notes or interpretations. The refinement of this was the group presentation.

All of these were put forth to make communications an aggressive management function for action, not as an end unto itself. In the next chapter, a special facet of communications will be covered…the use of the techniques of delegation in practicing the aggressive management style.

7

DELEGATE OR DIE

Like the exhortation, "Publish or Perish!" for college professors, the statement, "Delegate or Die!" was part of the lexicon of managers during the 1950s. The rationale in those days was that managers who couldn't delegate:

- were insecure.
- couldn't grow as the workload increased or the enterprise entered different arenas, requiring new and different work skills.
- limited the productivity of the department to the efforts and time of that single individual's capacity.
- thwarted his or her subordinates who saw only parts (usually the dull and routine ones) of the "big picture."
- caused a dissatisfaction among the ambitious and aspiring, since they were unable to gain experience from which they could assume a higher authority (such as the boss's job).
- frustrated superiors who were forced to wait or to rely solely on the work of a single individual, his or her physical stamina, competence, memory and, for that matter, his or her very existence ("Don't let a truck hit Marion.")

155

All of the above has no relevance to the one-person company, department or like enterprise. But it does relate to any condition where more than one individual is involved, even if the only other person is the manager's secretary. Think of the problems associated with:

- Only the boss can tell you where the paper is or the project's status.
- There is only one source for work distribution; when he or she is gone, everything waits to be dispatched.
- Only the boss can concur, sign, approve, pass-forward or reject the proposed action.
- You may call in a question (and it will be logged) but only "the oracle" can provide answers.
- "Only the governor can authorize the solution, but he's in Florida and unavailable."

THE "ONLY I" SYNDROME

All of the above are results of practicing the "only I" syndrome. This condition still exists, 30 years after being identified.

In this chapter, the reader will first be shown how to recognize the poorer practices of nondelegation. Then, some solutions will be offered within the framework of the aggressive management style. The purpose of limiting the solutions to those relative to AMS is to pick that which can aid in positive improvement for positive recognition. The subject of delegation, by itself, would be difficult to cover in one chapter, but those specific items relevant to AMS will be demonstrated.

The "only I" syndrome can best be diagnosed by applying a simple task analysis list to a week's worth of work. On a random sampling basis, fill in the following form, as honestly as you can.

Column 1 is a random selection of tasks performed. (If your job varies little from day to day, you could list every task; if you like the secretarial sampling described in chapter 3, use that technique.)

Column 2 requires you (or your designee) to check off whether (a) "only you" can perform the task, or (b) "others" (specify) could. This check mark is to denote "who could have," not just "who is" performing the task.

Column 3 is to have you honestly state either (a) "Why only you?" or (b) "Who else but you?"

The key to the success of this analysis is your personal objectivity, which forces you to at least be honest with yourself. (The following is also called "only I" Analysis.)

Delegation Analysis

Natalie
Kolder   4-16-79

(1)	(2)		(3)
	(a)	(b)	
Task	"Only I"	Others	WHY? or WHO?
Making travel arrangements	x		Secretary could do for me but I haven't yet shown her which way I like to travel
Arranging weekly meeting		x	One of "the troops" could do this, or my secretary, but I thought I would
Reorganizing office	x		Confidential nature of analysis precludes use of others
Editing Barnes study		x	Everyone else seemed busy and I didn't want to interrupt my people
Personally distributing recently typed memo		x	I wanted to; besides, the mail service is slow
Call restaurant to make lunch reservations		x	George, who is joining me, could do it, or my secretary
Complete set-up of Apple Project for Wilson and Carey	x		No one else can do it as well as me. Besides, I like setting up projects
Dictate answer to Sweeney letter	x		No one else is here at 8:30 p.m. It's due tomorrow morning, first thing, so here goes
Make "English" out of rough draft supplied by Ellen		x	If they'd learn how to write, I could read for content only. 'Till then, I must edit

Delegation Analysis (Continued)

Task	"Only I"	Others	WHY? or WHO?
	(a)	(b)	
Report on government fund utilization due tomorrow		x	Four others in this office could do it, but it's been on my desk so long that it's too late delegate
Getting desk supplies on way from getting coffee		x	Anyone could but I need a stretch break. I deserve it considering all the work I've done
Get answer to request by my boss	x		Only *I* can get answers for my boss. He expects that of me. It's the only way
Sign all expense vouchers	x		I've always done it. It's my job; isn't it?
Initial and sign outgoing correspondence	x		Who else can sign my memos and letters? I wrote them; I sign them
Keep tickler file current on due dates	x		I get a chance to see the work, all of it, by leafing through the project file
Get information from files		x	My secretary could do it, but I'd have to take the time to tell her what I want
Research work for chart data; make chart		x	My people could, but it's here on top of my desk so I guess I'll do it

The table columns above are labeled: (1), (2), (3), with (2) subdivided into (a) and (b).

As you read through the Delegation Analysis, some obvious problems and solutions become evident. Many of the solutions are merely related to self-discipline. But a look at the total picture — of why delegation is a problem — will give you more insights into possible personal corrective measures.

THE DELEGATION DILEMMA

As stated in the last section of this chapter, a look at the poorer practices resulting in nondelegation precedes the use of the communicative tools for delegation. (See chapter 6 regarding improved communicative tools to reach the receiver.)

The major reasons for nondelegation can be expressed in the following statements. See if your favorites are among them:

- "I like doing this task."
- "No one else can do it as well as I can."
- "I can finish the job by the time I tell anyone else what I want done."
- "Well, perhaps there is other more important work to be done now, but these papers are on top and have probably been here the longest."
- "I don't really have to be the one doing this, but it seems a shame to interrupt Harry or my secretary to get this done; so, I'll do it myself."
- "I know my time is very valuable, in fact too valuable to spend on this job, but it's here on my desk and I'll complete it rather than give it to someone else."
- "I was given this very rough draft by my senior engineer. I know there should be much more research, preparation, organization and editing before I should have seen it. But, here it is, so here goes."
- "I know I should show Harriet how to make these travel reservations, but I haven't gotten around to showing her how I want it done."
- "It's been on my desk for a week and it's due today, so I'd better just get on with it...too late to delegate."
- "Those 'dummies' can't do it as well as I can, so why bother the rest of the staff?"

The delegation dilemma is mostly a personal one. Should I or shouldn't I give the work to others? Why do I perform tasks that can be performed by others who work for me? Why do I do the work of other elements of the organization?

In adopting the aggressive management style, a manager should weigh the trade-offs involved. In practicing AMS, the end result, or a myriad of positive results, can more readily flow from a group of committed employees than from the total dedication of a single individual. Hence, the balance scale of savings weighs heavily in favor of more (and better) delegation.

To overcome the sentiments expressed in the negative (towards delegation) statements heretofore listed, consider the following principles in the practice of positive delegation.

THE PRIORITY CHOICE

When one chooses to perform any task, there is an implied priority of that job over any others. Otherwise, why don't you work on another task? Your answer may be that there are certain routine and shortlived jobs that you work on to get them out of the way. But even this relates to the aforementioned principle, since the routine and short duration tasks could also have been put off if their due dates were less than imminent.

Your choice to work on a short, simple task with a low priority elevates the priority status of that task when a long, complex job is imminently required. Action awaits, however, because of your preoccupation with the simple, non-urgent task. An example can better make this point.

You have two tasks that require two to three days each of concentrated work to be done by you. They are both due at the end of the week. The difference between the jobs, aside from content, is:

Job A — This is an interesting new concept that will be well received, since it addresses a major company problem with a simple solution. The report is being prepared for presentation to both your superior and your peers on Friday. Actually, the report is a compilation of your department's collective analysis, but you feel you are the logical one to put it together for presentation.

Job B — This work is also due on Friday, but it is your department's portion of Charlie's (a peer) proposal. You guess there is only a 60 percent chance of getting that job, even if Charlie's group gets the specification changed. Your department's work will be lost in the anonymity of the submitted proposal. Getting this job means a lot to Charlie (he told you so), but the company is having a good year and Charlie always presses his enthusiasm on others.

Given the above circumstances, the following will probably occur:

- Job A will be worked on first and will probably not be delegated to anyone else by you.
- Job B may be delegated to someone else in your department.
- Job A's due date will be met; Job B's may be missed and a logical reason will be forwarded requesting some delay from Charlie.
- You never considered both jobs of equal priority regarding due dates, personal involvement or delegatibility.

Let's add a few more jobs to "the pot."

Job C — It will take half a day to determine the reasons for failure on the Bratter job. You're certain the blame lies with the comptroller in how the estimate was originally prepared and the charges were accrued against that estimate. The "boys" are looking forward to you being able to "pin the donkey tail on that pompous bean-counter." In fact, Rich just called to ask (cynically), "How's the Inquisition coming? I can't wait to see the blood-bath!" One of your people could get all the facts together without being part of the conclusion, accusation or confrontation. No due date exists for this analysis (in fact, no one really requested this task, but it seemed like a natural for your department). Since you assumed the scrutiny, you will assign a due date relative to your department's workload, and have so stated this.

Possible Scenario — Job C will surely be elevated to a position of importance based on the collective vindictiveness (or righteousness) of your peers, who see their outlet in your analysis (the one with the foregone conclusion). It is a job worthy of your personal attention, not just to coordinate the fact gathering, but to have you personally gather the indictment of the comptroller. Although you can choose the due date, it seems logical to finish this one half-day job this week while the subject is "hot." This job will be fit in below Job A but surely above Job B, and will be your personal "objective" contribution to improved operations.

Job D — This must be completed each week and turned in on Friday. Simple job, quite routine, but when completed it gives you a definite feeling of accomplishment. You know how you are doing, cumulatively, each week and the results are good so far this year. It can be completed weekly by any member of your department, including your secretary, but you like to do it, although it has been delegated to others at various, frequent times. The job takes about two and one-half hours.

Possible Scenario — With jobs A, B, and C facing you, a certain amount of stress and accompanying anxiety is building within you. Some of the information you are collecting for the "prosecution of the bean-counter" (Job C) is not coming out as you expected; in fact, the comptroller may have done an exceptional job under the circumstances. Charlie is calling on everyone, including your boss, about the importance of both a responsive and on-time bid for Job B. Finally, a flaw has developed in the case you are going to present to your peers on Friday (Job A). A high degree of frustration has set in. You work on Job D because it's completable, the results are forcastable (and good) and the job takes only two and one-half hours!

Managing your priorities and your delegation requires both a drive to be more effective *and* the self-discipline to maintain a schedule of priorities. "Unfortunately, when anxiety and stress occur, we tend to neglect the more important items and retreat to the more familiar and less taxing items, where we bury ourselves in detail," states Dr. Vincent G. Renter of the Arizona State College of Business Management.

Delegation suffers the same fate as priorities. When under stress from anxiety or fear, we tend to hold work unto ourselves because it is routine, completable and breaks the frustration arising from the incompleteness we perceive existing in projects "not going our way." (Thus, we elevate the priority of Job D.)

We also tend to hold jobs unto ourselves where we feel quite certain of the outcome, which is either spotlighted by your peers, events, or where disclosure of your accomplishment will "add to your laurel wreath" (Job C).

On the other hand, there is a tendency to delegate the less important (in our minds) – the routine work that becomes a part of a larger endeavor where credit is least likely to accrue to the contributor (Job B).

As with prioritization of work, it is a human tendency to spend more personal time on the interesting, the breakthroughs, the jobs that warrant recognition by your peers and superiors (Job A). Hence, the priority of work, as established by you, determines the desire you may have to delegate that group of tasks. Even if the priority is a subjective perception, the delegation attitude will be based on that perceived (though subjective) priority.

THE PERSONNEL CHOICE

There are managers who weigh delegation on the basis of who is available. If Hannah is your choice to perform a delegatable task, but she is not available, do you then do the job yourself? It's Hannah or no one but you?

Do you worry about interrupting your employees? Do you know how much work they can handle, or do you assume they are overloaded? Doesn't it seem strange that you seem to fit in extra work (even with difficulty at times)? Is it because you are a boss and therefore have more time? Are faster? Better? More experienced? Or, does it seem easier to do it yourself rather than to interrupt Harry?

In chapter 2, a partial answer to the above managerial dilemma was shown. In that case, a secretary was given tasks with the required due dates attached. The secretary scheduled herself in accordance with her estimate of work duration. She could not change a required date; that was only the prerogative of her boss. However, if she could not perform a task by a desired completion date, she was required to notify her boss at the daily 1:30 p.m. meeting.

Since 80 percent of the tasks could be completed on time (her estimate), the 1:30 p.m. meeting was used to discuss only the rescheduling of
the exceptions (the 20 percent). Only the due date requestor could change
the due dates. This was based on the employee's ability to schedule the
multitude of varied tasks assigned through delegation both implied and
direct.

The personnel choice causes you to avoid delegation because:

- "No one is available."
- "The one person who can do it is busy."
- "It's Hannah or no one."
- "I can't interrupt Harry."
- "Guess I'll have to do the job."

To overcome this delegation dilemma, consider:

- Is it an excuse for my inability to schedule (by due date) my employees' work?
- Can I require my employees to schedule themselves, so that I may
  review this schedule on a sampling basis?
- Can I value my managerial time against the value of the task to be
  performed, its imminency and the importance of the tasks now on
  my employees' agenda?

When we examine our managerial style, we find that nondelegation is
many times related to this style. If we control our people's work, negotiate
reasonable due dates, sample work status and place a value on managerial
time, logical delegation will surely follow. Lack of delegation is an effect;
managerial style is the cause.

THE ECONOMICS AND LOCATION CHOICE

Remember the statement quoted earlier in this chapter..."I know my
time is very valuable, in fact, too valuable to spend on this job; but, it's
here on my desk, so I'll complete it rather than give it to someone else."
This dichotomy is a dilemma.

On the one hand, the manager recognizes that his or her time is too
valuable to be working on the task at hand (the economics choice). However, the job is on his or her desk, so it might as well be worked on (the
location choice). By this logic, the following is probable:

a. All irrelevant tasks that inadvertently get to the manager's desk
   have a good chance of being worked on by that manager because of
   that unfortunate circumstance.

b. All delegatable tasks that do not land on this manager's desk will
   not be performed by this manager.

One of the first places to investigate when you want to improve the
amount and quality of work delegated, is the function of placing obviously
delegatable work on your desk. Why do you get it first? Can other members
of your group, who are logical choices to receive the fruits of your delegation, receive the task without it being detoured through your "In Box"?

To begin with, perform the "only *I*" analysis described earlier on in
this chapter. Examine the delegatable tasks that have not been delegated
because:

- they are on your desk.
- you may as well work on them because they are on your desk.
- after all, "you could complete them by the time you gave them to
  someone else."

However, you *do* agree that the task is delegatable. Therefore, the
solution to the location choice dilemma is to set up a system of automatic
delegation (perhaps through your secretary) whereby obviously delegatable
tasks are given without your "middleman" services.

Next; look at the tasks which "only *you*" can delegate. Can you perform these delegations on a high priority basis? One of the most frustrating
experiences for the recipient of your delegation is when:

- The work delegated is already late.
- The time for completion has been reduced by the "sitting" time on
  your desk.
- During this "sitting" time you have not added to the accomplishment of the ultimate task...just let the project sit!

The use of the "To Do" cards described in chapter 6 can help. Note
that the task card calls for a consideration of delegating the task, a required due date and, of course, a control tied to the tickler file system.
However, this approach will fail if the priority of issuing the card causes
the recipient to realize the loss due to a late delegation.

As the reader can see, the location dilemma is closely related to:

- Why is this on my desk before being delegated?
- Why aren't most delegations performed automatically?
- Can I improve both the quality of the response, as well as the time-
  liness, by placing a higher priority on delegating the delegatable?

THE CRUTCH CHOICE

The purists among you will argue that the following is more likely related to the quality of your staff than your desire to delegate. I am referring to the work that is presented to you in a form that is not acceptable to be passed on...work that fails the minimum criteria for:

- logic
- clarity
- organization
- semantics and structure
- spelling and punctuation
- research
- legibility and/or neatness

Work is forwarded by the "children" to the "father" in a form that requires the "father" to partially redo or rethink the project. The "children" think:

- "He's the boss, so let him put it together; that's what he's paid to do."

The "father" thinks:

- "Well, they *are* my 'children' and it's my job to accept what they can do and then to help them rethink and rewrite the project. After all, what are 'fathers' for?"

This type of thinking by both the "father" and the "children" has a self-fulfilling prophecy and a self-perpetuating consequence. If we the managers expect incomplete work and the "children" grow to expect the detailed rework provided by the "father," this cycle will continue ad infinitum.

Work performed by you for others, which the others could (under most circumstances) have completed for your approval, is delegatable work. Are you an approver, a worker or a reworker for most work performed by your staff? What are your criteria for receiving work from them? Will you always be their "father" for all work? Can you break the mold, so that for 80 percent of work brought to you:

- The rationale is both logical and defendable.
- The conclusion based on this rationale meets your standards.
- The use of the "Mother Tongue" has not been discarded.
- The preparer believes he or she is bringing you a task completed

for approval signature, not a crude rough draft to involve your total input in initial preparation.

It is the duty of "fathers" to help their "children" reach "adult" status. Perpetuating their status as "children" is a disservice that with continuing practice will create a perpetual burden for the "father." The aggressive management style asks that you recognize the cost of doing (or redoing) the work of others...work that should be more completely performed by others. Recognize how the inefficiency of this occurrence is perpetuated by the acceptance of the "father/child" roles, and that corrective actions, from training to discipline, are available management tools to correct this costly situation. This is the crux of the "crutch dilemma."

ANOTHER CRUTCH DILEMMA

The previously described crutch dilemma involved the manager being more than necessarily supportive of his or her employees. Another version of this delegation problem arises when the manager feels and states, "I know I should show Harriet how to make these travel arrangements, but I haven't yet gotten around to showing her how I want them done."

The manager is providing a crutch because he or she has not created an alternative, many times due solely to the fact that the manager has not yet set aside training time. Obviously, the longer this training task is postponed, the more time that manager will be spending on performing possibly delegatable tasks.

As stated in chapter 1, where a management deficiency is recognized and still allowed to exist, the management style encompasses this deficiency. The deficiency is part of that management style. The practice of AMS requires an analysis of your style for positive improvements.

The crutch dilemma implies it is an acceptable management style to accept nondelegation until you get around to training. Is this a style or an expedient excuse? The practice of the aggressive management style requires:

- a realization by the manager of those tasks which are delegatable.
- an understanding of the reasons for nondelegation from the priority choice to the location and crutch choices.
- an action to consciously overcome a deficiency in delegation.

In the case of the crutch dilemma, caused by an inability to delegate to an untrained assistant, the manager both recognizes the need and understands the reasons for the problem's existence. It is time for an appropriate management action, such as:

- take the time to demonstrate the task required.
- delegate someone else to perform the demonstration and monitor the practice.
- ultimately have the delegation performed in lieu of the project arriving at your desk for delegation.

These actions should eliminate or greatly alleviate the crutch dilemma.

THE EGO CHOICE

The ego choice, as a reason for nondelegation, relates to *your* view of *you,* relative to *your* view of *you* relative to *others.* In this vein, the purpose of much assertiveness training is to reinforce the "number one" feeling about ourselves. In some cases, it is an approach to even convince us of our worth to *our* society at work or play.

Ego, or lack of it, relates to our view of delegation. Those with room-size egos have trouble delegating, since:

- "Those dummies can't do it as well as I can so why bother the rest of the staff!"
- "The same time that I spend in describing, checking and 'repairing' their work would be better utilized by me in just digging in and doing the job."

For those with thimble-size egos, the problem of nondelegation is relative to:

- "I'd like them to know that I can also do this type of work."
- "They'll think I'm delegating something I cannot do or that they do better than me."

The ego dilemma, in either of the above described situations, causes managers to cling to work that should definitely be delegated...work that:

- requires lesser skills than those required of you, the manager.
- could be learned by your subordinates, such that the group's interchangability to perform varied tasks is enhanced.
- keeps the manager from performing more highly valued functions.

You could use the "only I" Analysis described both in this and chapter 2. You could perform the 30 second test before starting any task (described in chapter 2, "I don't Have Time to Plan"). Then, examine the delegation specificity. (See chapter 6, "Communicating Specificity" and "Specificity with Routinization and Control.") The missing clue to solution is an honest-to-goodness search by you of what constitutes your ego as an obstacle to improved delegation. You should have a better answer for delegatable tasks performed by you, than, "I want to do them!"

THE DELEGATION OF INTERRUPTIONS

When discussing the nature of interruptions (chapter 3, "Interruptions Are a Part of Business Life"), the following points were made:

- Interruptions are and probably always will be a part of an executive's life.
- AMS envisages that they be reduced in quantity and improved in quality.
- A manager must learn (and practice) the difference between business and social courtesy.

To this list we will now add:

- Many interruptions, now being experienced, can be eliminated by a review of those that could have been avoided by the application of a delegation procedure.

This procedure establishes:

a. a review of delegatable tasks and "truthful" reasons for nondelegation.
b. an automatic delegation of those tasks that are "obvious candidates."
c. a high priority for tasks "only you" can delegate.
d. training of those who could be performing delegatable tasks.
e. using delegation tools (such as forms) to aid in specificity.

OVERCOMING THE JACK-IN-THE-BOX SYNDROME

Two of the delegation tools that can reduce interruptions are the:

1. *Personal Action List,* and
2. *Action Required* form

JACK-IN-THE-BOX SYNDROME

Before describing these tools, a look at the "Jack-in-the-box syndrome," common to many managers, may describe the "sickness" to which we are trying to develop a "cure." Every child has at some time or other seen the toy, which at a certain point (usually on the word "pop" in "Pop Goes the Weasel") has a clown's head pop up. The child is frightened at first, but after realizing the humor represented, starts to look for the "pop" with uncontrolled glee.

The manager evidences this same "pop" mentality when:

a. At the conclusion of dictating an answer to a letter, he or she jumps up, runs out and gives it to the secretary. There is usually very little relationship between the "quick surfacing" of the manager in the outer office to any degree of imminency in the reproduction of the dictated answer as hard copy.

b. Immediately after signing a memo or directive, the manager personally runs it down to the addressee. Sometimes the secretary is sent scampering down the hall with the just-signed missive. Does the missive deserve this expediting action? Suppose the receiver doesn't return to his or her office for four hours... even the internal mail service could beat that!

c. Every time a thought crosses the manager's mind, he or she runs out or uses the telephone to test this idea on employees or peers.

d. The secretary is besieged by the interoffice buzzer. It is rung at apparent whim, since three different items of the same type are never grouped, but are all handled on an emergency (buzz... buzz... buzz) basis.

THE ACTION REQUIRED FORM

A far more efficient approach to routine actions delegated to others might be to use a tool similar to the Action Required form on the next page. This form is a composite of the many I have seen, which allow a manager to spend 10 to 30 seconds to be specific regarding routine delegations. The form and accompanying materials are put in the "Out" box, which is emptied two times an hour by the secretary.

The form combines the request for the following routine actions:

- put-away information (file)
- retrieve information
- reproduce data
- distribute data
- request for reply
- routing of communications
- control of delegation (tickler file)
- issuance of "To Do"

Design your own Action Required form to meet your needs for routine delegation. Several secretaries in New Jersey were shown this form at my "Secretarial Time Management" program given semiannually for Rutgers University. Six months later, most of them had devised their own forms to receive and dispatch routine delegations for their bosses.

The main considerations are:

- reduce the "jack-in-the-box syndrome."
- delegate routine jobs expeditiously.
- if applicable, use a simple form to combine various routine delegable tasks.

Action Required BY: N. Kobert   Date: 4/5/XX   Time: 4:20 p.m.

A. File: #1841; #1916; _____; _____; _____
     ✓temporary; ✓permanent; ✓hold *19XX* date

B. Retrieval: _____; _____; _____; _____; _____
     _____ASAP; _____other _____when: _____

C. Reproduce: _____copies _____when
     _____type; ___ Xerox; ___other _____
     _____
     _____

D. Distribution: _____me only
     _____A. _____B. _____C. _____D.
     _____other _____
     _____
     _____plus _____
     _____
     _____minus _____
     _____

E. Confidential Status: _____yes; _____none

F. Reply: _____for me; _____from me; _____from you;
     _____from _____; _____special
     instructions _____
     _____

G. Miscellaneous: _____

H. Routings 1. _____
                     2. _____
                     3. _____
                     4. _____

Info Copies
1. _____
2. _____
3. _____
4. _____

I. Tickler File
Required
Date: _____
Delegated to: _____
Action Required: _____
_____
_____
_____
_____

ARF
NKA

THE PERSONAL ACTION LIST (PAL)

Many managers complain of an inability to get work done in their offices. They are either constantly interrupted or are easily distracted. Some of this is due to office layout, caused to a large degree by fatuous designers who put up short walls as room dividers, use potted palms and lump groups of people in human modules. These office planners should be made to work in the offices they design!

Even if external distractions are reduced (see chapter 9 on improving one-on-one work), the manager still has to contend with his or her personal discipline. For those who interrupt themselves by breaking in on a job with a random thought, and then pursuing same, the Personal Action List (PAL) may be of help. When I first started studying my work habits, I found that the biggest interrupter of me was *me!*

The Personal Action List was designed by me over 20 years ago to reduce the amount of time I spent on the "get ready" and "put away" phases of work. As an old industrial engineer, I was taught to maximize the "do" phase of the work cycle, whether this meant reduce setups in a manufacturing plant, or eliminate downtime at the end of any job in an office. The surest way to do this was to combine jobs, wherever feasible, to increase the ratio of "do" to the time required for "setup" (or "get ready") and "put away."

PERSONAL ACTION LIST						BY:		DATE:	

PERSONAL ACTION LIST

PRIOR — C | W | S | O — DESCRIPTION

- Call Harry regarding the Dole bid
- Set up the closing meeting on the Three Mile Island job
- Contact Richard on the tapes
- Write to Dean and John about their Diaries
- Call Jimmy about the loan from Burt
- Set up lunch with Raquel

BY: DATE:

PRIOR — C | W | S | O — DESCRIPTION

Figure 7-1

For example, it is easier to dictate four letters in a row, give out three instructions, place four phone calls or see four individuals in a row than to:

- dictate a letter   (1)
- call George   (1)
- see Harry   (1)
- dictate a letter   (2)
- call Dean   (2)
- see Richard   (2)
- call John   (3)
- give instructions to Mary   (1)
- see Karl   (3)
- call Phil   (4)
- dictate a letter   (3)
- give instructions to Mary   (2)
- see Pauline   (4)
- dictate a letter   (4)
- give instructions to Jane   (3)

Use of the Personal Action List allows for some combination of these activities. As you work through a particular project, the thought crosses your mind to call George. You do *not* stop what you are doing, interrupt yourself, and call George. Instead, you take the four seconds necessary to put a check in the "C" (for call) column and write "George Cole bid." You then return to your present project. You could have interrupted yourself and spent five minutes on the phone with George; and, if the information is vitally required at that time, you will. But since only 20 percent of your calls probably have a time imminency, 80 percent of the time you will avoid interrupting yourself.

The same routine is followed for a thought of writing (check "W" on the PAL) or dictating, seeing (check "S" on the PAL) or for other tasks (check "O" on the form) such as look up, check or assign a task. Use headings that you feel comfortable with in your daily work.

At an appropriate break in your work, review the PAL. You may have the 15 interruptive thoughts listed, as previously delineated. You now have the opportunity to:

- Combine like actions. It is easier to see four individuals in a row, dictate four letters concurrently and give out three instructions at the same time than to do them individually. You will have reduced the "setup" or "get ready" time as well as the "put away" time. The one and one-half

minutes (15 x 5 seconds each) of entry time on the PAL is what you have
traded off against these savings.

• Prioritize these requirements. The first column on the form is filled
in at the time you review the list. A priority number is placed, if you desire, next to the action item. Some of my clients use this column to ensure
they do the important things first, putting off items of a lesser priority until
a more appropriate or leisurely time. I have found this to be unnecessary
in my work, since the listed items are of very short duration for accomplishment. Remember, the PAL does not eliminate the detailed "To Do" form;
it is merely a "trigger" to make such a delegation.

• Routinely delegate that which you may have performed yourself if
you hadn't noted the item on the PAL. As you review the list at the work
break, note how many delegatable tasks are on the list. Did you indicate a
task postponed or a *delegation* postponed? This is the key. From my experience, I have set up a routine symbol "D" to be added to my Personal
Action List. When this list is turned over to my secretary, she pulls the
routine delegations (Ds) off for action. She is entirely capable (in fact overqualified) to:

- Call Harry regarding the Dole bid
- Set up the closing meeting on the Three Mile Island job
- Contact Richard on the tapes
- Write to Dean and John about their diaries
- Call Jimmy about the loan from Bert
- Set up lunch with Raquel.

The Personal Action List may not only help reduce *your* interruptions of *you* but may also improve your routine delegations in quantity and
in effectiveness.

USING YOUR SECRETARY TO IMPROVE YOUR DELEGATIONS

As you have seen, I have a very heavy reliance on my secretary to improve my use of a most important management tool — delegation.

In chapter 6 (Figures 1 and 2), the secretary is shown as a vital cog in
controlling plans, triggering a response on exceptions and handling the
routine and nonroutine act of physically delegating assignments. The use
of the Action Required and Personal Action List forms demonstrated how
the secretary can be utilized to perform routine delegations and supportive
actions. She can help reduce the "jack-in-the-box" syndrome and improve
the timeliness of your delegations.

For those of you who are "turned-off" by any discussion of using your secretary to perform administrative tasks, I'd ask, "Have you tried it?" Have you taken the time to train your secretary — the same amount of time you have taken to train others who work for you?

In the area of improving your delegations, both routine and non-routine, consider the help you can receive when your secretary helps you:

- control your "To Do" delegations
- physically handle the routine and nonroutine delegations
- control your "Tickler File"
- comply with the requests on the Action Required form
- handle routine delegations from your Personal Action List

Of the thousands of secretaries I have trained over the past 20 years for Clemson, Rutgers, North Carolina State and various industrial enterprises, I believe the vast majority can be exceptionally helpful in aiding the manager manage. In this chapter, we have looked at the aid secretaries can give regarding delegation, and how delegation without control is like planning without control. The secretary can be a vital aid in controlling your delegation function, which might otherwise be controlled by you in a half-hearted way — or not at all.

PROPER DELEGATION IS PART OF THE AMS

This chapter is based on the premise that well-performed delegation is achievable once the major personal management problems are overcome. These problems are highlighted through the use of the "only I" analysis, which emphasizes the amount of tasks that may be delegated and perhaps are not.

The manager has many dilemmas to overcome: the Priority, Personnel, Location and Crutch choices. The most difficult to overcome is the Ego choice, the one that causes us to feel, "I can do it better than the others and, by the time I tell them what to do, I could have done it myself." Since a large ego is one of the traits of a good manager, the problem is to weigh the nondelegated decision versus the ripple effects of delegating, especially routine tasks.

The simplest approach involves taking a few seconds prior to starting any task to ask, "Why am *I* working on this now?" The trick is to see only those tasks requiring your approval or notification for information and those that only you can delegate. If this is accepted, then techniques to assure routine delegations without the manager's direct intervention become paramount.

In this regard, the Action Required and Personal Action List forms, and their use in reducing interruptions and improving routine delegations, were covered.

Finally, the key to improving your delegations is your secretary. Her skill requirements and job knowledge have been expanded over the past 15 years, such that the title of administrative assistant fits her actual performance today.

To adequately practice the aggressive management style requires you to look at all the available tools to improve your management. Review the tools you now use to carry out and to control delegation.

8

THE KOBERT WHEEL

The reader has been taken through the aggressive management style as it relates to planning, control, problem-solving, communication and delegation. The framework within which AMS is practiced is the organization, with its myriad of line and staff relationships, authority and responsibility concepts, the formal and informal workings of committees and the personal and impersonal relationships of the "real people" who hold down those jobs "in the squares," — their hopes and dreams, desires and misgivings, skills and deficiencies.

Our management style may be formed or be dependent on those we either direct or persuade, sell or participate with, command or plead our case before. Since the aggressive management style requires a set of techniques that do impinge on others, it is important that organization be looked upon as a tool for implementing positive action.

In order to do this, we start with some simple "truths."

- People make organizations work.
- People are more likely to perform at what they perceive their jobs to be than what the organization says their jobs are.
- Informal relationships can be both constructive and destructive within the framework of an apparently sound organizational structure.

- What people perceive their jobs to be may be at variance with either their boss' concept or that of other organizational groups. This variance of perception can result in either a positive or a negative performance.

A knowledge of these "truths" forms the basis for both communication and analysis of the organization.

COMMUNICATING ORGANIZATIONAL DESIRES

As stated in chapter 6, the basic rules of communication between humans are:

- It's not what is *said* that's important; it's what is *heard.*
- It's not what is *written* that's important; it's what is *read.*
- It's not what is *meant* that's important; it's what is *understood.*

The premise upon which these rules are based is that the receiver is far more important than the sender if one is to effect good communications. These same rules apply to communications in analyzing how a particular organization works or doesn't work. An example or two will demonstrate this point.

For many years the problem of communications has been evidenced when there has been an organizational or procedural breakdown. This surfaces in statements similar to the following:

- "I didn't know that was my job!"
- "I did what I thought I was supposed to do."
- "Do you want me to do her job as well as my own?"
- "That is my responsibility, isn't it?"
- "You mean that performance was expected of me?"

The introduction of management-by-objectives concepts and annual employee evaluations brought many of these problems to the fore. When managers reviewed short and long range goals with their employees, they were frequently amazed to find a wide disparity between what they (the managers) expected and what their employees thought was expected of them. The largest differences occurred where the criteria for effective performance were initially established, especially where performance criteria were never previously detailed in any specific manner.

This chapter is not included as a review of personnel management techniques that exist today. Rather, the practice of the aggressive management style envisages certain additional insights and techniques to enable one to move quickly to a desired positive result. One of these goals is to determine on a current basis what:

- is perceived to be the job.
- is perceived to be the person or entity which can help you do your job.

I may perceive of my job as limited in scope. Does my boss think it's *all* in the job description? My peers? What people think relates to how they act or react.

If you think the comptroller is responsible for all internal audits, you may be surprised to learn that he or she expects to audit your paperwork procedure, but only from a financial checks-and-balances' viewpoint. The efficiency of the internal procedure, in terms of lead time, forms, delays and general efficiency, may be considered your department's internal problem. What you and the comptroller think the job is, and who is responsible, determines who does the job (or doesn't do it, as is more often the case).

A great deal has been written over the past 25 years about the formal and the informal organization, the implied and the stated functions, the perceived versus the specifically defined. Our point here is to analyze the problem and the solution to the communications problem that cause many of these organizational dilemmas.

TECHNIQUES EMPLOYED SHOULD MEET OBJECTIVES

A newly-appointed production manager was called into the office of the vice-president of manufacturing and asked, "Tom, what do you consider to be the most important job that you perform on a day-to-day basis?" Without hesitation, Tom replied, "Getting the orders out the door!"

Further querying revealed that the production manager accomplished this task by ascertaining the status of every single job and then physically tracking the jobs through the plant with his production planners, foremen, inventory controllers, materials handlers and stock chasers. When he wasn't there, which was a six-month period prior to his appointment, this work was carried out by no one.

His coordination and personal intervention into the day-to-day maelstrom of plant scheduling activities were welcomed, even though they duplicated the activities of his assigned staff. As often happens, when little or no delegation was exercised, everyone worked a bit less at their tasks, since they knew they were receiving assistance from "the chief expeditor", the production manager himself.

The vice-president was dismayed with the activities of the newly-appointed production manager. He wanted the production manager to coordinate the scheduling activities of his staff, and to reserve as his prime priority the improvement of operations: improved scheduling procedures, reduced cost and delays, lower work-in-process inventories, better house-keeping, shorter lead time from raw materials to finished goods, updated capital improvements, etc. This was all specifically delineated in the production manager's job description and in the initial discussions he had with the vice-president when they had originally discussed the job opening.

The production manager perceived a different priority when on the job. In the hectic days that surround a production manager, he was caught up in the work of his group…"When will I get it? Where is it? What's the problem? What are we doing about it?" Without changing much of the causes of the problems, the production manager had inserted himself into the position of helping to answer the questions and having the answers funneled back through him.

The vice-president wanted production systems improved; but he got another expeditor. When the vice-president's dismay was expressed to the production manager, surprise — complete and utter — resulted. The production manager had worked through five months on his new job performing functions:

- as he perceived to be the job of chief expeditor and coordinator of scheduling functions.
- as he perceived his boss wanted the job to be performed…even though different priorities were expressed seven months earlier by the vice-president (as he remembered it).

This is the crux of the communications problem in organization… what they perceive versus what you mean. A better method of communicating organizational goal entails:

1. a clearly understood definition of objectives and priorities (which exist in most major organizations with even a mediocre personnel policy)

   and

2. a method of continuously determining if those agreed priorities are being adhered to by the assignee (not merely on a once-a-year salary evaluation basis)

   and

3. an environment of "give and take", allowing the priorities and objectives to be renegotiated as the situation changes

and

4. a continuing review of the organizational services that exist or are required to efficiently carry out the assigned functions.

Since there is universal agreement on the need for clearly stated objectives (point one above), the main thrust of this chapter will be to explore a technique for achieving points two to four. Adherence to priorities and objectives should be monitored and an environment should be established in which to improve these self-same objectives and priorities. The help received or required from other organizational services will also be considered.

HISTORY OF THE KOBERT WHEEL

In 1957, I was asked by an Air Force General, at the Air Materiel Command at Wright-Patterson Air Force Base, to conduct a maintenance scheduling training program for the 1100 personnel who performed or were related to that function. This training was part of a contract with the Ohio State Research Foundation, which was charged with improving the skills of first-line supervisors at Air Force installations in the fields of human and work management.

I had the temerity to ask this general, "Do these supervisors feel that they are responsible for making the schedule work?" He replied, "I don't care; I just want the first-line supervisors trained in maintenance scheduling techniques." I persisted with, "Well, if they don't think they have the line authority to make the schedule work, they'll accept training as an appreciation of what other services, including production scheduling and control, can do for them!"

I face this same problem time and again with top managers in the civilian sphere. They constantly want to spend money on improving scheduling and inventory accounting systems, but rarely can see the need for training the first-line supervisor on how to make the schedule work and what to do when it doesn't (remedies that are available). When top management talks of increasing return on investment, I have to constantly remind them that the first-line supervisor controls most of that investment in workers, equipment and inventory...to the tune of $50-100,000 per supervisor.

I finally had my way with the Air Force training program and was allowed to poll a sample 100 Air Force first-line supervisors. The poll was to determine objectively:

- what they thought their job functions consisted of, and

- what organizational elements existed to support them in performing these functions.

The poll was, in reality, constructed to mask the real question, "Do you believe you are responsible for making the schedule work?" Had we just asked this question outright, we might have received answers they may have thought we wanted to get.

To gain a degree of interest, a diagrammatical tool was used that was promptly dubbed, "The Kobert Wheel." This name has clung to this approach to this day, and I recently saw an application of it in both Stavanger, Norway and Melbourne, Australia!

The wheel consisted of but three essential parts, in its original form (see Figure 1)...the axle, the spokes of the wheel and the tire (my British cousins refer to the Kobert Tyre). By reducing the analysis to a game-type diagram, I have long felt that a greater degree of cooperation was elicited than would have been with a cold questionnaire.

The following questions were then asked, to be answered on the wheel:

1. What is your exact job title? It has always been a surprise to me that some folks (six out of every 100) do not know their exact job title. This is not that significant, in that our concern is for what is done more than what you call yourself, but it is slightly revealing when related to the next question. The answer to question number one is placed in the "axle" circle.

2. What job functions do you perform? In addition, what functions do you believe are supposed to be performed by you, but (for whatever purposes) are not? The reason for expanding the question is to include the answerer's total perception of the job to be performed. In the Air Force survey, only 31 percent of the maintenance supervisors indicated they were responsible for making the schedule work...yet this was the group the general wanted me to train in order to improve the supervisory scheduling operations: The answers to question number two were fit between the spokes of the Kobert Wheel.

3. In order to help you perform these functions (detailed in the wheel's spokes), what organizations or people are available for you to contact directly for aid? The answers to this question relate to the answerer's concept of the organization as it works, not necessarily as it is drawn on the formal chart. The answers to question number three are placed in the tire section adjacent to the correlating function shown within the spokes of the wheel.

The early history of the Kobert Wheel consisted of this type of simplistic approach to determine:

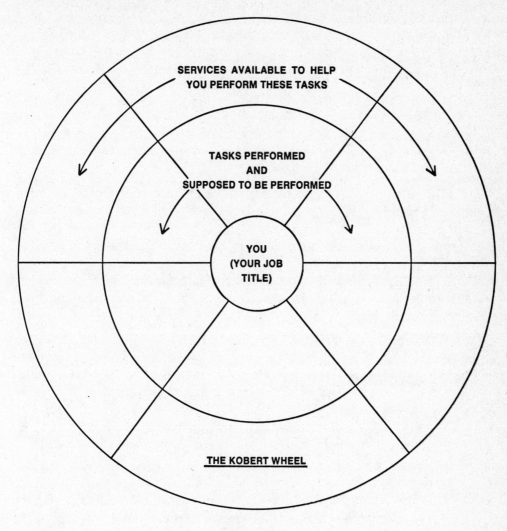

Figure 8-1

- what functions were performed or perceived to be required by the job.
- where aid was thought to be available in the organization to help carry out these functions.

The concept was to find out what the incumbent *thought* were his or her job functions, so that this could then be compared to the boss's perception or the problems with the present operations. Those were the first uses of the Kobert Wheel.

ANARCHY AT WORK — THE INFORMAL ORGANIZATION

All organizations — from the tightly disciplined, dictatorial ones to the free-form, open participative approaches — have some degree of anarchy practiced. My definition of anarchy includes:

- performing functions that should be performed by available services elsewhere in the organization.
- requesting and receiving services from organizations not established to perform same, while bypassing or neglecting the appropriate elements in the organization.

The defense of anarchy is often stated as, "I just want to get something done and 'their' quality of work and timeliness of response leaves me with no alternatives!" Anarchy actions establish a shadow organization...the informal one. That's the one that is rarely charted, but everyone knows exists.

Throughout the 1950s and 1960s, the informal organization was alluded to in the texts, but appended to the descriptions were the following admonitions:

- All employees shall have only one boss.
- Supervisors should not formally discuss employee problems with employees who work for another supervisor (especially for a junior supervisor in your organization), unless that supervisor has given permission.
- Staff employees may recommend, but line supervisors and their employees have the option to accept or reject any recommendation.
- Replies and notifications follow the same routing as information flow.
- When communicating outside the organization, matters of importance should be routed through your supervisor.

Strict adherence to these rules could create a shell around individuals, their creativity and their scope of contribution. Hence, the informal relationships that create the informal organization are recognized but not encouraged.

THE OPEN-DOOR POLICY

In the 1970s, managements wished to foster a freer climate for communication between all employees and appropriate levels of management. Thus, the open-door policies were born...policies that include such rules as:

- "Employees are invited to take their questions, suggestions and complaints to their supervisor or any appropriate level of management."
- "Employees have the right to a review of supervisory decisions on complaints at a higher level."

These policies are then followed by a procedure which invariably states:

- "Questions, suggestions or problems should first be reviewed with an employee's immediate supervisor."
- "In some cases, supervisors may refer employees to another member of management for assistance."
- "Occasionally, there are misunderstandings, questions or problems that cannot be resolved by discussing the matter with a direct supervisor. If an employee honestly feels a supervisor has not answered a question or provided a reasonable solution to a problem, the employee may seek the next higher level of supervision."

Finally,

- "No employee will suffer criticism, reprisal or discipline for exercising his or her privilege of using any or all steps in this procedure and all confidences will be respected."

Thus, the anarchy is controlled; the informal routes are formalized. Only a pure academic scholar in organization analysis will state that the informal organization:

- does not exist.
- exists, but is tightly controlled.
- does not greatly alter the workings of the formal organization.

A manager practicing the aggressive management style should learn to both recognize the informal organization as well as how to use it.

CASE OF THE TRACTOR EXECUTIVE WHO TREAD ON OTHERS

The Kobert Wheel was employed to analyze a morale-type problem at a farm implement manufacturer. The problem was evidenced by a general discouragement in the higher echelons of management about the value of individual contributions to the total enterprise. This discouragement surfaced when top management decided no job was "completed," all decisions were "second guessed," duplications of effort were constantly unearthed and any other organizational element could be asked to do "your job" or to add a "revered opinion" in your area.

Examples of a total disregard for who was responsible for what and whom were rife throughout the organization. Expediency ruled the day. On interview, the top managers agreed there were many instances that required an action-orientation, which was an outright disregard of the formal structure. They were frustrated that this exception had become the general rule for everything from major problem solutions to simple replies for information. Some of the frustration resulted in inaction. "Let Charlie handle this one just like he did that last one!"

The chief operating officer (C.O.O.) was given the Kobert Wheel to complete. Examples of the many statements he had listed under "Functions Performed or Supposed to Be Performed" follows:

- "Request design changes to meet market requirements." (At a trade show, some potential customers indicated that certain manual control locations might be placed differently on the console. He called the Research and Development group from the trade show and asked the vice-president of Research and Development to start testing a redesign of the control locations. The vice-presidents of Marketing and Engineering were not consulted. *Reason* — The C.O.O. had been promoted from vice-president of Research and Development. He knew that group and had selected his own successor.)
- "Correct production problems to improve operating efficiency." (While walking through the manufacturing plant, the C.O.O. stopped by an old, well-thought-of employee, who suggested an operational improvement to cut waste. The C.O.O. authorized the procedure on the spot. He told the production manager about the change as he left the plant.)
- "Improve corporate sales in units and dollars." (A letter from an independent sales agent was addressed to the C.O.O., who promptly answered same. In the reply, the C.O.O. announced a new sales policy regarding warranty return and replacement. A blind copy of the reply was sent to the vice-president of Sales, with a note attached requesting implementation.)

As you can see, the chief operating officer was a prime offender of the organizational rules...he disregarded organizational relationships when it suited his purposes. For those who argue that his action-orientation was for immediate improvement, in the long run, constant use of these "bypasses" leads to:

- procrastination on the part of those bypassed..."Let him do it, since he will, anyway, without consulting me."

- lowered morale by those who are constantly bypassed.
- emulation by managers who perceive these expedient acts to be the corporate policy and therefore adopt this management style (Pygmalion Effect.)
- confusion on the part of the lower echelons of employees as to who is in charge and what is the work rule or priority *today*.

The purpose of using the Kobert Wheel was to highlight the problem that:

- people work on what they perceive to be their job regardless of the formal organization, and
- aid, in carrying out real or perceived assignments, will be sought from those organizational entities the requestor believes can be most helpful, regardless of the existing and published work structure.

Again, the Kobert Wheel is merely an analysis tool; positive management action creates changes.

USING THE INFORMAL ORGANIZATION

As stated earlier on in this chapter, the AMS practitioner should understand the existence and the workings of the informal organization in order to use it. Two techniques, among many, should fit the average manager:

- "filling the void."
- "playing the game."

Both are aimed at giving the AMS practitioner an edge, not just for "politicking," but for positive results. As Richard J. Kendro, chief operating officer of the Aqua-Chem Corporation says, "Politics in business is a defensive strategy; seeking the best, proper way to achieve positive results is an offensive posture and one that is recognized by progressive executives."

Since most of the readers are not top managers who can impact the entire organization with their management style, the strategies chosen are far more useful for the strata of managers from which the average reader emerges...upper middle to first level executives.

FILLING THE VOID

The approach called "filling the void" is so named for the strategy of seeking out a needed task to be performed that is not now being worked on by the present organization. Examples of "filling the void" include:

- Establishing a pilot project in *your* organization, notifying the proper parties of this act and requesting that they monitor your scheme. Your action fills a void, notifies the proper authority and, if successful, will bring positive credit to you (an AMS objective). Ultimately, the proper authorities will take over the function if they are so inclined. They are now tacitly approving your pilot project because they either didn't conceive of it or do not have the resources to carry it out. You have taken advantage of the fact that no one wants to appear negative about an obviously good idea someone else is willing to try.

- Assuming a task with high-level recognition, that either has not been assigned or could be assigned under the present structure to a number of organizational entities. Upon volunteering to perform the work, you announce this is a temporary acceptance until a permanent home is found for the assignment. Chances are the same indecisiveness that caused the initial task to go unassigned will still exist during the time your work is taking place. Thus, by default, a formal assignment with high level recognition has fallen within your aura.

The "filling the void" technique uses informal organization to the advantage of the manager seeking positive results with high level recognition. The tasks assumed were resurrected from limbo...a not too uncommon location for many needed jobs in the usual formal organizational atmosphere.

PLAYING THE GAME

The approach called "playing the game" is so named for the strategy of playing by the rules of the formal organization...barely. No one faults a baseball pitcher who tests an umpire's strike zone in the pitcher's home ball park, a defensive lineman who can draw an offside offense by stunting, a tennis player who tests the foot-fault rule or a basketball center who elbows into position, without the ball, while under the boards.

All of the aforementioned athletes are weighing the advantage of the acts against the penalty assessed when caught. None of the acts are illegal, but they do relate to an interpretation of the rules of the game.

As a manager, you are complying with an interpretation of the rules of the game...the existing organization. You are still playing by the rules when:

- A contract of sale, requiring corporate legal approval, is approved by you contingent upon a legal audit, which in the past has changed or rejected less than 10 percent of the sales orders received. By risking the penalty of loss when bypassing corporate legal approval "up front," you may be shortening the lead time of order acceptance, manufacturing and procurement reaction, reserving a space to meet the committed date in the schedule, etc. If you could have received the legal approval (or comment) more rapidly, you should have; but your past experience on expedite requests has been exceptionally poor. The reward and recognition for gaining and fulfilling this order is large, the penalty through either material loss or censure by your boss is "in the livable range." You have weighed the downside risk and taken a positive recognizable action.

- The lead time for procurement of certain manufactured items is growing. Your examination of requirements for these items turns up shortfalls in the third quarter. You examine the forecast, which the sales group says is "firm," but a look at the firm orders on hand shows a very light shipping commitment for the third quarter. Corporate rules require that only the sales group may change the approved forecast, and that group is not about to do so. Should you order the required manufacturing items, or should you outguess the eternal optimists — the sales group? What is the penalty if the forecast is actually met? What if it isn't? You could "play the game" by any number of rule interpretations.

Both "filling the void" and "playing the game" are techniques whereby the manager, practicing the aggressive management style, recognizes and uses informal relationships within the structured organization.

PRODUCTIVITY IMPROVEMENT THROUGH OCCUPANCY

Professor Tor Dahl of the University of Minnesota, who also heads the Executive Development Corporation in Minneapolis states, "Occupancy refers to what the manager is doing with his or her time." In the October 1978 issue of *Corporate Report* he stated, "The percentage of time spent working — as opposed to waiting for work — is the occupancy rate...The goals of managers here is to manage their work and time so as to be fully occupied."

Two techniques may aid the manager increase his or her occupancy:

- use the Kobert Wheel in conjunction with a time allocation survey, such as an activity sample. (See chapter 3.)
- develop the Kobert Wheel for your employees to encompass tasks you believe that they can *barely* do.

By matching actual time allocation derived from an activity sampling study, to your concept of what your job functions are (or as depicted on the Kobert Wheel), the manager will find:

- Nonwork tasks, as well as tasks that could be delegated, amounting to between 35 and 40 percent of his or her time.
- performed tasks not contemplated when filling in the Kobert Wheel.
- an interesting disparity between high priority tasks and time spent on performing them.

By understanding your present occupancy matched against both your perception of occupancy and your expectations, a conscious effort and planned redirection of your efforts can be made to improve your managerial productivity.

PREPARING THE KOBERT WHEEL FOR YOUR EMPLOYEES

In working with your employees, there are some advantages to preparing the Kobert Wheel for them and including some tasks they can just barely perform. The goal is to improve the occupancy of *their* time.

It is incumbent upon any manager practicing the aggressive management style to express his or her level of expectations to the employees. Obviously, a low level of expectations will be met by a majority of the employees. In fact, most will settle back into complacency. On the other hand, if the manager's demands are set at too high a level, this has a self-defeating effect built in; the employee will sense that the likelihood of succeeding and receiving just recognition will be slim.

Success involves degrees of both certainty and uncertainty. The uncertainty portion may breed anxiety, while poor performance increases the certainty of failure. There are even some folks who prefer the certainty of failure to the uncertainty of success.

The manager, practicing AMS, will note that assigning tasks to the best qualified personnel sometimes involves providing work for which the employee is overqualified. You will get somewhat better results than if this same task is assigned to a less-qualified individual. However, the overqualified individual may take the assignment as:

- requiring less than "two hands on the wheel" to complete in an acceptable manner, or
- a sign that your task completion expectations are low.

On the other hand, assigning a task to individuals with qualifications that barely enable them to complete the task, has the opposite effect:

- the subordinates will have to strive harder and will learn something from that experience for future use, or
- they will see the assignment as an indication that you have higher

expectations from their efforts. (See Pygmalion Effect discussion in chapter 4.)

Instead of having your employees complete the Kobert Wheel, do it for them! This will be especially helpful to new employees and trainees. Gear your expectations to that which you feel they can "stretch" to accomplish.

In turn, gear your praise to your employee's capabilities relevant to the completion of the assigned tasks. You *know* Mary can do a better job, but Karen did the best within her capabilities to complete the task. Gear your praise to the individual's capabilities.

It has been said that employees measure their success by the praise or criticism they either receive or perceive. But this is on an individual basis, such that, as each person achieves the barely attainable (the tasks he or she must "stretch" to perform) praise geared to individual accomplishments can be a vital factor in motivation and in time occupancy.

The managerial control required increases as:

- work is given to less-qualified individuals, or
- managers err in overestimating the competence of their subordinates.

As described in chapter 4, managerial control involves a review of planned actions as close as possible to the action occurrence, in order to permit a measured response or corrective mode, if necessary. The frequency of performing this review will obviously increase in any of the above two delegation situations. But, the point here is that managers can set employee goals geared to their capabilities by using the Kobert Wheel.

SOME MISCELLANEOUS USES OF THE KOBERT WHEEL

The Kobert Wheel delineates the tasks that an individual feels he or she is responsible to perform, as well as those he or she is actually performing. In addition, the organizational elements one would go to for aid to accomplish these tasks are listed, in order to determine the individual's concept of organizational relationships.

Other uses of the Kobert Wheel are to ascertain:

- *a sense of urgency.* The employee ranks the functions he or she performs by his or her order of importance. Ties are not allowed, since similar to the "In-Basket Technique," you must choose one thing to do first. It is interesting to observe the difference between a boss' and his supervisor's choice of priorities. In this way, you can probe deeper than the mere matching of objectives approach, by forcing a time frame onto the decision to act.

- *organizational options.* This is done by asking the testee to follow-up the initial reactions to the questions asked by expanding the answers with a detailed analysis of the organizational chart. In this way, as he or she sees more possibilities for receiving aid, the testee is asked for second and third choices for aid to be selected from the organization chart. The testee gets to know the services available for aid, learns the relationships he or she has to these services and gains an appreciation of the procedures that are the organization's "life-blood." If the organization is the ectoplasm, veins, arteries and bones of the company, then the bloodstream of that living organization is its procedures of operation.

- *the informal organization.* A group of supervisors and employees meet to draw the informal organizational relationships. This is a very old technique for defining the informal operations of a company. Everyone knows that not all communications follow the formal path of the published charts and procedures. By discussing the variations openly, the group can voice its feelings with regard to:

  - those areas where the formal organization and procedures are not as effective as the informal ones.
  - hostilities, problems and losses, when the informal supersedes the formal approach.
  - recommendations for improvement, since it is usually found that people are much more likely to try to make *their* ideas work than *yours!*

Modifications of the original Kobert Wheel include formats where only narrative is required by the testee, or where the total statement is committed to paper by an interviewer.

On one occasion, the Kobert Wheel was completed through an oral discussion and taped for future reference, as well as face-to-face (one-on-one). Quite frankly, the answers appeared to be slightly changed by the process used to collect the information. The reason why is that most supervisors I have met are quite vocal about procedural and organizational relationships, since they feel their comments are usually constructive and will help the company.

Again, what "they" (those who make the organization "tick") think and do is far more important than what "we" think or draw on the organizational charts. Our management style is dependent on the concepts of organization held by those we direct. For this reason, it is important to understand what they perceive the organization to be. Part of what is perceived is related to our manner of communication...how we express our expectations.

To help define the existing problem of making organizations perform effectively, you should understand the working of both the formal and the informal organization. This is done by examining objectives and priorities, continuous monitoring of these objectives and priorities, creating an environment for negotiating changes and relying on a knowledge of those organizational elements that can aid in meeting both the objectives and the priorities.

The Kobert Wheel was devised to help perform this type of analysis in a "painless" manner. The first application showed a vast discrepancy between what management thought and what their first-line supervisors perceived was their job. Further analysis showed an even greater schism between these segments as to how the organization operated.

The informal organization exists in all areas of work...the working arrangement created by either a desire to "get something done" despite the constraints of the formal organization, or by practice. Even the "open door" policy, a product of the 1970s, recognizes and uses the informal organization so that the relationships to accomplish work fall far short of total anarchy.

The manager, using the aggressive management style, should understand the workings of the informal organization in order to use them. Accordingly, two strategies were put forth..."filling the void" and "playing the game." Both strategies involve using the existing informal organization to achieve a positive result and high level recognition.

Finally, the Kobert Wheel is used to compare job functions and priorities to the actual time spent on these tasks. Occupancy is the amount of time a manager spends on managerial functions. The Kobert Wheel, coupled with activity sampling, can measure the degree of occupancy presently existing in the manager's work area. Likewise, the occupancy of your employees can be improved by setting goals that cause them to stretch their capabilities in order to gain positive accomplishment and to receive praise.

The purpose of presenting the Kobert Wheel was to provide another tool for analysis. The manager, practicing the AMS, should review the techniques of using this analysis tool. However, analysis without a planned control and action can be just an interesting academic exercise.

9

USING THE AMS TO IMPROVE
ONE-ON-ONE RELATIONSHIPS

In the previous chapter, the workings of the organization were covered as they related to the problems and opportunities of employing AMS techniques, such as "void filling" and "playing the game." The analysis tool was the Kobert Wheel.

As stated in chapter 1, a proper analysis of managerial techniques should go from the macro down to the micro. In the next three chapters, microanalysis will cover techniques for dealing with one-on-one situations (9), small groups in meetings and on committees (10), as well as motivating individuals (11). In my training sessions for managers, I always try to structure material coverage in this descending order of analysis. This never pleases those who want "a quick fix." These "quick fixes" are generally contained in the microanalysis section of my programs...the last hours of the last day. So, too, microanalysis and techniques consume the last three chapters.

I urge you to consider "working with a giant earthmover before using a teaspoon." Since the highest form of improvement is elimination, consider how many work processes can be modified by a macro look that may eliminate the task one can only improve with a microanalysis!

In chapters 1 through 8, a macro look has been taken at planning, time management, managerial control, problem-solving, communications, delegation and organization. In this chapter, your managerial style relevant to individual actions will be covered.

Personal management devices will be shown, such as:

- decreasing energy spent on worry or regret.
- promulgating change from the status quo.
- decreasing double approvals and unnecessary concurrences and signatures.
- receiving information relative to criticality by distinguishing between need to know and like to know.
- encouraging grouping versus individual discussions.
- providing the questions you will ask...before you ask them.
- defining a completed stage and/or a completed task.
- saying you're busy when you're busy.
- making the chain of command work for you.
- rapping with your secretary to improve office management.
- using the telephone as one of the communicative tools available to improve operations.
- communicating with hard-to-get parties.
- controlling time spent with visitors for maximum benefit.
- understanding and using your physical metabolism.
- maintaining a "survival kit" in the office.
- maintaining a filing system for *retrieval*...not just for *putting away* information.

The list is obviously endless. As a regular contributor to the magazine, *Boardroom Reports* (as well as a member of its Panel of Experts for Productivity), I have counted as many as 68 ideas for improving personal management style in just one issue of this semimonthly newsletter. What I have culled out on the following pages are those ideas related to the practice of the aggressive management style...the bold ideas for positive gain and high level recognition that I have contributed over the years.

WHAT COULD HAVE BEEN ISN'T

The world of business is full of those who "rail against the gods" for things that could have been or should have been, but aren't. We can wish we looked differently, had a better speaking voice, were taller, thinner or even cleverer. However hard we try to change what is, we mainly succeed in modifying the worst aspects, while adding some lustre to our best features. Very few of us are capable of, or willing, to *completely* change ourselves over to a sought-after image.

It was along these lines that this book was written...not to change the average manager into an assertive "tiger," but to attempt to persuade the reader to recognize some available techniques for modifying his or her management techniques.

If the manager uses aggressive techniques, this does not necessarily mean it must be done through an assertive personality. The aggressive management style was defined as a group of aggressive techniques, seeking positive accomplishment and being coupled with recognition.

An important trait to modify is procrastination. One of the signs of a procrastinator is that worn by the person who keeps telling you why things didn't get done and why they weren't done in the past. This is an obvious groping for an excuse to cover indecisiveness or inaction.

The not-so-obvious display of procrastination is evident in the amount of effort and time spent on describing the "if onlys":

- "If only sales were up in the Northeast, we'd have met our budget."
- "If only the needed part had arrived on time, we'd have met the shipping schedule."
- "If only they weren't caught in the Watergate offices of the opposition party."
- "If only Memorial Day didn't shorten the amount of working days in May."
- "If only the snowstorm hadn't hit us in mid-February."

"If only" alludes to a fact that "is" or "was." No amount of discussion will change the fact that it "is" or "was." But, it is interesting to discuss and to postulate on what could have been, might be now or could occur "if only"...

You will note this type of thinking, not only in meetings with peers, but also creeping into your employees' thinking. Note how much of a meeting's time between you and one of your employees is spent by the employee explaining what might have been, "if only..." Is this an excuse, or just a time waster? Regardless of the discussion, "what was, is," and your action or decision will be based on "what is."

There are some exceptions to consider:

- If a discussion of "what was" discloses a situation to be overcome by a future plan of action, seek this out. However, separate the search for a reason to be considered in future actions from a rehash of "what was" and cannot be changed, such as the weather, a fact, an act of God, etc. This is the subtlety between honest fact-finding and procrastination-type discussions.

- Allow for some discussion of "if only..." as it discloses information not heretofore known. But, keep informational discussions to a purposeful objective...to inform, explain, focus. The procrastination creeps in when the conversation drags in an attempt to excuse, blame or defend an action. This, too, requires a knowledge of the subtlety between useful information and mere excuse formulation.

To employ the aggressive management style requires:

- a separation of informative writings and discussions from excuses, cover-ups or accusations.

- a drive to focus on what to do (or not to do) based on what is, thus

- reducing the procrastination and indecisiveness associated with long-winded writings and discussions prefaced by "if only...."

This approach should obviously lead to having you recognized as one who is action-oriented, not just one searching for excuses. This type of recognition is sought by aggressive style managers and is a "positive" observable trait when noticed by your superiors.

"WE'VE ALWAYS DONE IT THIS WAY"

The introduction of change constantly flushes out the defenders of the status quo. This is acceptable if the defense is logical, based on cost savings, safety, business logic or a relatable prior experience; it is not "reactionary," "too conservative" or merely "playing it safe." However, a defense of the status quo based on, "We've always done it that way" should be an unacceptable business posture.

As in the previous section on "if only...," there is a fine line between the obvious procrastination and indecision and the subtle. Subtle ways of proclaiming, "We've always done it this way" are expressed as:

- "It doesn't seem different, so why change a successful formula?"
- "You've proven your point, but they won't buy it!"

- "The tests sure are statistically conclusive, but let's make certain... really certain."
- "It looks like you made the facts fit the predetermined conclusion."
- "You're so obviously correct; there must be something wrong with the conclusion...otherwise why haven't others thought of it?"
- "Let me think about it."

In all of the discussions of AMS so far, techniques were introduced that brought about positive change. To institute change is to recognize and to work with those forces allied against change. The first person to observe is *you!* See if you write about or state positions that reject or modify well-documented, suggested changes based mainly on a defense of the status quo. This type of defense is usually based on such factors as:

- the new idea changes a procedure that *you* had installed (false pride of authorship).
- you know what you've got but are uncertain about what you're getting. (Look at probability of gain versus downside risk.)
- insecurity and fear (would the fear of *not* changing help you to make the correct decision?)
- peer pressure (weigh being the "first on the block" with a new idea versus always "running with the pack").

YOU AND YOUR PERSONAL ETHICS

The final factor, the most difficult one, is personal ethics. If you are really convinced on an objective basis as possible that the change is correct for the entire entity, then you should examine your lifestyle concept of doing what is right. How far should you push for adoption? Based on the value of the change? Your fear of rejection? Is the fight worth the effort... is it either win or lose? What affect does time have on the ultimate adoption? Is compromise better than rejection? Do you put aside your personal ethics when you come to work each day?

There are no pat answers to the above questions. They relate to your lifestyle at work. The Sunday Christian casts personal values to the wind at work. However, your workplace is a microcosm of society. What society accepts from its members does not change right from wrong, as perceived by the individual, but it may modify his or her behavior in striving to conform within society.

The basic weakness with this whole argument is that every one knows individuals who have succeeded to the highest levels of business and government with little regard for even the minimum of personal ethical values. Yet, a moral corporate or governmental "micro society" has elevated them in spite of this personal shortfall. Should we examine their traits to emulate? If this were true, *Mein Kampf* and the personal diaries of Idi Amin would receive more attention from those desiring to achieve success in business than the works of Peter Drucker, Earl Nightingale, Hertzberger, Caroline Bird or Alec McKenzie. The main body of rewards to managers have been accorded to the talented, hard working, aggressive, good looking, efficient and well spoken, who also happen to possess an average level of personal ethics.

CONVERTING OTHERS TO CHANGE

After a self-evaluation of your motives regarding change or the defense of status quo, we can now look at those we wish to influence...our peers, superiors and employees. Of this group, it would appear that the easiest group to convert should be your own employees. Point out their defensive posture, the advantages of seeking positive change, and — most importantly — what you believe is the best approach to evaluating change. Your input as the boss is the most important element in modifying employee behavior relative to the status quo...right or wrong.

Your peers are usually not too excited about receiving constructive criticism from you, and they are not about to change an attitude or behavior because you think it will help the overall enterprise. You are their peer and that relationship is fraught with respect, jealousy, understanding, suspicion and "back-stabbing"...all the positive and negatives of human behavior in the larger, real world.

To get your peers to accept change — especially a change recommended by you — requires an understanding of their attitude toward the status quo as well as toward the suggested change. Remember, they have a stake in both.

First, look at what "is." A little research can turn up how and why we are doing what we are doing. If the research turns up that George is the initiator of the procedure you are preparing to change, you had better first check our George's "pride of authorship syndrome." Will he look at your suggestion for change as a criticism of "his" procedure? If not, fine; however, if this does pose a problem, why not consider asking for George's advice on an idea, getting him involved with the credit for the change, seeking his support, or at least lowering his possible resistance to the recommendation? Remember, selling is not a dirty word in AMS.

To practice the aggressive management style requires that recognition be received for your efforts. Shared recognition of an accepted change is far superior to exclusive recognition for a rejected recommendation.

For those peers who will fight for the status quo because it is more comfortable, you must seek a way to promote change without upsetting their "security blanket." Answer the asked or mostly unanswered questions with enough supporting detail to allay fears caused by:

- potential exposure to the unknown. Be specific, not elusive, as to the exact impact of the proposal on their future actions, jobs, etc. If possible, put this specificity into commonly accepted terms such as the budget, the organizational chart, the procedures manual, staffing pattern, career pay ladder, job description, capital budget proposal and the like.

- fear of loss of control. Cover the hidden question, "Will I have less of an empire?" If they won't, say so; if they will, seek substitutions in functions to be performed and recognized after the change. If the peer is not worthy of selling, then say so, and allow the unsupportable negatives to sink the position of this individual peer.

- fear that *you* are the prime beneficiary of the change. No matter what you say or do, some peers will think this anyway. I have found that a direct statement as to the benefits to you, expressed honestly and "up front", can deflect this negative. Now that you have stated what's on *their* mind, try to see if there are any other major objections. If not, you have reduced the position of the potential objector to, "It's a good idea, good for the enterprise; therefore, can I reject it solely on the grounds of who is the prime beneficiary, especially if this was honestly stated 'up front'?"

DECREASING DOUBLE APPROVALS

Just as it is necessary to consider your boss, peers and workers when seeking change from the status quo, so too must you look at tasks that you consider "necessary." You've always done them, so you will continue doing them. Elimination means no one will do them; delegation indicates it will be done for you.

A ripe target for such analysis is the area of double approvals. If one asks, "Why must you approve?", this question is best preceded by, "Why is it necessary to require an approval at all?" These two questions have been discussed in the narratives preceding this chapter under such headings as "elimination is the highest form of improvement" and "delegate or die."

A practitioner of the aggressive management style must also look at double approvals...those actions or correspondence requiring more than one creditable authorization. Some examples are:

1. Dictated correspondence reviewed by your secretary or the word processing pool and then physically signed by you. Why? Do you often change what you have dictated? (I refer here to content

changes, not just to correcting punctuation as a result of proof-reading.) Is your signature the only accepted authorization for *every* piece of correspondence? Can you isolate the significant few items that require your personal signature and so annotate the tape or paper when sent for typing? In this way, all other correspondence, memos, informational statements, meeting calls, reports and the like can be "proofed" or signed for you, if necessary, and then dispatched. What does your personal signature (the double approval) add to a majority of your communications?

2. Replies to routine questions, answered by your employees in letters needing your signature before being sent off. Does *all* of this correspondence require the approval of both your employees and yourself? The answer is obviously yes for the new employee or on vital matters. But why are you double approving routine correspondence or actions? Can you determine the level of work requiring double approval? And, then can you describe the difference to your employees? If you can, you can reduce double approvals to the vital few requiring your personal attention. You can still sample-read items going out without your concurrence to check on how well the system is working. Those employees who cannot "hack it" after explanation, training and follow-up by you, should be replaced, transferred or dehired. No company should have to pay two people to do the work of one.

3. Correspondence forwarded to you by your peers or supervisor can be classified as:
   a. requiring your personal concurrence.
   b. that which can be routinely delegated to your people to provide a recommendation for your acceptance.
   c. materials that should *not* have been sent to you for approval by your peers.

It is this latter point that is the most difficult to resolve. You may be required to ameliorate the situation by confronting the forwarder as to why your group needs to approve the materials. A childish reaction may result, "Well, if you don't think this need be approved by your department, we'll stop sending items like this in the future!" You are asking for more discretion in the practice of forwarding materials, and you receive a "total embargo" reaction. Try to indicate the advantages of requiring less approvals; suggest specific items for exclusion. Indicate how you will help initiate the "project"; describe the support you can provide with his or her peers.

In all of the above, the key is to recognize double approvals that are redundant, nonproductive and targets for elimination. In practicing AMS, you are indicating a positive attitude towards expediting work authorization, concurrence and cooperation with your peers.

THE "AT-YOUR-LEISURE" APPROACH
TO RECEIVING INFORMATION

Most managers today can make the distinction between "need to know" and "like to know" relevant to information. In the previous section, a portion of this philosophy was covered in regard to double approvals. If you don't have to approve something twice, consider the criteria for *not* having the matter brought to your attention at all. If something is brought to your attention as information, what form and priority would fit your management style?

In my youthful era as a manager, I had inherited a secretary from my predecessor, whom I promptly dubbed, "Chronological Mary." Her concept of order in the office was to put everything in chronological order, date stamp everything coming in and going out, including the junk mail, and to always present calls, memos, messages and visitors in a strict chronological sequence. First was always first; a lifo (last in, first out) system was considered heresy.

I would return from a five day trip and receive five folders marked, "Monday, Tuesday...Friday." I had very little choice but to start with the first folder, "Monday", and work my way through to "Friday." I had tried scanning through all the folders, but found it quite difficult to pick out other than the very obvious materials of a higher priority than that which was ascribed to it by the folder, namely, "Thursday."

Invariably, I would be finishing "Tuesday" when a caller would ask, "Have you decided yet? The most important decision of 1980 has to be made by 10:30!" I would then scramble to find the documents buried in "Thursday."

I soon realized that a chronological order was more for my secretary's convenience than for mine. As a manager, information was best handled by me if presented in some priority order; the receipt of information usually had little to do with the priority required to handle it. I could have received news of an impending disaster at the same time as Harriet requested Tuesday afternoon off for a visit by her nephew.

With a little training on my part, I introduced the manufacturing scheduling concept to my office routine. In manufacturing scheduling, an individual work order is related to:

    a. its own demand due date, relative to the need to balance that individual work order completion with other manufactured or

    procured items and the customer demand as expressed by the
schedule.

b. the time capacity requirements of all other work orders to be
balanced in the same way as in "a" above.

Chronological Mary was shown how to master schedule all of my
work in large work groupings (research, follow-up, planning, budget,
information, etc.), and then to prioritize the individual tasks or requests
within these categories. In this way, the whole pile of "Information Only"
was given a low priority; the "Action or Answer Needed" pile was given a
high priority. Then, within the grouping, all work was prioritized from
"urgent" down to "needed." Of course, it was never in the *exact* order I
would have wanted it, but it was *always* close enough.

I had traded a frantic, priority selection for a more leisurely and
logical work pace in which to review information crossing my desk. Production managers weigh skilled and expensive direct labor and equipment
utilization against the costs of such indirect services as set-up and maintenance. They know the cost of having their talented skills and assets
directly involved in preparing for work. So, too, an executive should understand that his or her management skills are being diminished by performing
indirect services of sorting, prioritization, double approvals and routine
delegations.

OTHER ONE-ON-ONE AMS PRACTICES

The aggressive management style is practiced by Dr. Marvin B.
Glaser, Mgr., Environmental Programs, Exxon Res. & Engr., by the following one-on-one actions or expectations:

- encouraging his people to group questions and discussions with him
  instead of receiving a steady stream of disconnected requests and
  statements.

- constantly reviewing the types of questions *he* will ask, so that they
  come prepared with the answers.

- defining a completed stage or completed task so that advice, concurrence and ideas stem from a knowledge of the entire project,
  not just a narrow view of an isolated incident. For example, a decision or recommendation on an *individual* bugetary item is related
  to the status of the *overall* budget; so, too, are logical decisions
  reached in an acquisition, major procurement or contractual negotiation.

Your management style, when expressed or demonstrated to others, reflects your view of action versus procrastination, analysis versus "fishing", determination versus indecision. When you go one-on-one with your employees, peers or boss, it is important to express by your actions a positive approach to handling the work. The three approaches used by Marv Glaser show this "face" to his employees. By the Pygmalion Effect, his employees will emulate Marv's approach; sometimes peers and bosses will also do the same. In any event, the manager practicing AMS practices techniques receiving positive recognition and even emulation by others.

MANAGING YOURSELF

There are positive, recognizable actions that merely require self-discipline — the ability to manage oneself. For example, can you:

- say *yes* when asked if you're busy?
- say *no* to those who bypass the chain of command?
- change your mind about a decision you had previously reached based upon fragmentary or insufficient information?
- admit to a prejudice in the distribution of work?
- understand why you accept or reject ideas, not just based on facts or experiences, but on pure "gut-feel?"
- accept information or logic from a previously unreliable source?
- accept suggestions or even criticism from lightly regarded sources?
- modify an objective even though much time and effort has already been expended in another direction?
- state a valid objection to an almost unanimous position taken by your peers and bosses and then accept rejection without petulance?
- invest time to train others instead of continuing to complain about *their* shortcomings?

The list of self-discipline questions is obviously endless. However, unless we as managers perceive that our management style is a partial reflection of our self-discipline, we will continue to grasp individual techniques, singular "eye-catching" acts and isolated dramatic statements as a way to improve our management style. The overview look at your style — from macro planning to micro self-discipline, one-on-one actions — is a superior approach.

"STEALING IDEAS" FROM OTHERS

Whenever I use the word "stealing" in any discussions with managers, they tend to cringe. That just isn't a proper word to be used amongst sophisticated folks. Most people feel better with such words as "borrow", "modify", "incorporate", "fuse", "extract", "select" and the like. To steal is to take unto yourself that which belongs to someone else, for your own purposes and without appropriate consideration or recognition given or even offered to the provider of the idea. If a pistol is used, it's armed robbery; if threats are employed, it's blackmail; if you take it from a competitor, it's strategy; when the boss takes your idea unto himself or herself, that's teamwork!

A "good soldier" is an employee who provides a stream of positive actions and ideas for the "team", regardless of the absence of recognition or other reward. He or she is not discouraged by a lack of recognition for his or her ideas as they are passed on and adopted by others. The reward is in knowing you have contributed to a job well done; in fact, a "good soldier" sacrifices self-interest for the good of the enterprise.

The trouble with all of the above is not the self-sacrificing concept, but in finding the people to adopt the "good soldier" attitude. In time of "work or starve," the "good soldier" attitude may be fostered by the community's economic position. When an employee reaches a stratospheric level compared to his or her perceived abilities, or relative to similar opportunities elsewhere available, "good soldiers" are born out of fear of losing that attained position. Finally, "good soldiers" may be developed by rewarding their efforts and successes.

Let's put the "good soldier" and "stealing" concepts together. You can create a "good soldier" by rewarding, in either a direct or obtuse way, the originator of the ideas that are ultimately adopted. This is an acceptable form of giving credit.

"Stealing" can be reduced to buying, if a proper (though not necessarily immediate) reward is provided to the victim.

A "kissing bandit", especially a moustachioed one, will not assuage *my* feelings over the loss of money or other valuables. But I can be turned on by a multiplicity of rewards to replace the "money" removed from my wallet. The reward makes for "good soldiers."

There is a literal mine of ideas all around you. Some are presented willingly; some have to be dredged out. These ideas can help you do your job better, and may provide positive recognition for you by your peers and boss.

Consider keeping a personal file or scorecard per employee for proposed and adopted ideas. These can be accumulated for the appropriate salary review time. Make sure your employees know you are "keeping score."

Now you can have the type of teamwork where ideas are presented to be incorporated. You have encouraged teamwork. In a church, it is offered with a hope of a distant reward; in industry, the reward just has to be a little closer to our time on earth.

RAPPING WITH YOUR EMPLOYEES

During the 1960s, a whole segment of our population, mostly in our colleges, revolted against an establishment (government, home, industry, society in general, schools) that did not appear to be listening to them. Their central themes were the Vietnam War and the military draft, but they could have been toothpick length and napkin size. Not that the war and the draft were not the most serious issues of the decade, but nothing infuriates and antagonizes more than the feeling that no one is listening.

Most companies represent "the establishment" to their employees, who feel the managerial staff is involved with perpetuating past practices while slowly evolving and instituting new practices. It has been established that three-quarters of the offices in this country do not use (or have ever heard of) word processing equipment more than 20 years after its introduction; 80 percent of sizable installations do not use materials requirement planning, shop floor controls or capacity planning. The order entry systems, accounts receivable tallies, cash flow statements, credit checks and the like have been done the same laborious way, in many companies, since Scrooge used a high desk and quill pen.

Are you listening? Do you really take the time to encourage your employees to participate and then follow-up to implement a good idea? This is best accomplished on a one-on-one basis. Some folks will not open up at a meeting, in public or in front of visitors. "Write me a memo," seems like an easy task (for you) but may be difficult for your employees.

Start with one employee...your secretary, if you have one. Tell her that you are going to set aside 15 minutes per week to rap with her on ideas she may have for improving operations in the office. Set it up a few days in advance. Put it on your calendar. Tell her to start putting items in a folder for this discussion. She can bring in specifics as examples, but you don't want a meeting solely on the Barnes project; you want a discussion on improving the management of your office. Make her responsible for the agenda.

Start the meeting on time; don't put it off, if possible, for another job; give it some degree of priority. Have calls and visitors deferred, just as you would if you were in the office with an important customer. This is significant. Take notes on important decisions. Put them into practice. Give credit where necessary and where possible. Make sure you meet again on a regular basis. Encourage a free flow of ideas, criticism and opinions. Make the meeting productive by zeroing in on solutions and positive steps to improvements.

Now try this approach with another employee. If you have seven people directly reporting to you, this described practice, rapping for 15 minutes a week, will consume about two hours per week dedicated to "fire prevention," leaving at the very least 38 hours for "fire fighting."

SOME IDEAS GRAINED AT RAP SESSIONS

I should like to "sell" the reader on the advantages of the above, not just by restating the advantages to your image as an executive practicing the aggressive management style, but also by listing some actual improvements that I have experienced.

Jumping the Queue

Telephone calls tend to cause the receiver to act more expeditiously than memos or letters. When the phone rings and the party asks for you, it is not uncommon to have the call "shoveled" directly into the called party. Do *all* calls require such a time urgent handling?

I worked in a British company where the managing director saw visitors and internal personnel by appointment only. Only six officers and his own secretary had direct access to him. Yet, when you met with him (by appointment) he would receive a host of calls, "shoveled" in by his secretary, that were jumping the queue. If you called, you gained access immediately; visitors had to make an appointment and wait to be summoned. You can guess how great the quantity of calls were as employees and visitors learned how to "play the game" and jump the queue.

At a rap session with his secretary, they worked out a scheme, as follows. No caller who wished to speak to the managing director should be refused. However, alternatives were provided by the secretary, who when asked, "May I speak to Mr. Clarke?" responded, "Certainly! However, he is busy right now; shall I interrupt him or may I be of assistance?" Nearly 60 percent of the callers (a) received information the secretary was authorized to give, such as the time of the next meeting, (b) were diverted to parties that the managing director would have himself called to get the answer, (c) left informative messages such as the new price, the contract revision, a comment or two, all of which were passed on to the managing director at his leisure, (d) left questions. When presented in a group to the managing director, they were mostly answered by "Tell George that the new price is all right," or "Tell Beverly that 10:45 tomorrow would be just fine." You can guess at what the questions were and realize the callers wanted information, not necessarily the managing director.

Using the Blue Note

In line with jumping the queue, another solution to constant telephone interruption and call back for left messages was devised. People call because that is the quickest way to contact someone in the office. People don't answer their mail in any urgent manner and a visit is time consuming. Therefore, the telephone is mostly used for any answer or information required within four hours.

At a rap session with one of his managers, a vice-president of a Southwest company developed the "blue note" system. For all information to be supplied in less than one day and requiring less than an immediate communication (thus requiring the telephone), the information or information request was put on a "blue note." All recipients of "blue notes" had to respond as soon as possible on that day and at their convenience. The reader can see the obvious advantages:

a. The provider of the information gets the request in the proper time urgency — that day — instead of at a possible interruptive time.

b. The information can be absorbed or gathered by the provider without having to be done while on the phone.

c. The task may be delegated.

d. The reply may be delegated.

e. A mass of requests, handled by telephone only, is reduced to the proper time urgency — less than "immediately," but in the work day and usually within four hours.

Reducing Paddle Tennis with Left Messages

At a rap session with his regional sales manager, a group sales manager selected a solution from some possible alternatives to the "ping-pong effect." The ping-pong effect exhibits itself by messages which read as follows:

a. "Henry called" on a call report form on your desk.

b. "Norman returned your call" on Henry's desk.

c. "Henry called again" either noted on the original call form or on a new one.

d. "Norman called again" now reported on Henry's desk.

Before showing the reader the improvement in the above, let's first consider another situation. The sales manager is out-of-town. When a regional manager calls, his secretary replies, "He'll be calling in at 11:30, can I ask him your question at that time?" Most of the time the secretary will be provided with the question because the boss is out-of-town! When the boss calls, the secretary asks the question, the answer is given and the secretary is told to give it to the questioner.

The reason for interjecting this story was to demonstrate one of the accepted conditions for the secretary to question the caller, as well as one of the situations where the boss authorizes the secretary to provide an answer in his or her name! At the rap session, where the "ping-pong" effect was discussed, it was determined that the main reasons for the many calls, recalls and messages were:

- the caller didn't leave a question, a request or any information other than that he or she had called.

- the secretary didn't ask or even suggest, "Can I be of help?"

- the called party had no other choice but to leave the following message when his returned call found the original caller out, "returned your call."

- bosses many times didn't allow their secretaries to provide answers ...except when they were out-of-town, at a meeting, etc.

The rap session outlined a Sales department approach, requiring a training and indoctrination program for all bosses and secretaries on how to prevent "paddle-tennis" messages. Obviously, the program contained "how to call" practices as well as "how to respond" rules.

Controlling Your Calendar

At a rap session with his administrative assistant, an engineering manager found that when someone wanted to either set up a meeting or visit the manager, the boss's calendar had to be checked, since only the boss could authorize the appointment. This meant that the administrative assistant would either have to sneak in and interpret the boss's calendar or simply take a message for a call-back if the time was all right.

The administrative assistant suggested the following:

- a list of appointments that the administrative assistant was authorized to commit for the engineering manager was drawn up. The administrative assistant could say, "yes" for the boss and the boss was merely informed of the commitment for these situations.
- the boss's calendar was moved to the administrative assistant's desk. A copy of the commitments made and future appointments was put on the boss's desk, but, the official calendar was on the administrative assistant's desk.

Maintaining a Survival Kit

A constant source of expected inefficiency was experienced by a manager in a suburban Maryland office. This related primarily to outside visitors. They made requests that would tie up the office staff for such things as stamps, bandages, cleaning fluid, button-sewing, antacids, etc. The manager felt that every visitor was an honored guest to be treated with the "courtesy of kings."

At a rap session, she was informed of an alternative by her office manager. Why not collect and maintain a "survival kit" of the items most frequently asked for by visitors? The survival kit was put together from a tally of visitors' requests made over a three month period, containing over 80 percent of normal visitor's needs. A great deal of interruptions to satisfy visitor needs was thus reduced.

The above examples were intended to motivate you to practice having one-on-one rap sessions with your employees. They should be formally structured and scheduled. Your style will reflect the fact you are listening, and in return you'll have a host of new ideas to "steal."

THE PURPOSE OF FILING IS RETRIEVAL

The purpose of filing is retrieval, not just filing. You can improve your managerial efficiency by understanding this powerful message. Obviously, the system you will use will be the company system. Where one does not exist or is working poorly, in terms of retrieval, the following could be of value to the aggressive style manager.

You have a distinct advantage in most companies, hospitals or government services, in that the usual pressure in these offices is to "put it away." Hence, the drive is for the use of "little pictures" such as cartridge microfilm and microfiche. In such an atmosphere, the improvement in retrieval is related to the speed or accessibility one has to *everything* in the files.

Think about the advantages you can propose that accentuate the screening process of (1) what goes in at all and (2) where it is to be filed. Let's start with the latter...where it is to be filed. As you will see, part of the solution is "why file it at all?"

The first question to answer is "Will it be needed in the future?" You have *no* choice with certain records of a legal or contractual designation. This question is mostly directed toward the mass of information filed under the nonspecific category, "general information."

Note the "Action Required" form in chapter 7; the first question is missing, but is the most potent in file information retrieval systems, "Will it be needed in the future?" It is the first question to be asked.

LET THE BOSS DO THE FILING

For this reason, I have introduced the "let the boss do the filing" system into some companies. Before you slam this book closed in disgust, let me explain how it works, how little "boss time" it takes and some of the advantages.

The system works as follows:

1. All paperwork that can be delegated, destroyed, approved, filed or otherwise handled prior to being seen by the boss should be defined in a working and perhaps documented procedure.

2. The options available to the boss on receiving the remainder of the paperwork, should include (as one of the highest priorities) "destroy." This requires a discipline to understand the future use of information need and to act accordingly. "Destroy" suggests that there is a slim chance of future need and no serious loss if there is such a need for retrieval with no document to retrieve.

3. Determine who is the most logical person requiring the information to be retrieved. This will vary from office to office, but in a majority of times it is the boss who needs the retrieval rather than the secretary (although the retrieval request is most often passed on to the secretary for action).

4. Maintain a filing guide at the convenience of the person in paragraph three above. If your offices don't have any documented filing system at all, consider the Standard Industrial Coding (SIC) system published by the Government Printing Office, or the system as published in the free literature of your favorite data or word processing companies.

5. A majority of correspondence, memos, informative documents and notes (worthy to be filed) can be selected from the file in less than

15 seconds by the party chosen in paragraph three. Since the boss is only receiving materials that are *not delegated* to be routinely filed by others, perhaps only 10 to 15 items a day need be file-selected and marked for filing. Therefore, the opening phrase, "let the boss do the filing" infers a *three to four minute* process each day by the party most likely to require retrieval (the sole purpose of filing!).

This procedure is most advantageous for the documents relegated to "general information" and has the least impact on obvious filing (and retrieval) papers such as:

- customer accounts (by name or number)
- students, patients and the like (by social security or assigned student numbers)
- project papers which are filed by project name or number
- committee reports (same handling as project papers)

SOME AMS TIPS TO IMPROVE F. & R.

In case you have forgotten, F. & R. stand for "Filing and Retrieval." The manager practicing AMS realizes that F. & R. is the most expeditious way to discuss information storage concepts (this is basic computer science dogma as well). For those of you who have observed or participated in office "safaris" ("Who has the files? Where is the information?," as the searchers stumble from office to office, desk to desk, searching, ever searching...), you appreciate tying retrieval practices to filing procedures.

The following is a further listing of data retrieval techniques that complement the "let the boss do the filing" concept:

1. Use a "filing slip" or "Action Required" form (see chapter 7) to indicate both filing and retrieval requests. This allows others (your secretary, the mail crew, etc.) to file for you. Some offices make the files one of the mail "drops." It also makes the file requestor think about cross-file categories, need for confidentiality and the distinction between temporary and permanent.

2. Make the distinction between temporary and permanent when requesting information storage. This saves the massive effort generally required for file purging. Establish a time-held criterion, say one year, on temporary information. As you can see in Figure 9-1, (C and D) this allows for a routine purge and discard of temporary items. This temporary or permanent distinction can carry over to that which is or is not photographed for cartridge tape or micro-

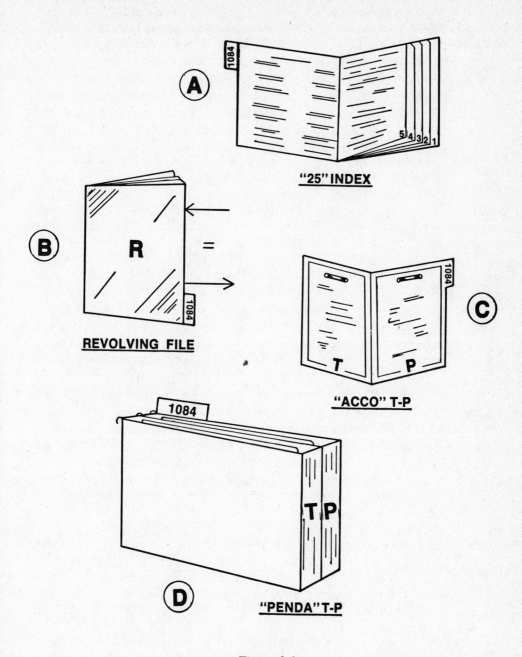

Figure 9-1

Retrieval Time-Savers

fiche. Imagine storing a letter, "Kobert will arrive at the Ft. Lauderdale Airport at 5:10 p.m. on Wednesday, 5 August 1980, on a "little picture" in a Utah mine shaft! Imagine the geologist's expression when he or she finds this letter in the year 2480!

3. For minutes of committee meetings, as an example, why have 15 duplicates of *all* the 10 year data in the files of *all* the members? The chairperson could be designated as the recipient or keeper of the files. The individual members need only have pertinent and current information at their fingertips. An "R" file, denoting a rotating or revolving file, can be established for the 14 members other than the chairperson. (See B, Figure 9-1.) This type of file requires the purging of the oldest item when the newest item is entered. Hence, if a six month file horizon is set up, it will be maintained, more-or-less, by this information rotation (oldest out, newest in) with the information retriever knowing full well that the complete file exists with the chairperson. Other applications include project portions performed by you that are submitted to the whole, information files of temporal value, etc.

4. Maintain "over 25" indexes on file (Item A on Figure 9-1) that collect over 25 entries (or pick another appropriate number). This will save retrieval time if individual files become quite large. You are trading off the time for notation on entry against the time for search on retrieval. Consider entering this information on the "file slip" or "Action Required" form. Remember you are noting items entered, not pages filed.

5. Cover withdrawals by discouraging the discourtesy of nondesignated withdrawals. Use a copy of the "file slip" or "Action Required" form as the "living" receipt for the extracted item.

6. Consider eliminating or reducing personal files. When Ehrlichman, Haldeman and Dean left the White House during the Watergate affair, I was reminded of all the corporate employees in the nation who spend their last hours before termination removing "their" files. Who paid for them? The next time a university professor backs up a truck for "his" files when he leaves office, have the campus security police ask this question. Who paid for the travel, the conference registration, the books, etc? One of the main reasons for office safaris is that there is not a sharp distinction made between business and personal files. Can you apply this discipline in your office, on a good business or at least on an ethics basis?

ONE-ON-ONE INCLUDES SELF-APPRAISAL

At the micro level, a manager looks at techniques involving individual relationships. These relationships include how others can be positively motivated by your individual actions. Your management style should include bold, aggressive ideas that result in positive gain for the enterprise, as well as higher level recognition.

The key in this chapter was to present a multitude of ideas and techniques that could be used in one-on-one situations. But in order to employ them, the manager must first practice a form of self-appraisal…an audit of gain versus expenditure and commitment. Consider the subjects covered, among many:

- decreasing the time spent on worry or regret.
- promulgating change from the status quo.
- decreasing double approvals.
- establishing the priority of information received.
- placing priority on retrieval over filing of information.
- "rapping" with your employees.
- controlling visitors.

Many of the micro improvements need only be put in place by a personal commitment on your part, whereas many of the macro analyses discussed in previous chapters require concurrences, approvals or, at the very least, notifications. This is not to draw a fine line between the two, since this is not the case, but rather to point out that the one-on-one techniques covered in this chapter are *less* susceptible to the usual rationale for no-action, "they wouldn't let me!" One of the quickest ways to gain the positive recognition of an AMS manager is to put in place aggressive actions that require little or no other party for approval.

10

OUR MEETING IS MISSING

As stated in chapter 1, the aggressive management style requires high-level recognition of a positive nature. An ideal showcase for this type of recognition is the meeting. It is in this arena that judgements, rightly and wrongly, are made by your peers and superiors. In these cauldrons, new stars rise and some perennials diminish in the glow light. The main elements of the meeting are:

- get ready
- attend and participate
- follow-up

A fourth and very definite step (a step that eludes the authors of texts, who are usually so preoccupied with improvements that they miss the very first step)...is to question why the meeting is even held!

THE "WEAKLY" MEETING

This is not a typographical error; it is an attempt to focus your attention on the effects of managerial inertia. The weakly meeting is held weekly because it has always been held then. I remember telling one of my employees that I had to leave to go to the weekly meeting. He asked, "Why is it held weekly?" I lamely replied, "We meet weekly because it's the weekly meeting."

Yet, many times it could just as well have been called the "weakly" meeting because:

- Very little was new to the attendees, since we all saw each other during the week and got copies of each other's memos.
- A few people presented a few new ideas, which could have been sent out in a memo instead.
- Some used the meeting as a form to castigate or "outshine the others."
- For 15 minutes of information that was vital or helpful to my function, I had to sit through over 90 minutes of rehash on items of little relevant interest.
- We were told there was an agenda. (You could have fooled me.)
- There was peer pressure to attend. If all the branch chiefs were there, then you had better be there as well.

Charles Kettering, inventor of the auto self-starter and a founder of Dayton Electric (DELCO), was reported to have said upon learning of Lindbergh's solo Atlantic crossing in 1927, "Humph! Like to see him do it with a committee! That would be a feat!" He was obviously referring to the advantage of individual action over trying to move an entire group of disparate interests toward a common goal. In this way, many weekly meetings do become weakly meetings.

But this creates the atmosphere for the manager practicing AMS to achieve recognition. If the regular meeting justification is just plain inertia (We've always done it this way!) then a change which affects this method of communication will have some clearly noticeable results.

DON'T PUNCH THEM IN THE NOSE

For the overly assertive in the audience, I would like to provide some "don'ts" before we cover the specifics of positive AMS actions relevant to meetings. Under the previous subheading, the weekly meeting was used to describe the results of inertia. Let us expand this discussion now to include all get togethers that require us to meet with others at a formal or informal business meeting. Here the inertia is not evidenced in the need for a regularly scheduled meeting, but is seen in the inertia that causes meetings to be held where none might be required.

You could gain recognition by "punching them all in the nose":

- don't attend when invited
- leave if you think the meeting is unproductive
- tell everyone what you think of the meeting as a timewaster, including whoever called it
- tell others what you think of the meeting *and* the attendees
- write nasty memos to emphasize your opinion
- all of the above...or pick one really good one!

The cost/benefit ratio in "getting it off your chest" and "really telling them" is akin to the byproducts of childish vindictiveness:

- feeling better, briefly, and
- surprise when others are hurt or strike back at you, albeit quite a while later.

We propose an evolving plan of improving the conduct of meetings that gains positive recognition for the reader. Others should work with you — not because they are intimidated, but because the logic of your approach to holding productive meetings reduces the alternatives to continue the unproductive past meeting practices.

ANSWERING THE FIRST QUESTION FIRST

The very first question to be considered when a meeting is called, is, "why are we meeting?" (The second question is, "why me?," which we will answer in the next section.) By assuming that all meetings are necessary, we blindly attend them and focus on improving their productivity. Yet, the first question is concerned with the rationale behind tying up those high-priced executives at a meeting. Is there an alternative and has it been considered?

I once was asked to write a publisher's review of a book on making meetings more effective. The book was written by a professional colleague of mine with whom I was friendly on a social basis as well. My comment was never published, despite this close relationship. The comment was, "The first chapter is missing...the one that addresses itself to the justification of the meeting or a listing of possible alternatives." Yet, this is a logical first question to ask as an AMS practitioner, if it can be done without "punching them in the nose." Remember, from chapter 2, the highest form of improvement is elimination of the function. So, too, the elimination of a meeting has got to beat improving the conduct of the meeting!

SOME AMS TECHNIQUES TO "ELIMINATE" MEETINGS

Let's start with that which is totally under your control...*your* meetings with *your* employees. How many are called under the guise of communication but result in you giving out *the word* to your troops? Are you practicing communication or ego enhancement? Do your employees have any other choice but to attend? Can the objective be met in a more efficient manner by:

- a smaller meeting with a selected but involved group.
- eliminating the meeting in favor of a memo.
- staggering attendance on a "need-to-be-there" basis. (More on this concept when the use of the Meeting Call form is described.)
- combining meetings and calling them on an "if needed" basis.

If we are preparing to propose to others that meetings can be eliminated, then we should be practicing this premise in areas *we* control, if for no other reason than to confirm our own commitment to our own proposal. Those you wish to sell are not impressed by "do as I say, not as I do" types of demeanor.

THE ON-CALL APPROACH

An effective method of reducing attendance or eliminating meetings is the on-call approach. This involves notification of those who may be required at a meeting to be on-call, that is, immediately available if required. In that way, the person may be located immediately and advised of a need to be in attendance, or never called at all if no need arises.

Compare this with the "Hail Mary" approach that requires inviting everyone possible to a meeting because:

- if you invite *one* branch chief, you invite them *all.* (The inefficency of politeness.)
- "you never know..." when something of interest will be covered. (You also never know if *nothing* of interest will arise!)
- what if the uninvited party has something to contribute and he or she is not available when required at the meeting (the down-side risk gamble).

This latter point caused the on-call system to be developed. In determining the potential attendees at a meeting, list those who *must* be in attendance for almost all of the topics to be covered, and, separately, list those whose attendance *might* be required for certain subjects. Notify those who *don't* need to attend of the approximate time they may be required. (See on-call notation on the Meeting Call form in the next section.)

For those on-call times, it becomes the responsibility (of that party so notified) to be easily located, prepared and available if called. He or she is to notify his or her secretary or coworkers when leaving the office, the premises, involved in a distant project, etc.

The on-call party is motivated to be available...motivated by the knowledge that the success of the on-call process will reduce lengthy attendance, or *any* attendance, at many meetings.

This approach can be used in two other ways:

1. to reduce man-hours of time spent with visitors, where the host requires the so-called courtesy of the availability of many organization members with the visitor for brief, individual periods of time, and

2. as a *nonspecific* requirement relative to a perceived need for the alerted party. In place of asking that party to sit through an entire meeting, he or she is put on-call for the total meeting time. Remember, the on-call notification can be either specific *or* nonspecific.

Try the on-call approach with your personnel. Then, allow others in the organization to see the benefits of this system before suggesting a wider adoption. Offer to aid others apply the aforementioned principles and practices. The overall adoption of a proven method, introduced in your area, will gain for you the type of positive recognition envisaged in the practice of the aggressive management style.

THE MEETING CALL FORM

A number of years ago, I developed the Meeting Call form for a client who was determined to make her meetings more productive. She was president of a division of a high-fashion clothing firm. Although the results of using this form proved inconclusive at the time, the form itself has since gained in popularity from Sydney to Stockholm in those organizations where it has been adopted.

To understand the use of the Meeting Call form, depicted in Figure 1, look at the concepts for better meetings:

- limit the meeting to a definable objective, or eliminate the meeting.
- invite only required attendees.
- use information copies of the meeting's results for those who need to know but need not participate.
- practice staggered attendance through the use of the on-call system.

- provide an agenda to allow participants to come prepared, to send or to bring others as required.
- estimate the time required for each item on the agenda as it relates to a cost/benefit ratio. (Don't spend dollars to save pennies.)
- allow conclusions and assignments to be promptly communicated. ("What to do.")
- provide the format for follow-up "by whom and when." (Specificity versus "Do you mean *I* was supposed to do *that, now?*")

The Meeting Call form allows for the application of these aforestated principles. You will note in Figure 10-1 that:

1. The "Requested Attendees" list is immediately followed by on-call and "Information Copies." Hence, the person calling the meeting is immediately confronted with options to requiring attendance in the usual "Hail Mary" or peer pressure manner. Usually, without options to attendance, Messrs. Perl, Klein, Brandt, Carter and Lyndtt would have probably been invited to attend the full-blown meeting. Now, however, there is a good chance that only Perl and Klein will arrive for item two on the agenda, with only Klein staying until item three is also covered. These options to attendance may have reduced this meeting's man-hours by 50 percent!

2. The agenda is listed as a practice of a time-worn management theory, "Tell 'em what is to be covered to allow (or force) preparation as a requisite to attendance."

3. State the objectives of the meeting. Unacceptable objective statements include: the weekly meeting, to hear the report on Harry's trip (send a report) or to better communicate. (With everyone?) Try some one-on-one, or select those who don't understand or even want to; does everyone need to "receive *the word?*"

4. List the time estimate for each item on the agenda as a guide to the chairman and attendees to evaluate on a cost/benefit basis, and to allow for staggered attendance by Perl and Klein. They can arrive at 9:50 a.m., and Perl can probably depart at 10:30 a.m.

5. Since most meetings follow the agenda, provide for "minute taking" on the same form, adjacent to the items on the agenda. This is superior to providing yellow "doodle pads" and relying on the individual members to either track progress by margin annotations to the agenda, or to simply wait for the publication of the minutes. In fact, the use of the Meeting Call form essentially eliminates the need for publishing minutes or having a secretary in attendance. (In many companies, the minutes of the previous meeting are distributed at the opening moments of the next meeting, causing some

MEETING CALL

PAGE _1_ OF _1_

CALL DATE: _10/14_

MEETING DATE: _10/22_

START TIME: _9:30 A_

LOCATION: _Conf. Room C_

REQUESTED ATTENDEES: _CARLSON, BLANDE, RYAN AND STELLOVICH_

ON CALL: _PEEL (2) AND KLEIN (2+3)_

EQUIPMENT REQUIRED: _O.H. PROS. W/T. ROLL_

INFORMATION COPIES: _BRANDT, CARTER, LYNOTT_

OBJECTIVES: _CONCLUDE PARIATT ASSIGNMENTS AND AGREE SCHEDULE_

VISITORS: _L. PARIATT, M.H.I CORP (1)_

CALLED BY: _KOBLET_

FOR CONFIRMATION, or INFORMATION CALL: _HARRIET SLATTERY #318_

ITEM	AGENDA FOR DISCUSSION	TIME	CONCLUSIONS AND ASSIGNMENTS	F/U
1	PROGRESS ON PRE-AWARD PLAN	20	STEP 4 NEEDS EXPEDITING (BLANDE)	10
2	TO START AND COMPLETE ASSIGNMENTS THROUGH 12/31	40	SEE ATTACHED LIST OF ASSIGNMENTS	#3 NR4 #11 NK12 #12 NR 4/25
3	EXPANDED PROGRAM POSSIBILITIES LETTER OF 9/3 (ATTACHED)	15	NONE	—

TOTAL: _75_

ONE COPY MUST BE SENT TO DESK #1

Figure 10-1

attendees to exclaim, "I was supposed to do *that* in time for *this* meeting!")

Look at the completed Meeting Call form in Figure 10-1 and note it has all the elements required of typed and distributed official minutes, such as who was there, what was discussed, concluded and assigned. Except for certain legal requirements or governmental regulations, the completed Meeting Call form *is* the minutes of the meeting! The participants, by consensus, fill in the conclusions, assignments and follow-up (F/U) columns. The latter information is immediately assigned to the Tickler File for scheduled follow-up or action. (See chapter 4 discussion of the Tickler File.)

Some added advantages of using the Meeting Call form were described to me by a secretary to the vice-chairman of a leading auto parts company. She was amazed to find that:

- when her boss now planned 75 minutes for a meeting, he returned in about that time, thus allowing for better planning on his calendar for other needs.

- meetings started on time, even if all the requested attendees were not yet present. Participants felt that if you could start on-time you might have a chance to finish on-time.

- all the participant's secretaries were no longer involved in lengthy drafts and revisions to minutes. (She was most appreciative of no longer being required to attend those "boring, endless talk-a-thons.")

As stated earlier on in this chapter, try this form out in your organizational area; let others examine your successes; then offer to aid them in establishing the idea elsewhere. Recognition should flow from acceptance and positive results...both of which are objectives of practicing the aggressive management style.

SOME DRAMATIC IDEAS

Some readers of this book may be in the higher stratosphere of the managerial hierarchy or may have the overly assertive personality traits to carry out one of the following ideas. These are not to be used by the timid, slightly-built, vulnerable or idle poor among you.

An Iowa company was desperate enough to try out the first idea. Its desperation stemmed from personnel spending 43 percent of working time at company meetings. Company officials tried exhortation, slogans, and went so far as to buy a Danish clock that openly recorded the cost of the meeting while the meeting was in progress. The clock was actually used by one participant "to see if we can beat yesterday's record!"

Finally, they did the unthinkable. Over a weekend, the G.M.O. removed *all* the furniture from *all* the conference rooms and mandated that all the meetings of more than three people had to be held in these denuded conference rooms. Consider attending a meeting, standing up, while holding your notes, drink and cigarettes in one hand and your pen and ash tray in the other. Those meetings went faster!! The theory is that if you make people comfortable, the meetings would last longer; hence, discomfort would shorten the meeting length.

Two other ideas are now being tried:

1. Meetings are held after hours or close to eating and quitting times as a motivator to ending lengthy and perhaps unnecessary verbiage.

2. The conference rooms have carpet in an ivory-colored, fragile fabric, to keep the smokers and drinkers both alert and uncomfortable. Those who ban smoking altogether are just making the compulsive smokers unhappy; the ivory-colored rug is designed to make *everyone* uncomfortable, especially those who use the floor for holding their ashtray, drinks, writing instruments or files.

A Massachusetts firm is experimenting with conference room door locks. The room is locked at the appointed hour for starting the meeting. All latecomers must knock to achieve entry or wait until the next item on the agenda is reached. It is hoped that peer pressure (or ridicule) will bring some order to those who practice a discourtesy on those who *do* arrive on time.

This idea was developed as a result of a rather funny situation. An important contract applications meeting was about to begin, when one of the attendees noticed Harry wasn't there. He suggested, "Let's wait for Harry." After 15 minutes of business chit-chat had ended, the attendees decided to go ahead with some minor topics until Harry arrived. When Harry still hadn't arrived another 15 minutes later, they called his office to learn that Harry was on two-weeks vacation. At that point, they decided not to wait for Harry any longer.

The next time someone says, "Let's wait for Harry," consider the possibility that Harry may *never* come to the meeting. This has forever crossed my mind when a group is told to wait for someone. Will he or she ever arrive? Should we check? Or, should the courtesy of our society prevail? The "non-attendee" should inform us of his or her intentions to be either absent or late. Otherwise, why not start all meetings on time regardless of who is in attendance?

I use this technique at my "time management" seminars throughout the world. An agenda and text with which to follow the speaker (seminar notes) are provided. In the front of the room, I post the seminar times, such as:

Begin	9:00
Break	10:45-11:00
Lunch	12:30-1:30
Break	2:45-3:00
Adjourn	4:15*
Close	4:30
	*3:15 on the second day.

I begin speaking promptly at 9:00 a.m., even though some of the enrollees are still socializing or finishing their coffee. About 10 percent have not yet arrived at all. Everyone is a stranger to me, but they feel guilty being caught standing around while I have begun at the posted time. They scurry for seats, while I seemingly pay them no heed. After all, it *is* a "time management" seminar, so they think I am making a subtle point.

I break promptly at 10:45 a.m. for the first break and announce that we will resume at 11:00 a.m. The group departs for coffee; some come up to speak to me; many scurry for the available telephones. Some of the latecomers actually come up to me and apologize for their tardiness. (It is always somebody else's fault, or those uncontrollable elements such as, "I awoke late" or "I didn't know that you started on time.")

At 11:00 a.m., I begin speaking, sometimes with the slide projector on. I once began in a London hotel with only four out of 70 enrollees in place. The frantic return of the "lollygaggers" is exceptionally amusing, especially the actions of those who cut off the light to the screen with their bobbing heads making shadows. When the chaos ends, (during which I am calmly speaking on a point of the program) I merely state that if we are to teach time management, we must observe it ourselves. To begin on time means:

- We will end on time (applause).
- Attendees can count on the break times, as posted, to schedule their necessary calls to be placed or received; this is my responsibility.
- You can count on catching the getaway flight without having to leave early on the second day of the program (waves of applause).

The difference between "adjourn" and "close" allows me to adjourn the group and stay to handle individual questions that may not pertain to the total group's interests. Thus, we drive for completion by taking away the speaker's excuse, "I didn't expect so many questions." The attendees are alerted to ask questions that require answers relevant to the entire group, knowing that time has been set aside to also answer their individual questions. But, *their responsibility* is to ascertain the difference. Think about the meetings you have attended where two people partake in a lengthy discussion that is of no interest (other than mere curiosity) to the rest of the attendees.

By the start of the afternoon session (1:30 p.m.), everyone is quietly in place and ready to begin. No other start time is again missed. In fact, if I should be even one minute off on my watch, it is brought to my attention that I am late. Sounds silly? It isn't. I have posted the agenda and I mean it! The group accepts my oddball behavior of starting on time without awaiting their arrival, because they see the obvious advantages. The rest is easy; I have demonstrated and established a facet of *my* AMS.

STICK-TO-ITIVENESS

Much has been written about the need to stick-to-it, avoid distractions, control interruptions, end on time and the like. But, these are merely exhortations. How does the AMS practitioner put these exhortations in practice?

(I attended a time management seminar given by the leading writer in this field. He told the attendees to control interruptions by not allowing them, to say "yes" when asked if they were busy, to avoid distractions by noting them so as to avoid them. ... Yet, he is not alone in the exhortation management seminar and publication business. A recent publication on running better meetings suggested, "they should be run more efficiently," and if papers crowded the conference table, then "get a bigger conference table." As Casey Stengel would have said, "Amazin'; simply amazin'!")

The major effort by either individuals or a group to stick-to-it is made when an agenda with time estimates is provided. Notice the heavy black, vertical line on the Meeting Call form. (This does not appear, so emphasized, on the actual form.) The caller of the meeting, before it begins, is required to fill out all of the heading information and the space to the *left* of the heavy black line. The Meeting Call form can be forwarded weeks before the meeting or it can be handed out at the meeting. The discipline is that *no* meeting can start without one...even a meeting that is hastily called!

The caller of the meeting owes it to the attendees to delineate what is to be covered and the time frame for discussion. What if you don't know? If you don't know what is to be covered, why are you calling the meeting? If you don't know how long the meeting will take, estimate the time required (cost/benefit ratio) of the items you do know and guess at the others.

Remember, you are asking for an investment of time and talent at the meeting; the least you can do is try to plan it wisely...at least as wisely as the circumstances will allow. How do you feel about being called to open-ended meetings where, seemingly, *no* effort has been made by the meeting caller to prepare for the management time expenditure?

For those who say this is an impossible request made of a caller of a hastily called gathering, let me relate that filling in the top and left sides of a Meeting Call form takes an average of two and a half minutes! Try and tell the expensive attendees that you didn't have the time to spend on the agenda or the time estimate; so you called the one-and-a-half hour meeting that cost $375 of their time. Reverse the situation; as an AMS practitioner, consider showing the courtesy and organized approach of spending two and a half minutes of *your* time to overcome expensive, frustrating, open-ended meetings.

Flexibility is not ruled out. If items must be added, the group adds them, including the appropriate time estimate. However, be careful to add only items of *group* interest, delegating items for individuals to resolve between themselves to *those* individuals.

Stick-to-itiveness begins with a plan to stick to. It is aided by estimates that turn a plan into a schedule. It works because there is an evident goal, coupled with a benefit for those who stick-to-it. If someone calls a three-hour meeting, it will last at least that long. If the caller breaks down the items and provides reasonable time estimates for same, this very same meeting may only last two hours! Most itemized listings result in less time required than gross estimates.

CONTROLLING AND STIFLING

We all laugh when Archie Bunker says, "Stifle it, Edith!" But he isn't saying it to us, and Archie is both a lovable and harmless character. The humor derives from his tone, his foil's reaction (Edith, with lips turned down at the corners, condescendingly answering, "Awwwr, Archie; You don't mean thaaat.") and the overall situation that has driven Archie to use his last remaining "bullet," "Stifle it, Edith!"

At meetings, there are participants whose actions and antics cause disruptions or obstacles to stick-to-itiveness. For the simple "wanderers," it may require only a reminder that the agenda defines the subjects of this time slot and the objective won't be met by continuing in the wanderer's direction; however, "if this is a different and pertinent topic, perhaps it should *also* be put on this or a subsequent agenda?"

In this way, you have been the one to point out the wanderer's meandering, but the group must now decide to either get back on track or put the item off for a more relevant time...that is, more relevant to the group. At your prodding, you have gotten the group to say, "Stifle it!...for now." This sure beats your saying this directly to the wanderer.

A subtle but disruptive force at meetings is caused by the actions of those who could best be described as the "interpreters." These folks interpret what others have said, by stating, "Let me tell you what Marv means." Marv speaks English; the group has a grasp of the Mother Tongue; yet the interpreter now proceeds to tell us what Marv meant. The problem is that Marv now agrees to this redundancy by stating, "Yeah, that's what I meant."

You would like to say "stifle it" to both Marv *and* his interpreter (and perhaps you are in a position to do so). For most of us, this would be considered rude, especially since Marv, himself, did not object to being interpreted.

I have found that a more effective method is to continue the wasteful behaviour, which the group seems not to object to when practiced by Marv's interpreter. "Well," you continue, "I thought you meant..." as you pick up where the interpreter left off...but now you are interpreting the interpreter's remarks.

Sounds zany? Well, it is, and it will be noticed by the others, who should become frustrated with the whole direction of the meeting. Someone will ask for the interpretations to cease (not you). But the end result will be that the ridiculousness of encouraging interpreters will be recognized by the group and the process will be discouraged in the future. It is more important that the meeting group stifle the offenders than one individual (you).

One of the most frustrating actions at any meeting is usually associated with the "gate keeper." The attendees are about to close on a point whereupon the "gate keeper" rises to say, "Wait; we haven't heard from Josephine." Even Josephine is caught by surprise. She doesn't have a single thought on the matter...but now everyone is looking at her. So, she proceeds to hem and haw, restate what was said and finally fumbles her way to the same conclusion reached before the gate keeper took hold of the meeting. Remember that participation at a meeting is not just limited to those who speak. Listening is also participating. Josephine may have been participating in her own way...by listening.

To harness the "gate keeper," try emulating him or her. After Josephine bumbles her way to a conclusion, jump in with, "Wait, let's hear from Kenny." Surprisingly, there is no Kenny at the meeting. There is a sweeper named Kenny; the boss's son is named Kenny. But, they are not at the meeting (in fact, they weren't even invited!). If you still haven't made your point, ask any member of the meeting who hasn't spoken to give a comment. By this time, you may be coming through to the group by demonstrating the absurdity of the "gate keeper's" actions. The group should move to stifle that member in the future.

CONFLICT MAY BE PRODUCTIVE

There are those who believe that conflicting opinions, staunchly defended by their individual advocates, is a nonproductive exercise at a meeting. These people feel that conflicts should be resolved outside the meeting place; the meeting should constitute a smooth transfer of ideas leading to consensus decision and action. Perhaps so. This is a pleasant approach which may very well be applicable to long-established, profitable enterprises, academia or governmental agencies that control large funds in undramatic regulatory areas. But what about dynamic companies in highly competitive fields, dealing in technical breakthroughs, absorbing unforeseen losses or any myriad of circumstances that create the excitement of business adventure? Does it pay to stifle any conflict out of which may come a better idea?

Hegel's concept of thesis and antithesis leading to synthesis applies to meetings as well. The "mediator" may do more harm than good when he or she states, "Let's not argue; what do the majority of you think?" If the majority stifles the minority as a basis for avoiding conflict, you may be cutting off some good ideas or counter-arguments that, if expressed plausibly and fully, could sway the majority. It is when conflict breeds wild accusations, irrational discussion or just plain antisocial behavior that the "mediator" is right to attempt to stifle conflict by appealing to the majority.

Recognize the proper role of the "mediator." If you feel the "mediator" is merely attempting to stifle what may be productive, conflicting opinions, ask the group, "Should we move to settle this matter without considering the counter-argument? Should we consider it now, or have it resolved by the next meeting? Surely, we cannot reach a decision before this is reviewed!"

You are appealing to the group's logic, while forcing them to consider the thrust of the "mediator's" move — not on the basis of avoiding conflict, but rather on the basis of avoiding the presentation of another idea. You will lose some, but your logic will establish your businesslike approach toward focusing on the best decisions, not just the expedient or popular.

USING YOUR SECRETARY AS YOUR AIDE

An important factor in applying AMS to improving the conduct of meetings is the utilization of your secretary, not just as your administrative assistant, but also as your deputy. Your secretary can be your aide (with an "e") to:

- Write-up most of the Meeting Call forms for you in advance of a meeting.
- Help establish and carry out the rules for meeting interruptions.
- Handle visitors, calls and urgent requests in your absence.
- Sign, delegate, issue or postpone matters while you are at a meeting.
- Prioritize your calls, mail and messages for your return.
- Follow-up on the decisions reached at the meeting for you.

Obviously, this depends on the qualifications, training and motivation you provide...but this holds true for *all* of your employees. I cannot accept the statement, "Well, she was there when I arrived, and she's nice but untrainable." Would you allow incompetence to be overshadowed by seniority, personality or even "looks" in other areas? If your answer is, "yes," skip to the last page of this book. It is there I state that the practice of AMS will not overcome basic incompetencies in your application of management principles...one of which is, if you can recruit, hire, pay and promote, you must be able to train, motivate, plan and control. Failing in this, you must be able to punish, transfer, demote and fire (now called de-hire and outplace). The secretary can be one of your most valuable employees. Treat her like one.

During the Korean conflict, I shared a secretary with five other individuals in the Pentagon. She was the model of a shy, timid but darling person. Because of her "sweetness," the six of us put up with absolute, gross incompetency. Instead of instituting the proper managerial action, we deviously plotted to get her pregnant, somehow. No one of us could face up to telling that sweet Virginia flower child that she was a gross incompetent.

One day, the six of us were at an important meeting with many of our peers when she walked into the conference room and announced she had received a very important call. The meeting halted as all eyes were riveted on this child-like countenance. Silence followed. I filled the breech by asking, "Who is the message for?" She replied, "I don't know. They didn't say and I forgot to ask." I pressed on, "Well, give us the important message and we'll figure out who called." To that she eagerly responded, "The message is, 'Bring home a bottle of milk.'" Six managers brought home a bottle of milk that night. (One only had a cat at home, but he figured it had gotten desperate and had somehow dialed.)

That secretary disappeared into the oblivion of old secretaries. Since that day, I have forever insisted that managers and their secretaries have a detailed plan for interruptions to a meeting. I know it is impossible to cover all bases, and you could never put up with an ignorant secretary, no matter what he or she looks like. But a plan for interruptions is a definite plus in practicing AMS.

This plan should include:

- Handling of certain calls from important parties.
- Visitors, both planned and unplanned.
- Urgent requests.
- Signature and concurrence requirements.
- Delegation of certain work, so that it does not have to wait for you to personally do it. (See chapter 7 on improving the timeliness of delegations.)
- How to postpone actions until your return.

ACTIONS AND FOLLOW-UP ARE MORE
IMPORTANT THAN MINUTES

Follow-up to assure action starts at the meeting itself. Each action item is assigned a "who" that is to do "what" by "when." Your Meeting Call form lists those items you are required to act upon.

Take five or 10 minutes on your return from a meeting and make believe you are still away. Don't just jump in and start returning calls, dictating memos and the like. Instead, use the extra five or 10 minutes to set up action on the items assigned to you. Schedule the work to be done, dictate delegations, use your Tickler File, begin work...if you do all this while the meeting is still fresh in your mind, your initiation of action should be both specific and logical...at least better than doing the same tasks two days later.

I learned the above trick from an old salesman, who knew that once he got into the office he would be deluged with paperwork and visits from his compatriots. Since he had to show up sooner or later, he would come in and give out instructions to his secretary, which indicated to others that he was still out during the first hour of his return.

While she handled matters as if he was still gone, he worked as though he were still on travel. His comment was, "I just made believe that my trip was one hour longer!" You could do the same for five or 10 minutes, working as if you are still attending the meeting. You could then buy time to get actions started.

All of which brings us full circle, namely, the purpose of a meeting is to reach a conclusion, followed by positive action. If there are alternatives to the expense of a meeting, these should be examined first. Elimination of a meeting beats making the meeting more effective.

One of the tools of the AMS practitioner is the body of meeting philosophy contained in the Meeting Call form. Who should be invited or placed on-call? How can we allow for staggered attendance in order to decrease man-hours at meetings? The use of a time estimated agenda allows for attendee planning. But, just as important, it allows the organization to practice cost/benefit analysis. Let's not spend $400 on a $50 problem!

Meetings are more effective if stick-to-itiveness is encouraged and practiced. The "wanderer," the "interpreter," the "gate keeper" and the "mediator" should be stifled...not in the crude Archie Bunker manner, but by a series of actions by you to turn the attendees onto those who do not practice stick-to-itiveness.

There must also be a drive for action and follow-up, so the time spent at meetings is not wasted by significant time elapsing between the end of the meeting and the plan to accomplish the necessary follow-up and actions. To the practitioner of the aggressive management style, the well-planned, efficient meeting is a showcase for your talents displayed before your peers and superiors.

11

RELATING MOTIVATIONAL TECHNIQUES TO YOUR AMS

There are methods to improve every performance. One hundred percent ratings on performance have always been suspect, whether it be the rating of a gymnast, an ice-skater or a foxy lady or gentleman (1-10). Just as the four-minute mile was once considered impossible to achieve, a manager's performance, even at his or her peak, also leaves open goals for higher performance.

There are levels of satisfaction that give the AMS practitioner a chance. In some organizations, perfect performance is the meeting of goals such as the budget or attendance or a sales quota. But who sets the criteria for this performance? On what is the performance based?

A macro look at our society discloses that our culture defines success. Sometimes this creates impossibilities. Only one politician becomes President. Should all 900,000 politicians in our country be rated against this ultimate criterion? In any organization, only one or a very few become the chief executive officer. Yet, should this be a criterion for judging the maximum performance for every one of the ten thousands of M.B.A. graduates in this country?

These criteria of ultimate success create a sense of dissatisfaction among those who either aspire for or have given up aspiring for that "top rung." Practically speaking, the paucity of "brass rings" makes the total performance reward an impractical goal...at least against the odds. For those of you in your 20s, the odds may appear insurmountable. Yet think of the middle managers in their 30s and 40s who have settled for a more reasonable career path, as well as those in their 50s and 60s who *know* where their careers will end.

For a manager, dissatisfaction with self or with circumstances may lead to either greater motivation or despair, or somewhere in between, such as a qualified acceptance. When you are told, "You are the 'top of the tree' in our accounting group," do you accept this as the ultimate compliment, or do you look for the "bigger pond?"

There are those who will work their hardest when dissatisfied with themselves, no matter how their performances have been rated by their company. New goals may be set and new frustrations may set in. The higher you aspire, the less positions are open to aspire to, and the greater the competition for those fewer opportunities.

RAISE THE BRIDGE OR LOWER THE WATER

The problem for the practitioner of the aggressive management style is to relate:

- performance criteria, with
- motivation, with
- satisfaction.

There is no true 100 percent. The budget can be beaten; the sales quota is based on vague assumptions; the very criteria for evaluating individual performance are subjective and judgmental at best. (I could name two chief executive officers who run major companies with the managerial intelligence and reasonableness of a cat in heat...and I'll bet you could too.) If the criteria are man-made, consider the fallacy of basing your performance on a set of criteria whose basis you may question.

Let's examine some managerial criteria. The budget is a negotiated instrument, usually based on past performance, mandated actions and prejudiced forecasts, all wedded to the limitations imposed by such realities as product problems, service deficiencies and past failures. Strategic planning is a broader view of where the enterprise is headed, but is also based on the prejudice of the planners and the bias of the historical viewpoint. A management-by-objectives dialogue with your boss is a subjective view of your accomplishments versus a negotiated list of objectives. What was your input as a percentage of the objective?

All of the foregoing relates to our management rating system, which formally or informally establishes the "height of the limbo stick"...our performance criteria. Recognizing the inherent fallacies in the rating system, we can assert ourselves to aggressively petition for either a "raising of the drawbridge or a lowering of the water." Both of these are not as potentially fruitful as:

- accepting the basis of evaluation within reasonable limits, and
- concentrating our efforts and the time associated with them on individual motivation. We then may derive satisfaction from our performance against our subjective criteria.

Of all of life's frustrations, none ranks as high as "tilting at windmills." Cervantes' hero could have plagerized from Kismet by stating, "Don't look at apples if you have no teeth!" Concentrating on the possible, *your* motivations and *your* satisfactions, seems to be a more fruitful application for the AMS oriented manager.

MOTIVATING THE MANAGER

One of the most difficult tasks of any manager is to understand the motivations of his or her employees:

- "Why don't they work as I do?"
- "I don't understand them. If that were my job I'd have done it another way (better)."
- "Don't they know how to do a good job? Why don't they care, as I do?"

The major problem is that the manager is assigning his or her objectives to others. Chances are the manager became a manager by listening to a different "fiddler on the roof" than his or her employees. Most employees want to do an acceptable job and go home. They are satisfied by being compensated in some relationship to the value of their jobs and their perceived financial requirements in an inflationary economy. The manager wants to be recognized for the good job done in his or her department, more pay based on a fair evaluation, and a promotion possibility when there is an opening. These are not what one would call congruent goals.

If a manager wants to read the mountain of literature on motivating employees, there is a good chance that the application of those principles may be lost. Most managers became managers by:

- being motivated by an inherent drive to achieve a higher position, more pay and recognition.
- desiring to be a "peg above the rest," not just "one of the boys."
- a quest for power that goes with position, as well as the status symbols represented by the perks of office.
- a need for recognition as an achiever in the community, the company, the profession or by family and friends.

These goals are not necessarily related to the psychology of motivating workers, who are generally seeking recognition, security, pay, "fringes", parity and equality, while performing at their present tasks. Therefore, productivity discussions abound with talk of "quality of life," "vocal and written recognition" and "participation." This list is barely congruent with the list of a manager's personal objectives previously listed.

THE GRAVESTONE OF MANAGEMENT

The AMS practitioner should develop individual and personal motivations based on private goals. These are developed from a truthful statement of what *you* require of *you!* Don't tell me. Don't tell your religious leader, your psychiatrist, your wife, lover or best friend. Tell yourself! Be truthful. The basis of personal motivation is a personal goal that is realistic, practical and achievable within the limitations of time and inherent skill.

Phil Rizzuto, a slightly built and aggressive man, and former player for the New York Yankees, once aired a very interesting story. When he was a permanent fixture at shortstop for the five time world champions, he was visited by some old friends from his sandlot days. They were all amazed at his stature in baseball, because, as Phil stated it, "They had far more talent and were of big league physical dimensions when I played with them."

Yet here was Rizzuto — the premier shortstop of the invincible Yankees of the early 1950s. The answer was a single-minded drive to do the best possible job with whatever talent he had. Sacrifices, in terms of education, low pay in the minors and constant practice year-round had to be made. His compatriots took the usual summer jobs to earn enough to date, to drink and to have pocket money for college. Rizzuto chose a child's game played by men where size, skill and determination provide a very small minority with five to 10 years of limelight and related compensation.

Now, very few of us have a life plan, much less a plan for the next three years. This doesn't mean we can't have a flexible plan that varies with circumstances, but I am referring to a specific, thought-out *and* documented set of goals.

I have them...but I'm not about to show them to anyone. Yet, by having them, I can relate my progress, status and efforts to a longer range objective than "get the kids through school," "get a bigger or second house," "retire early," "live in Florida" and "just fish." The previous statements are really only rewards for having life goals or the results of living in America during prosperous times.

A West German radio station starts off each day with the proclamation, "Happy Birthday! Today is the first day of the rest of your life!" What are you doing the rest of your life? If you answer honestly (and that is best done *by* you, *to* you) this can help focus on what is really important to you in your lifetime. It can help you sort out your personal priorities and motivate you to overcome minor, daily or temporary obstacles. This creates the foundation for satisfaction.

What could be said in your obituary, on your gravestone or by a "knowing" man of God? One technique for getting managers to attempt to set managerial goals is to start with life goals. Write your own obituary! Today and five or 10 years from now:

NAME: _____ AGE: _____ DIED: _____
TODAY FROM: _____
SURVIVED BY: _____
MEMBERSHIPS: _____
ACHIEVEMENTS (SOCIAL): _____
_____

(CONTRIBUTORY) _____
_____

(POLITICAL) _____
_____

(BUSINESS) _____
_____

At the time of his (her) unfortunate passing, he (she) was working on becoming: _____
_____

He (she) will best be remembered for: _____
_____

He (she) will be mourned by: _____
_____

The world will suffer the loss of his (her) contributions in the following areas: _____
_____
_____
_____

One of his (her) main unfulfilled ambitions was: _____
_____
_____

Instead of flowers, please send contributions, in the deceased's name to:
_____
_____
_____

Quite a few of the goals portrayed in your obituary will not be related to your career. But how many will be related to this year's (fiscal, or otherwise) objectives or corporate actions? As a famous king of ancient Lebanon remarked, after learning that it takes 100 years for a cedar tree to attain full plumage, "Well, don't wait; we'd better start planting them right now!" If you have devoted your life to the organization's goals, but very little to your own, start your personal planning now!

If you take the time to honestly establish your personal goals, you will have created the greatest single human motivator that will ultimately lead to job satisfaction. You will have put your job in perspective with your life objectives. You will find motivation varies greatly from almost all of your readings on motivating your employees, especially the majority of those that hear a different "fiddler on the roof"...those whose self-written obituaries will contain a stream of words on "getting by," "getting the most for the least," "awaiting the lucky break" and "wishing for the impossible."

REWARDING THE MANAGER

The bibliography of books on managerial compensation is filled with words such as "performance/remuneration ratios," "finding the hot button," "value of perks and fringes," etc. Yet, the literature on supervisory management principles is far more heavily weighted in terms of "human relations," "quality of life," "understanding people," "participation," "improving the work environment" and "the art of listening." The terms just mentioned are covered in five to six times as many pages as those on money (as both a reward and a motivator).

The justifications for this ratio are simple. When asked, managers rarely rate money as their chief motivator. After all, that is a *crass* answer. Can you imagine conducting an interview with a prospect, who when asked why he or she is applying for the job states, "I am really impressed by the pay, benefits and fringes you are offering and believe my talents will be adequately rewarded when I demonstrate in the future, what I can do."

Instead, you'll hear:

- "Just the challenge I'm looking for."
- "You've got the name I'd like to be associated with."
- "I want to help your firm grow and grow with you."
- "The synergy is right."

One famous author, in the area of management writings, interviewed 416 top and upper-middle management executives (including some managers in the governmental and hospital service areas). The executives ranked compensation as fifth amongst factors of job satisfaction. Of course they did! Why?

- How many would rank it truthfully as number one, when they felt either their board of directors, the shareholders or *their* bosses would hear about it? You are supposed to salute the corporate flag, not the corporate pay check.
- Most of them had already received a high remuneration relative to the industry, the job title or their predecessors in the same position.
- It is not a subject to rank high because of the constant negotiation with all who work for you, from those who report directly to you to those in the bargaining unit.
- We are conditioned by society to rank pay and sex as low on the list of stated desires by creative, talented and contributory people.

The professional athlete lives in a more honest atmosphere. He wants to be paid for his talent during the few years he has it on display. He is, however, castigated by the press and the fans for holding out for more money, asking to be traded, just sulking, or even daring to compare his or her ability with some other figure in the sports world. Woe unto the player that asks for more money and, after receiving it, gets injured. Yet, society would decry a corporate organization that would fire an executive after a heart attack or a nervous breakdown...both of which may have been brought on by an inability to cope with the job.

In his frequent speeches on "Improving Productivity," Mitchell Fein, a personal and professional friend, often states, "Money may not be the number one motivator, but it sure is near the top." He proves this time and again in the over 200 installations of his copyrighted *Improshare Plan*.

The point of all this is to discuss money as one of the prime motivators of people from workers to top managers. It may not be openly discussed or even admitted...but it certainly deserves to be more than ignored by the manager who is to practice AMS. After job security, money ranks as one of the top three motivators for most of the managers I have met who practice the aggressive management style. Consider the drive for employment contracts, the discussion of payment, relative to previous compensation, the amount of options, etc.

Try hiring a manager away from the competition without paying more than his or her current pay, without a contract, separation terms spelled out and the like. If you get away with it, you are probably hiring someone who is unemployed or about to be. Instead of money, offer challenge, potential growth, recognition or the like...those items mentioned five to six times more than money. Then write a book on managerial motivation.

USING PROPER REMUNERATION AS PART OF YOUR AMS

Consider the advantages (to you) of retaining and attracting the best employees. I have seen AMS practicing managers who devote abnormal amounts of time trying to reward their employees. In a very structured environment, this means:

- constant rewrite of job descriptions to truly reflect the job requirements both desired and being performed by the incumbent.
- challenging the area, industry or job scales used for the base or norm. Is the sample truly representative of the job you have in mind, or as it is being performed?

In an unstructured environment, try to have the right to pay within budgetary restraints on a total basis. If you have $100,000 for salaries and four people receive an average of $25,000 each, there isn't much you can do if the individual's pay is related to the cost-of-living index and/or seniority. However, as personnel are retired, laid off, promoted or transferred:

1. Use the difference in the total salary account to negotiate with the three remaining employees. Can you offer to split the difference with the remaining three, by asking if they can make up the slack in work required and performed, paying 50 percent to the three (and you) and 50 percent to the company? Is this too revolutionary for your company to handle? What if *two* of the three ask if you'd like to split a larger difference as "the pot?"

2. Use the difference to *unequally* reward the three remaining managers relative to their past performances. With the diminished remainder, hire or promote, at a lower level of pay. Call this your starting level salary.

If you don't believe money is a prime motivator, the above are meaningless actions. So, let's list some *demotivators* relative to money:

1. If everyone receives approximately the same pay for dissimilar performance *and* work content, the group may adopt a performance that is barely acceptable enough so that they are not discharged.

2. If all are paid approximately the same (within plus or minus 10 percent) for the same job, but for *dis*similar performances, this may act as a productivity leveler. (Ayn Rand wrote startlingly successful novels on numbers one and two above.)

3. If the size of the reward is meaningless, the group will perceive this. Sure, they'll work for a new set of golf clubs. Or is it a foregone conclusion as to who the winner will be, such that true performance is not affected? (John Toble is a contractor-representative for the Texas Refinery Corp. In 1979, he won a silver tray for a $1 million dollar plus performance. John and his wife, Louise, love the tray, but John would have brought in the 1980, as well as the 1979, sales without it. He likes to be recognized for his accomplishments, but the tray acts as neither a motivator *nor* demotivator. It just makes him feel good to be recognized. One of my clients runs sales contests for its sales agents. Year after year, the period following the contest depicts a sales order entry drop! This means that those who know how "to pull up the orders" get the prizes. Otherwise, their sales levels, on an annualized basis, are steady and predictable, by units not dollars.)

4. If the reward is difficult to relate to the performance, it may have little significance to those who are supposed to be motivated by the reward. An outlandish example is from a company in the Midwest, whose profit sharing plan showed substantial gains for two successive years...of corporate losses! The fund administrator did better than the management of the firm!

If you can reward the performers with significant pay increases, you will have gained:

- the retention of the high performers (and, conversely, probably the loss of nonperformers).
- the attraction necessary to recruit from both within and from the outside talented, ambitious high-performers.
- recognition as a productive manager having built a performance-oriented organization.

As I have been stating throughout this book, the foundation of the aggressive management style is positive recognition by others of a true contribution to the particular endeavor. Monetary rewards, both meaningful and relative to performance, may gain such recognition for you.

CONTROLLING AND MAINTAINING IMPROVEMENTS

Arousing the will to work ranks second to maintaining it. The corporate history books are filled with ideas that worked dramatically for brief periods of time. The Hawthorne Studies at Western Electric, the Short-Interval-Scheduling installation at Montgomery Ward, the Job Enrichment and Enlargement work at Volvo, the Employee Suggestion Plan at Maytag, Job Restructuring at Texas Instruments, the experiments in improving productivity at GM's Lordstown Plant, the Medford Works of Corning Glass and the General Foods Plant at Topeka all were "media events" at the time of the installation of productivity improvement concepts. But how many are continuing as successes, or are even in existence at this reading?

Les Lippy, vice-president of Martin-Marietta stated, "I'd rather muddle along with the slow evolution of improvements rather than commit all my resources to a grand plan that folds in a short period of time." Hence, he rejects solutions that do not include monitoring, controls and preplanned reactions to the unexpected...which should be expected. (See chapter 5 discussion on controlling the installation of the problem solution.)

As stated in chapter 5, anyone can plan and then review the performance of others. Most reporting is along these lines, with the addition of variance and management-by-exception data. Management control requires receiving data close enough in time to the actual occurrence to allow for corrective action. But, what corrective action? Some examples will expand on this theme:

1. A tool manufacturer reported the missed plans of all supervisors one week after the occurrence. The supervisors culled what they could from their memory and made up that which they thought were acceptable excuses for these schedule misses. At the production meetings, all logical excuses were accepted. The continued use of this technique resulted in much time being expended on explaining away misses, with a minimal amount of effort to resolve the problems. If you could explain them, why bother to solve them?

2. Many managers were overworked in a Southeastern lumber mill because they not only had their work to do but assumed that which their employees "assigned" to them. These so-called "assignments" came from employees who brought problems without solutions to their supervisors. In the course of these discussions, the manager would say, "Well, leave it with me; I'll have a look at it." As William Oncken, noted management consultant and lecturer, might say, "They just passed the 'monkey' from their back to the supervisor's." It then became the supervisor's problem, having been "assigned" to the boss by his or her subordinates.

3. A Philadelphia company had sent all its staff and administrative officers to a top Eastern school to learn better management of office personnel. One of the key elements of their training was to learn to listen, to encourage employee participation in problem solution and to incorporate good ideas from everywhere for the common good. The training was great; everyone came back enthused. Then, after three months, the same problems seemed to exist, even though proposals for improvements were sought after *and* forwarded. The problem was that there were many ideas:

- management refused to accept...for good reason, but this seemed to turn off the sought after suggestors. They weren't unhappy when they weren't asked, but were furious when they were asked and their ideas were subsequently rejected (for whatever good *or* silly reason).

- accepted by the first-level of supervision, but they didn't know how to implement them.

- accepted orally by management, after the proposal was orally forwarded (at a meeting or one-on-one), but the manager forgot or postponed the implementation of the solution.

AROUSING INTEREST RANKS SECOND TO MAINTAINING IT

To overcome the three company problems presented above is to consider that arousing interest in improvements or problem solutions ranks second to maintaining interest through controlled implementations. Consider:

1. Information that requires action must be in the hands of the party authorized to act as soon as possible. If your present information retrieval system cannot accomplish this, see if you can separate historical from action information...one can proceed at the normal "turtle's pace" through your present system, while the other is culled out and forwarded as soon as possible to a party authorized to act. Information is important, but timely information, forwarded to an action-oriented party, is vital for management control.

2. Employees, at all levels, should understand their level of action, which they can take without a higher level approval (or even without notification). Where a higher level approval *is* required, the employees should be trained to present problems with potential (or optional) solutions. "Trained monkeys" can bring you problems; managers practicing AMS must encourage the presentation of options for solution. This will go a long way towards preventing

the "monkeys" from being passed indiscriminately from the presenters to the listeners.

3. Finally, management should have plans to implement ideas before calling for them. Lester Lippy, vice-president of operations of Martin Marietta Aerospace in Baltimore believes, "My job is to see that improvements are implemented...to turn informal meetings, discussions and off-the-cuff ideas into resolutions. If I don't, I had better stop asking my 1100 people to come forth with ideas, which, when not put into effect or logically modified or rejected, can lead to a mass frustration."

Try encouraging your people to write up the action instrument to back up their proposal if accepted. Therefore, when you are presented with a problem *and* viable options, all you need to do is sign the memo prepared for your signature *prior* to the meeting. Consider on how many occasions you had agreed to a solution but nothing came of it because you, or the suggestor, went on to other things and never "put the solution to bed" by instituting or authorizing action?

Consider the maintenance of a flow of ideas "fertilized" by a structure for implementation. By collapsing the time frame for information that cries out for action, you promote action orientation in the usual historical-information environment. By establishing levels of independent action, you are encouraging responsible reactions to problems at that action level. By requesting that recommendations (not just problems) be brought to *your* action level, the AMS practitioner will promote participation, accentuate areas for his or her own concern and thus maximize the organization's brainpower by having everyone take care of his or her own "monkeys" while also helping you with yours. Finally, by having the action instrument provided with the options presented, you will be catching most of the informally presented ideas that may today be "slipping through the net and drifting out to sea."

CONTROLS SHOULD NOT COST MORE THAN THE CONTROL IS WORTH

In chapter 4 this concept was discussed. You may remember the controls on expendable tools costing more than the loss reduction they were designed to control. On a broader basis, we find managements willing to spend mega-bucks for control systems, with the idea that more (and costlier) information leads to more control. You can sell most top executives on:

- a larger and more detailed data base.
- reports that can massage data in various ways.
- simulations of events that are both possible or improbable.
- exotic formats, terminals, regenerations, displays, remote entries and the like.

But how much of the corporate expenditures are devoted to cost/benefit ratios relevant to the manager's use of data? This is not a call to return to the days of clerks and tub files, but rather a review of user capabilities and training expenditures. "More and better information does not produce more and better managers," states Phil DiPerna, president of Mid-America Consultants in Milwaukee, but, "It does guarantee more and better information."

The computer consultants or staff are concerned with the cost of information versus the value of the information. To this end, they proclaim and insist on user involvement at all phases of installation. Do you really think you would be that much better a driver if the automobile manufacturer had you tour his plant and tack on a few weldments? Management must invest more time in developing controls to:

- React, reassign, reschedule or reject a plan or schedule miss. Don't just look at it and hope that "fairy dust" will blow it away. Invest in training to uncover and implement options, actions, approvals and notifications.
- Accept the majority of on-target information and have a defined level of organization reaction to the exceptions. Who does what when? "If everyone is responsible then no one is responsible" is a favorite saying of quality assurance consultant, Harmon Bayer of Detroit. This means that action information not only goes to the party authorized to act, but he or she knows the parameters of execution, approval and notification. "You're good and you're bad" is the 1930s approach; fostering and defining action should be the 1980s dogma.

ZERO-BASED APPROACH TO IMPROVING PRODUCTIVITY

As Alice in Wonderland found out, you have got to run to pass the trees; if you just trot, they'll keep up with you. The level of today's productivity may be kept level if we continue our present management style. Productivity has been increasing at a decreasing rate in America until it finally fell negative in 1979 after 32 years of fits and starts fostered by industry and governmental exhortations. Labor blames management; management blames government; government keeps the statistics while the public pays for inflation. Whatever the political, socio-economic or emotional causes are, we are "barely keeping up with the trees!"

Don't look for an answer to this dilemma in chapter 11 of a book on the aggressive management style. But there are some lessons that may help us in our micro look at society...our place of business.

"Where are we?" may be a most appropriate question for the AMS manager to consider. We should study the history of how we got here, but *only* if it's relevant. Santayana made a generalization that has been used time and again by high school graduates and history department professors, "Those who do not study history are prone to repeat it." To the foregoing statement let me add that one must separate the pertinent from the interesting in order for history to have relevance.

Just as our environment has changes, so have our attitudes and reactions to the unforseen. Our involvement in Vietnam fit the 1960s scheme of things; our lack of interest in the invasion of Cambodia fit our concept of the 1970s. Historians blame Chamberlain and Daladier for a spineless reaction to Hitler's moves in the Rhineland, Austria and Czechoslovakia in the 1930s, as a prelude to World War II. These same purusers of history commended President Jimmy Carter for his restraint in Iran, Afganistan, Cambodia, Angola and Eritrea. Only time will tell if the lessons of Chamberlain and Daladier were worthwhile.

Hence, companies, which are merely microcisms of society, may learn little from history, unless its relevance can be helpful in guiding future actions. Would your company learn much from reading of the unionization of the auto industry in the 1930s? Of the attitudes toward the introduction of technocracy in the 1920s as it applies to today's computerization of office functions? Perhaps, but I doubt it.

A more fruitful approach may be to read of and listen to the current experiences of managers in handling today's problems: the new workforce of women, blacks and Hispanics, the motivation of suburban earners of a second income, drug and alcohol problems during work hours, security and the impact on personal prerogatives, taxation that creates both problems and opportunities, etc. There may be some relevance in reading of how the waves of immigrants were brought into the work force at the turn of the 20th century...but I doubt it can help resolve the problems of workers in the 21st century.

I recommend a zero-based approach. We are where we are and *may* gain some insights if we examine the history of how we got here. But, we have a six-person accounting staff that evaluates the budget, plans cash flow and predicts profitability problems. This is where we *are!* Can we do the same job, with five, when Mary retires? Do we really get 20 percent more usable output by hiring on another senior staff accountant in addition to our staff of five? What is the value of the present output versus the present input? These are the questions that are more fruitful to pursue by the AMS manager...not that the 1971 manager hired Max because he is married to Carrie's sister.

The zero-based approach requires:

- A start from a base of no input, but with a statement of a desired output. We really need some of the accounting services, down to "it would be nice to continue these tasks." But, the zero base is the absolute minimum we build upon.
- Matching the desired and calculated outputs to the inputs of manpower, equipment, space, support, outside services, etc., by matching the desire with a management asset by plan.

The major problem with the zero-based approach is that folks get bogged down and defensive about what is in existence. We tend to try to justify the six incumbents because they are *our* six incumbents. "I'll cut my group if you'll cut yours" sounds childish, but has proven to be the death bed of zero-based budgeting in practice.

Input/output analysis can also be conducted from a base of where we are now. For the majority of the readers, your company, hospital or governmental agency will survive next year without major or even drastic "surgery." Where you are is pretty much where you will likely be next year. If you do nothing drastic, you will probably have your same job next year. If you are lucky, someone will die, leave or be promoted, or the firm will expand and you will rise in the management ranks because of it. Just hang in there.

Let us assume that the status quo *is* the zero base. This is our input; this is our output; therefore, this is our base. Now, if we can positively affect this ratio and gain recognition for it, you have lived up to the criteria for the aggressive style manager.

The ratio of input to output can be improved from this zero base by:

- more output from the same input
- the same output for less input
- a combination of input to output, either plus or minus in both areas, which affects the ratio in a positive way

This is easiest measured in the production areas where there is a count of output by units, standard hours, dollars, return on investment and other unique values. In all areas of business, the difficulty is not so much in measuring the *input,* but nowhere is it as simple as in production areas to measure *output.* This accounts for the success of such productivity improvement by measurement plans as Rucker, Scanlon and Improshare in the manufacturing arena.

The entity produces 100 widgets, 600 wachets and 400 jockos. This value can be expressed in estimated hours, cost dollars, standard hours, mix profitability, total revenues or any other finite number. During this period, 6,000 man hours, $800,000 of depreciation and 2,000 staff support hours were input. Thus, one can compare hours produced in product out the door (output) to hours or costs expended during this period (input) and arrive at a ratio. This is where you are; this could be your zero base. When the ratio is bettered by increasing output, decreasing input or by a combination of both, you have positively affected productivity in your area. All one needs now is the recognition for this gain.

For the manager of a staff function, an administrative service, a creative function and the like, this is a more difficult base to establish and improve upon. Again, the input will not prove to be difficult; measurement of the output, in meaningful terms, will be more difficult than for your management cousins in a manufacturing industry.

The trick is to have a *meaningful* measure of output. A traffic cop who is measured by the amount of moving violation tickets that are issued can easily fudge the output if so motivated. An auditor can cover more ground during an analysis by lowering the quality of the questions or the depth of the probe.

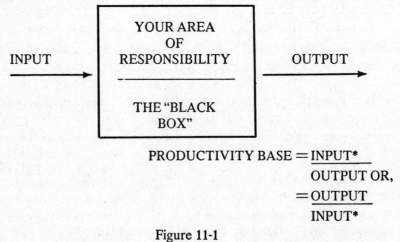

$$\text{PRODUCTIVITY BASE} = \frac{\text{INPUT*}}{\text{OUTPUT}} \text{ OR,}$$

$$= \frac{\text{OUTPUT}}{\text{INPUT*}}$$

Figure 11-1

Note — one usually chooses the fraction that provides a whole number instead of a decimal; hence, the larger figure usually goes into the numerator.

As can be seen by the preceding figure, the output should be meaning-ful as it relates to the job objective. In nonproduction areas, the following may be of help to the reader:

1. Tie the input to an output that your group supports. As a staff service your group may support a sales effort by providing cost estimates. Tie the man-hours input to the number of successful bids or the potential profitability from gaining these contracts. The base is your past input versus output. Although your group's efforts are not the sole reason for all the contract awards, it still is a *better* measure than "We're doing a good job; everyone can see that," or "Our manpower budget for bodies and salaries ought to go up to match the cost-of-living-index."

2. Relate your output to a recognized company objective, or one of your own that would be readily understood as a corporate objective if it were formally stated. A hospital administrator tied the dietary groups' budget to a drive for nutrition dollars per patient day, assuming a standard mix of special, extreme and normal diets served. A parks and recreation manager related appearance and facilities upkeep to dollars for staff and equipment.

Again, the measure of output is the key to establishing the input/output base. Consider that where you are is but a foundation for where you want to go...but, it's a good zero base. In this world of "gimme," "get me" and "I want," you will be providing a more solid base from which your efforts and requests may be judged. The use of a measurement will set you apart from most managers. The planned increases in productivity will give your group more direction and a better motivation than your peers and their organizational elements.

TRAINING THE AMS MANAGERS

There are various theories about training and its effects. Some of these are:

1. *The Shotgun Approach*

   Set a budget for training. Out of all the people who participate in public seminars, conventions, society meetings, attend schools, receive in-house instruction, and the like, *something* good will come of it. If you fire a shotgun, surely some pellets will strike an appropriate target sometime, somewhere.

2. *The Rifle Approach*

   Find an area that is either obviously lacking or mandated for im-provement by the boss. Fire a well-aimed shot with all your fire-power at one or a limited group of priority objectives. If the single shot misses, or merely grazes the target, try another rifle shot, if you have any ammunition left.

3. *Combination of Shotgun and Rifle Concept*

   Fire a rifle at some and a shotgun at the rest...and hope the combination pays off.

4. *Count the Nostrils and Divide by Two*

   This is sometimes called "training-by-the-numbers." If you send 100 nostrils to school (50 hot bodies) and you sent 80 nostrils last year (40 breathers), then it is obvious your training program is 25 percent better than last year. If they don't believe you, tell them to count the nostrils!

5. *All Training Is Valuable*

   This theory starts with the idea that some training is better than no training and graduates to the premise that everyone can benefit from some training all the time. These are valuable philosophies to justify the job *and* the staff of training directors. They are now called human resources developers, generally playing the same numbers games as their predecessors...the oldfashioned training directors.

For the AMS oriented manager, who is seeking positive results from any management endeavor, there are some questions begging for answers. For one, what is the zero base? If we discontinue the present training procedure or retain it, what are the results we have achieved and reasonably expect to achieve? Do our people work better or get more work done through others? Do they just feel better? Is the training, itself, given as a sign of recognition or reward? What is the value (output) versus the total men, skill and dollar investment (input)? If you cannot track it, should you do more? The same amount? Less?

I have vented exceptionally strong feelings on my clients even before they became my clients. Ms. Jodi Johns, manager of Human Resources Development at Martin Marietta's Baltimore Division, recalls, "I asked Norm to give a presentation to our senior production managers on a program for improving production scheduling. After presenting a two-hour dry run of 80 pages of materials for production schedulers, industrial engineers and our production supervisors, he asked the assembled top management if that's what they *really* wanted. After a very short while, they agreed they wanted improvements and accepted that training was *one* of the ways to get there."

I do that regularly. You could too...set down your objectives and you'll find that training is but *one* of the ways to get there. It is the easiest way to show action; "See, I'm doing something!" But, is it the best alternative from the "shopping list" of ways to meet the objective? (It might be, if you are the training director and you have a training budget to be expended.)

After you have gone through the exercise of defining your objective and made a "shopping list" of alternatives, you will probably find that training *is* on the list. From my experience, it probably belongs, but always in combination with other management actions. For example, should you demand specific training relative to your company's very specific problems? If so, why send someone to attend a three-day seminar in Los Angeles? For the same cost, you could train 10 people, on site, on the specifics of your defined problem.

What should you do to prepare for the trainee, who returns with a fistful of ideas and notes? Ask for a trip report? Request a proposal for even the simplest and smallest idea, which, when implemented, pays for the total cost of the training?

All of the above relate to some steps to assure that training is more than a reward or an expenditure one must live with:

- Choose and get agreement on the objective of the problem to be resolved, especially as it relates to other outstanding situations needing resolution.

- Establish some criteria for success, as well as some limits for expenditure to meet these criteria.

- Make a shopping list of actions, which will more than likely include training.

- Schedule necessary training as part of the overall solution.

- Have all training directed towards the problem solution (unless you are a school, where the end product is broadbased education for all).

- Allow for some investment of time and other resources by the trainee upon his or her return. If you don't do some *one* thing with your new knowledge, you may *never* get around to it again. Take a poll of those who have returned from most public seminars. You will be lucky if they can still find their notes. As a part of the Great American coverup, those who wined and dined in Mexico City cannot say they aren't now better managers. The training director has to agree. So does the division vice-president who authorized the trip, or he'd have to answer to the corporate controller (or the IRS). However, if one small step is taken immediately, upon the trainee's return, the "disease may be catching." Do one small step yourself and allow your employees to do something on their return.

- Finally, tie the training results to the overall problem review. This will not only assure a control has been established, but will also lay the ground work for making future training more specific and more effective. Obviously, the value of the training is in the results of this endeavor, not just in the number of nostrils divided by two. (Note the similarity of the above-described steps *and* the steps in problem-solving detailed in chapter 5.)

WET YOUR TOES BEFORE JUMPING IN

Just as picking an area to implement a training idea is a good first step, "wetting your toes" is a good way to implement the aggressive management style. If you just put this book down and put off trying one of the ideas herein presented, you may never do *any one ever!*

I suggest you examine the initial premise of seeking high-level recognition through positive actions in the business environment. The majority of the readers probably track with the generalized profile of managers. Hence, a good number of you are middle or lower managers seeking some guide to increased pay and promotions.

"Wet your toes" by taking a simple task that is completely under your control, such as *your* meeting, *your* desk control, *your* visitors, *your* telephone handling or *your* training program and try an idea presented on these pages. Or, put in one that meets the criteria of improvement. Then show or tell others.

Of course there will be some rejection. But by "wetting your toes" you have not committed anyone else but yourself. Even a rejection by another is a form of recognition, if the rejection is not of the idea and the results you have achieved, but merely a rejection such as, "Well, yes, it may work for you; but it won't work elsewhere." Couched in those words is an acceptance that you did do something of value ("but, of course, there are no other applications").

Don't stop now. Get bolder. Set an objective; think through alternates and put in another idea. Ask others to participate in your success. Give credit. Get bolder still; suggest ideas in the larger arenas, such as among your peers. Document objectives, cost/benefits and the like. Use "simmer times," the Personal Action List, recommend "the blue note," the 10-50 curve, triangulation, etc.

The beginnings create the end. Wet your toes; let success breed on minor attempts that succeed because they have a high probability to succeed. Monitor and publicize these successes.

Finally, write your own book on the aggressive management style. You must by now realize that this book is an orderly compilation of techniques related to an underlying series of management philosophies. The only one that I believe is "set in cement" is the very basis of AMS — the aggressive search for results, of a positive nature, that culminates in recognition within the management hierarchy.

Put in your action plans, instead of mine, as they relate to the management philosophies in each chapter. Your personal application will commit *you* to *your* own AMS book...your aggressive application of management techniques for positive results. By "wetting your toes," you can begin writing your own book today.

INDEX